VANCOUVER
CONFIDENTIAL

VANCOUVER CONFIDENTIAL

EDITED BY
JOHN BELSHAW

ANVIL PRESS | 2014

Anvil Press Publishers Inc.
P.O. Box 3008, Main Post Office
Vancouver, B.C. V6B 3X5 Canada
www.anvilpress.com

Library and Archives Canada Cataloguing in Publication

Vancouver confidential / edited by John Belshaw.

Includes bibliographical references and index.
ISBN 978-1-927380-99-4 (pbk.)

1. Vancouver (B.C.)--History--20th century. 2. Vancouver (B.C.)--In art. I. Belshaw, John Douglas, editor of compilation

FC3847.4.V34 2014   971.1'3304   C2014-900730-2

Book design by Derek von Essen
Cover painting by Tom Carter
Map by Eric Leinberg

Represented in Canada by Publishers Group Canada.
Distributed in Canada by Raincoast and in the U.S. by Small Press Distribution (SPD).

The publisher gratefully acknowledges the financial assistance of the Canada Council for the Arts, the Canada Book Fund, and the Province of British Columbia through the B.C. Arts Council and the Book Publishing Tax Credit.

Printed and bound in Canada.

TO THE PEOPLE
OF VANCOUVER
WHOSE STORIES
REMAIN TO BE TOLD.

CONTENTS

INTRODUCTION
JOHN BELSHAW

W hat follows is an intentionally distinctive history of Vancouver. It is based on the first principle that stories exist to be told. Even—perhaps especially—the confidential ones.

When Diane Purvey and I began work on our book, *Vancouver Noir*, in 2004, there seemed to be very few local writers interested in the city in the mid-twentieth century. By 2012 we found that a fast-spreading meme had been let loose. It was Lani Russwurm's *Past Tense* website that provided a photograph of the notoriously camera-shy pimp and bootlegger, Joe Celona. Eve Lazarus's book, *At Home with History*, became dog-eared and beaten up from overuse. Aaron Chapman found a groove about the storied Penthouse Nightclub and its patrons that had seemingly waited for his arrival on the scene. Will Woods's "Forbidden Vancouver Walking Tours" and Cat Rose's Vancouver Police Museum–sponsored "Sins of the City" tours are celebrations of the zeitgeist we had hoped to capture in *Noir*. Finding James Johnstone heading up our neighbourhood association meant that we thought of him first as the "Strathcona guy" before we realized he was the "house history guy" whose excitement for the layered fabric of the East End knows no peer. An exhibition of Tom Carter's work at a Gastown gallery revealed a brilliant visual imagination of the era. We couldn't wait to bring a few of these individuals together and propose a common project.

On any given spring day, there are more people learning about Vancouver's history from the contributors to this book than there are in every undergraduate British Columbia history class in the world combined. Between the bloggers, the book authors, the journalists, the artists, the museum speakers, and the historic tour guides, together they might encounter a couple of hundred interested parties in an afternoon (weather permitting). They shape public understanding of this city and, at the same time, nurture curiosity about Vancouver and its people in a way that is very ecumenical. They reference one another's work and share tidbits and antiquities. Every one of them shows up for public lectures. They are all supporters and benefactors of heritage and historical societies. To my enormous delight, I have discovered that a few know how to gain access to the sacred sites of local history: the private trove of artifacts, the dependable curiosity shop and dealer, the venue, the lost work of art, and—most wonderfully—the carefully hidden living sources of our city's past. These individuals contribute knowledgably to the civic life of Vancouver precisely because they are historians familiar with the habits, people, and textures of the city.

Needless to say, a history tour guide delivers the goods in ways that are different from the classroom history teacher. So, too, the blogger and—very obviously—the musician and the painter. What matters in their respective narratives is necessarily different from what matters in the lecture hall or the refereed journal. The message they wish to convey conforms to different principles and goals; the manner in which they tell the story adheres to the expectations and needs of the audience. Many of these individuals are entrepreneurs, and so their storytelling style reflects a need to deliver the sizzle as well as the steak.

Perhaps it is not especially amazing to say that few of the contributors to this book had met one another before we gathered together several to discuss the embryonic concept of *Vancouver Confidential*. This is, after all, the twenty-first century, the age of social media in which one may combine fame and anonymity in hitherto impossible ways. Face-to-face encounters engendered genuinely collaborative work and unforeseen partnerships. This ethos of sharing is perhaps best exemplified by Jason Vanderhill's near-mystical ability to divine gold from garbage in used bookstores, antiques auctions, and the like . . . and then to dole out his wares to his co-authors. Everyone began looking out for everyone else. We met and exchanged drafts, swapped ideas and suggestions. We also took an interest in one another's projects. The Police Museum has hosted several of the contributors as speakers, as has the Vancouver Historical Society. Vanderhill has had a Museum of Vancouver exhibition. A well-attended evening panel discussion at the downtown Vancouver Public Library included Aaron Chapman, Cat Rose, and Diane Purvey along with Vanessa Richards from the Arts Club Theatre Company. Contributors found themselves taking the walking tours, and some of us show up on Stevie Wilson's film on the 1930s, *Catch the Westbound Train*. Jesse Donaldson's *This Day in Vancouver* and Lani Russwurm's *Vancouver Was Awesome* were launched together at the Portside Pub with several team members on the scene. Even Toronto-based Terry Watada waded into the fray; an accomplished writer with a daunting resumé, Watada forged connections to several other contributors and demonstrated generosity and splendid encouragement where needed.

And, indeed, support from a distinguished writer was something this group valued. For several, this is their first venture into published work. Readers (and reviewers) will find styles that benefit from being read aloud or imagined as anecdotes, reportage, or poetry. These are the voices of individuals who make it their business to speak the stories of the city. If you're looking for scholarly analysis and burnished prose, look elsewhere. There is a wealth of stories in the Big Smoke; here are fifteen of them.

Sharp-eyed observers will notice the connections between various chapters. James Johnstone draws attention to the links between the Pantages (aka: the State) Theatre on Hastings and the East End community in which it stood; Tom Carter (whose artwork graces the cover of this book) describes the changes in ownership of the State and how it was pivotal in making the careers of entertainment czars in Vancouver. Chapman's exploration of the militarized, fearful city that emerged after Pearl Harbor alludes to the dangers of vice in Hogan's Alley and the Left, a theme that is touched upon by Johnstone, Rose, and Russwurm. The city's underclass of unemployed is explored in very different ways by Russwurm and Wilson. Vanderhill's liquor dealers are the legit side of the criminalized booze cans that show up in several articles. The proliferation of sidearms, gunplay, and violent assaults comes up in the contributions from Purvey and Donaldson. Gangsterism, racism, illicit gambling, and police corruption are threads that run between and across many of these accounts, including Rosanne Sia's, which is one of two that add misogyny to the mix. These elements become common denominators of life in a harbour city (the visuals of which I discuss in my own chapter), a berg where a mayor like L.D. Taylor could shrug and say, it's not going to be a Sunday-school town.

Speaking of legendary mayors, Gerry McGeer turns up like the proverbial bad penny in one chapter after the next. He was a dramatic individual who spent his career grandstanding. Like him or loathe him, the city's history is ornamented by his contribution. Three chapters in particular draw attention to McGeer's involvement in corruption investigations and crackdowns on crime. McGeer was also an inveterate enemy of socialism and was front and centre in the struggle between the authorities and the unemployed in the Dirty '30s. Was he motivated first and foremost by his strident morality in the battle against corruption or, as Will Woods suggests, did he use law-and-order rhetoric to garner political success so as to better attack the Reds?

Academic, scholarly history has its own axes to grind. The analysis of patterns and data, developing broad interpretations of motive and mentality, exposing a new perspective on an old theme . . . this is all grist for the university mill. Since the 1970s the number of BC historians on campus has grown significantly, and the range of their interests expanded dramatically. I am very proud of my colleagues who have followed in the footsteps of Margaret Ormsby and Jean Barman (who, as if it needs to be said, continues to be a powerhouse in the field outpacing the rest of us). All of these academics are supported by a network of peers in the post-secondary sector locally and nationally, and also by amateur and volunteer organizations like the BC Historical Federation and the Vancouver Heritage Foundation.

Equally, one has to point to the independent scholars and writers whose books crowd the shelves belonging to history professors and buffs alike. People like Dan Francis come immediately to mind. Without Francis's extensive and ambitious work, the city and province would be infinitely poorer. The late Chuck Davis was another —no, *the*—encyclopedic exemplar of dedication to the field. Across the province there are many other local historians whose small books and hefty tomes contribute to the sum total of our knowledge of British Columbia and Vancouver. Beyond this, however, there exists a parallel universe of understanding of our regional past.

Some years back, I taught undergraduate courses on BC history at Thompson Rivers University in Kamloops. Every year, I'd pile two- to three-dozen fourth-year students onto a bus for a visit to Vancouver. We'd start at the Casa Gelato (get them sugared up a bit) and wend our way on foot through the East End, Chinatown, and Gastown to the Marine Building, then up to West Georgia. As learning experiences go, I'm told it was great. As teaching experiences go, I learned quickly my limitations as a tour guide. I developed a real appreciation for the John Atkins of the city, people whose knowledge of every street corner seems inexhaustible. What's more, the ability to turn that knowledge into a story replete with characters, tensions, and meaning is a substantial and necessary skill. It populates a city's past with real people and imaginable lives.

The chapters collected here do one thing in common and several uniquely. First, they all describe some aspect of early to mid-twentieth century Vancouver; in each case the subject is either known to very, very few—perhaps it is being explored for the first time—or it is one that has rarely seen the light of day before. And this is the distinctive thing: each story is being told in its own way by a historian whose job it is to see the city in ways that defy orthodoxy. What does a house historian hear that a crime researcher does not? What does the musician notice that is not on the radar of the journalist? There are three chapters written by card-carrying academics: even in these cases the focus is on something other than theory. In every case, the focus is on some aspect of the *essence* of Vancouver.

Collectively and individually we'd like to thank the following individuals and organizations: Jim Wong-Chu (who provided good advice and introduced Terry Watada and Rosanne Sia to the project); Catherine Plear whose editing helped to no end; Derek von Essen for layout work extraordinaire; Tom Carter for the fabulous artwork on the cover; everyone at Anvil Press; Eric Leinberg for the map; the professional and deeply engaged staff at the City of Vancouver Archives and the downtown branch of the Vancouver Public Library; archivists at Pacific Press and the Vancouver Police Museum; supportive folks at the Vancouver Historical Society; and Vanessa Richards and the Arts Club Theatre Company, whose production of *Helen Lawrence: Vancouver Confidential* was a happy coincidence. We are all grateful, as well, to the city's many historians and historical writers whose works inspire us to explore more nooks and crannies. These include but are not limited to Kay Anderson, John Atkin, Jean Barman, Bob Campbell, Dan Francis, Stan Douglas, Michael Kluckner, Bruce Macdonald, John Mackie, Peter Moogk, Becki Ross, Paul Yee, and the late Chuck Davis. Finally, we would like to acknowledge the generous financial contribution, towards research and writing, made by Thompson Rivers University, Open Learning.

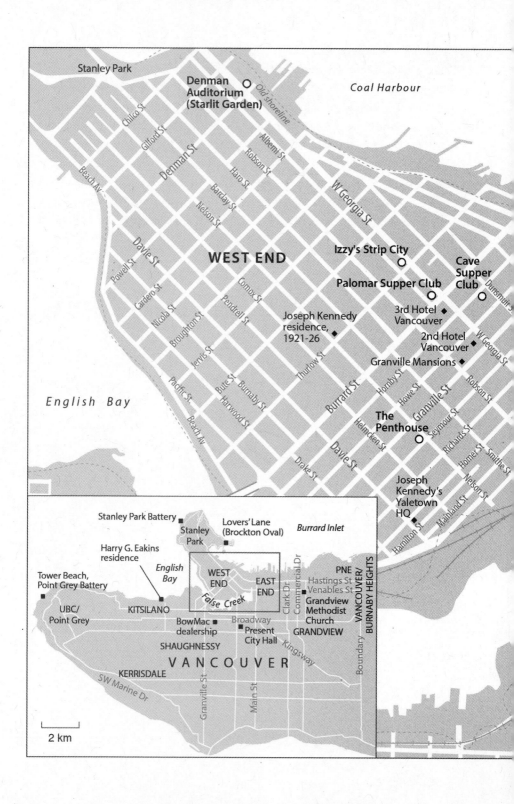

Stanley Park

Denman
Auditorium
(Starlit Garden)

Coal Harbour

Old shoreline

Chilco St

Gilford St

Denman St

Alberni St

Robson St

Haro St

Barclay St

Nelson St

Beach Av

W Georgia St

Davie St

WEST END

Powell St

Cardero St

Comox St

Nicola St

Pendrell St

Broughton St

Jervis St

Thurlow St

Izzy's Strip City

Palomar Supper Club

Cave
Supper
Club

Dunsmuir St

3rd Hotel
Vancouver

Joseph Kennedy
residence,
1921-26

2nd Hotel
Vancouver

W Georgia St

Granville Mansions

Bute St

Burnaby St

Pacific St

Harwood St

Beach Av

Burrard St

Hornby St

Howe St

Granville St

Robson St

Seymour St

Richards St

Homer St

Smithe St

Helmcken St

The
Penthouse

English Bay

Davie St

Drake St

Joseph
Kennedy's
Yaletown
HQ

Nelson St

Mainland St

Hamilton St

Stanley Park Battery

Lovers' Lane
(Brockton Oval)

Burrard Inlet

Stanley
Park

Harry G. Eakins
residence

English
Bay

WEST
END

EAST
END

Clark Dr

Commercial Dr

PNE

VANCOUVER/
BURNABY HEIGHTS

Tower Beach,
Point Grey Battery

False Creek

Hastings St

Venables St

UBC/
Point Grey

KITSILANO

BowMac
dealership

Broadway

Present
City Hall

Grandview
Methodist
Church

GRANDVIEW

SHAUGHNESSY

VANCOUVER

Boundary

Kingsway

KERRISDALE

SW Marine Dr

Granville St

Main St

2 km

Vancouver, Mid-Twentieth Century

△ Hobo Jungles   ○ Entertainment Joints

■ Other places mentioned in text

Burrard Inlet

Canadian Pacific Railway Yards

W Cordova St

Old Police Station

Coastwise Longshoremen & Freight Handlers' Association

Harbour Board/ Hastings Mill △

Sandy's ◆ Billiards

Relief Camp Workers Union

Nihon Jinkai ■

World Hotel

Alexander St

Dominion Building ■

Flack Block

Carrall St

Showa Club ■■

JAPANTOWN

Powell St

Victory Square

Abbott St

W Hastings St

Majestic Theatre ○

Columbia St

Maple Hotel ■

Main St

■ City Morgue

Powell Street Grounds

E Cordova St

Toronto Apartments

Daily Province ■

W Pender St

BCER Depot ○

Carnegie Library & Museum ■

■ First United Church

E Hastings St ■

Sun Tower

Mandarin Gardens ○

Hamilton St

Cambie St

Dunsmuir St

Beatty St

Pantages/ State Theatre

Old City Hall ■

C H I N A T O W N

EAST END

E Pender St

Keefer St

Gore Av

Dunlevy Av

Jackson Av

Heatley Av

Hawks Av

Campbell Av

793 East Georgia

Old Georgia Viaduct △

E Georgia St

Holy Trinity Russian Church ■

Old shoreline

Brothel ■

HOGAN'S ALLEY

Princess Av

Union St

Prior St

City Dump △

False Creek

Great Northern Railway

Terminal Ave

Main St

Canadian National Railway

False Creek Flats △

200 m

Map by Eric Leinberg.

NIGHTCLUB CZARS OF VANCOUVER AND THE DEATH OF VAUDEVILLE

TOM CARTER

W hen the old State Theatre on East Hastings Street was torn down in 2011, it erased the setting of several epic entertainment stories. It was the place that brought together some front-office heavyweights who became Vancouver's nightclub czars: Hymie Singer, Jack Aceman, Charlie Nelson, and Isy Walters. It has been said that "Vancouver was the place Vaudeville went to die," where its footlights finally flickered out. These were the guys who kept it alive here longer than anyplace else. They were also the ones to finally pull the plug.

They ran some of the hottest nightspots of the '40s and saw vaudeville's transition to modern entertainment. The term "czars" may be a bit over-the-top and definitely immodest, but that's exactly the kind of guys these were. They were brash, tough, self-made hustlers from immigrant families who overcame poverty and prejudice. Like everyone who came to Vancouver then (and many still now), they weren't settling for the scraps they could get back home. To set their stage (so to speak) in the 1930s, we should look at how things were in Vancouver 20 years earlier.

Long before the Granville Street clubs of today, even before the much-missed cinemas and theatres they replaced, before there was a Theatre Row, there was an even wilder and much more exuberant night scene in Vancouver: the Hastings Great White Way. Gilt-plaster-and-plush palaces, covered in light bulbs and stained glass ran continuous shows up and down Hastings, from Gore all the way to Abbott, interrupted only by pool halls and restaurants. Every last one had live music and a constant din of orchestras, pipe organs, and nickelodeons spilled onto the street to mix with the heavy traffic and rain. While the CPR Opera House over on Granville was playing up to the Englishmen of the West End and Shaughnessy with high art and oration, the East End was run by Americans, mostly San Franciscans having left the destruction of the 1906 earthquake, lured north by the cash of the miners and loggers. These showmen (as well as the madams and girls that moved up with them) knew what the people of Vancouver wanted. And no one set the tone in this era like The Great Charles E. Royal.

San Francisco's Charles E. Royal came up to play various Vancouver theatres after 1903, eventually running the Empress, Royal, and Orpheum, and giving Isy his first job in showbiz. AUTHOR'S COLLECTION.

A legendary American showman who'd transplanted himself and his whole theatre troupe from San Francisco, Charlie Royal arrived like an entertainment whirlwind in the midst of the Great War. Charles Elven Elliott was born in 1880 to a family of pioneer settlers in Monmouth, Oregon. Twenty-one years later, he was in San Francisco selling songs in the *New York Clipper* magazine, having changed his last name to Royal and adding "The Great" for good measure. Royal wrote songs by the bushel and published with the top ragtime sheet-music company of the day. Acts in *Billboard* and *Variety* magazines were performing his material everywhere. Charles and his wife, Edythe Fletcher, formed their own musical family, which included Edythe Royal Elliott, whose stage name was Baby Royal and who was billed by her market-savvy father as "America's Favorite Child Actress." In the nineteen-teens they were all touring extensively, playing out of a circus tent with a 30-piece troupe.

Royal's connection with Vancouver begins in December 1903 when he shows up on a bill at the People's Theatre in the 800 block of Pender. In 1906 he and Edythe played the Opera House on Granville. A few years later Alexander Pantages called upon him to open a new theatre on Hastings Street. Royal had played Pantages' venues elsewhere and he had managed theatre houses in Washington and Oregon. Royal's time with the Pantages was brief, but he returned to Vancouver three times: in 1911 he played the National (on West Hastings near Carrall), the Panama Theatre in 1913 (very nearby to the National), and then, in 1917, Charles, wife Edythe, and daughter Baby Royal would begin a five-year-long stay in Vancouver, one that would leave a lasting legacy for the entertainment business.

The Royals and their entourage became the house act at another theatre on East Hastings (at Gore) from which they took their name, the Empress Players. They were a huge hit, and local celebrity status followed. The Royals moved into the Regent Hotel at Hastings and Main, which was Vancouver's swanky showbiz hotel; the location was important—it was between the best theatre in town and the Carnegie Library and City Hall. Royal gradually managed more of the business of the Empress Theatre itself. When the old Pantages Theatre—the very venue Royal had opened back in 1908—came on the market, he grabbed the lease. He added more gilt plasterwork to the interior and changed the name, with characteristic humility, to the Theatre Royal.

The spotlight remained on Royal until, in 1925, he—and what was left of the Empress Players—decamped for California.[1] Long after Royal's star had dimmed and his contribution eclipsed, his effects were still being felt across the Vancouver entertainment landscape. His style was broad and brash and shameless. He reinvented himself time and again, was relentless in his pursuit of success and celebrity, and was larger than life in a great many ways. He was a frontier-era entertainer who never met a limb onto which he was afraid to climb. No one was as great a model, no one so set the context for Vancouver's next generation of entertainment czars as The Great Charles E. Royal. Charlie Royal's was an older style, but his successors naturally wanted to be every bit as royal. Indeed, it was Royal who brought Isy Walters into the entertainment business, selling candy in the Empress and Royal, and it was the Royal Theatre that linked the entertainment czars' careers.

By the mid-1930s the city was as economically paralyzed as the rest of North America, and the scene had changed enormously. The Columbia and National (beside each other at 63 and 58 West Hastings) were converted into retail stores by 1931. The Strand on Georgia was padlocked in 1932 due to the Depression, so the only places for variety onstage were the Orpheum (and the days for vaudeville there were numbered) and the Royal on Hastings, which still featured "vodvil" around the B-pictures. For Vancouver in the Dirty '30s there was only cheap movies, a few legitimate stages limping along, and some dance halls—that was it.

The first of Charles Royal's successors to arrive on the scene was also the first to leave, albeit briefly. Isadore Waltuk was born in Odessa, Russia, in 1906 and, in 1908, his family moved to Vancouver. Young Isadore, "bitten by the showbiz bug," changed his name to Isy Walters and was learning the ropes in the late 'teens from Royal. He left Vancouver and the candy-sales business at the Royal in about 1920 to spend much of the next two decades in the carnival business. He travelled the US and Canada with Browning Amusements and Conklin & Garrett Carnivals. Walters took what he learned in the Vancouver of Charles E. Royal and added to it the world of exotic ladies and "freak shows." As Walters was on the road, two of his future partners would arrive in Vancouver from Alberta—Hymie Singer and Charlie Nelson.

Andy Snider would recall "Charlie Nelson as a Damon Runyonesque character." Long-time band leader Dal Richards agreed and, with a laugh, added "and Hymie Singer even more so!" Singer came from parents used to throwing everything on the line and making it work—they came from Poland in 1905, and in 1906 Hymie was born in Toronto. Mother Bella and Hymie went back to Europe while father Abraham worked across the country for the railway, finally landing in Calgary, where he set up a home for them to return to in 1910. With Bella scrubbing floors and Abraham building a string of small businesses, they scraped up enough money to buy a rooming house and then another. It's the classic tale of immigrants taking risks and working hard—something they passed on to their boys. By the 1920s Hymie and brother Jack were put to work collecting rents and helping to maintain the apartments. The Singers were building a real estate empire that continues to this day, with holdings throughout Western Canada and the USA, including numerous shopping malls and skyscrapers. In the Depression years Hymie and Jack were in their twenties and exploring the glamour of Hollywood. About 1936 Hymie came to Vancouver, filled with ambition to build a ballroom named after, and as glitzy as, the Palomar in LA. He took over L.B. Wing's produce market at Burrard and Georgia and, with all the money he could borrow, started building "Canada's most beautiful ballroom."

Not much is known about Charlie Nelson's early years, apart from the fact he came from Edmonton. Nobody seems to know how he came to be in Vancouver or how he hooked up with Singer. All we know is, when the Palomar opened in 1937, Charlie Nelson was MC and manager. Also there on opening night was Vancouverite Sandy DeSantis, leading his hot swing band. The club was a smash hit, but beneath that veneer of cool glamour, things were tight financially. In 1939 the club closed to add a kitchen, and Dal Richards remembers how Singer routinely had tradesmen threaten to walk off due to unpaid wages. Singer would lend them personal items like his expensive wristwatch until he could scrape up more cash.

Being fast-footed was a trait of both Singer and Nelson. The Palomar wasn't just a Vancouver venue—it was a national institution. In 1938 Singer scored a promotional coup when he landed a weekly half-hour spot broadcasting coast-to-coast on the new CBC. A red neon sign was installed in the ceiling above the art deco stage that would light up with "On The Air" during the live broadcast, starting with the announcement: "It's Springtime along the network of the CBC as we present the music of Sandy DeSantis and his Orchestra from the Palomar, Canada's most beautiful ballroom, located in downtown Vancouver . . . " Young Dal Richards was ready to take his clarinet solos while Charlie Nelson and Hymie Singer watched over the crowd of revellers in black tie and ermine, served by an army of waiters, cigarette girls and other attendants.

In 1939 there was a blow-up between Singer and house band leader Sandy DeSantis, which was common enough, but this time it ended with DeSantis being fired, or walking out, depending on who's telling the story. Singer took aside young star clarinetist Dal Richards, who had just joined the band, and asked "Hey kid, you think you can lead the orchestra?" Dal replied, as any 20-year-old would, "Sure, why not?" He says he took the position more seriously after he saw Hymie Singer advertising his new leadership of the band: "starring Dal Richards, Canada's Artie Shaw." Dal went and quit school right there and then, and taking Hymie Singer's word as gospel, he started a legendary career.

After Dal was poached to lead the dance orchestra at the Panorama Roof of the brand-new Hotel Vancouver across the street, Singer and DeSantis buried the hatchet, and DeSantis returned to lead the orchestra to the end of the Palomar's days. DeSantis would take over the club in 1940 when Hymie Singer left to serve in the war. He'd lead it through some of its most glamorous, star-studded years, only to lose it to the Penthouse's Joe Philliponi to settle gambling debts.[2]

While Hymie Singer was taking a little break from civilian life, his compadre Charlie Nelson also left the Palomar. Instead of heading to Europe, he moved across the city to Chinatown. The south end of Columbia Street used to terminate at Pender, beyond which it became an alley that disappeared into the murky waters of False Creek, an oily cesspool of trestles and log booms. In the middle of the street and running from Pender to Keefer, sat Charlie's new club: the Mandarin Gardens. It was a grimy old brick building festooned with red and gold faux-Chinese ornamentation and a huge neon rooftop sign in the shape of a Chinese temple running across the entire length. The club took up the whole top floor above a few shops and one of the countless chop suey houses in Chinatown, all covered in elaborate neon and the whole works glowing and buzzing ominously in the foggy night air.

Charlie Nelson's Mandarin Garden at the end of Columbia on East Pender. Columbia Street now goes right through it.
CITY OF VANCOUVER ARCHIVES, CVA 447-64. PHOTOGRAPH BY WALTER E. FROST.

Charlie took over the place with his friend Jack Carveth one night in February 1943 rather on a whim. Nelson was talking with one of the three owners, Alec Lee, who complained of poor business and just wanted out. His other partners had abandoned him, so he offered it to Nelson and Carveth for what they had between them: $67.39. Charlie Nelson hadn't made a lot of money working for Hymie Singer at the Palomar, and Carveth—who ran the Narrows Supper Club in North Van— was similarly poor, but they obviously saw potential in the Mandarin. Soon, Charlie Nelson was using his Palomar contacts to put together full floorshows, variety acts and showgirls. He called on Sandy DeSantis's brother Carl to assemble the orchestra. The Carl DeSantis Orchestra would play for Nelson not only at this venue, but at his second Mandarin Gardens in the late '50s.

Nelson and Carveth inherited not only the furniture but also the ghost of Chan See Wong. The owner of the building died in the club in 1938, and his spirit decided to stay put. Dishes clattered in the drawers, cups and china rattled, and there would be laughter. The big floor polisher would repeatedly get unplugged, to the annoyance of the custodian—and the ghost would laugh. One afternoon, while making out the bank deposit, Charlie saw a disembodied hand floating feet away from him. He bolted for the police station, saying afterwards "I didn't run three and a half blocks because I was scared. Let's just say I was a little nervous." The ghost didn't seem to want to bother customers though, and through the late '40s there were lineups spilling down the stairs and out onto Pender.

Jack Aceman (left) with his wife, Hymie Singer's sister Diane, along with other sister Rose, at the Palomar, October 24, 1945. ACEMAN FAMILY COLLECTION.

During Hymie's absence to serve in the war, his sister Diane and brother-in-law Jack Aceman moved to Vancouver from Calgary, where they'd been married in 1934. Jack and Diane's son Byron tells how when Uncle Hymie returned to Vancouver, the two men went into entertainment ventures together. Hymie, the charming connected "man about town," would be the public face, and Jack Aceman was the behind-the-scenes business brain and financial muscle.

With the war over, and the economy booming all over North America, Vancouver was bursting with an energy it hadn't seen since the '20s. Not surprisingly, the demand for entertainment was huge. It was even greater than in Charlie Royal's day, and Singer, Aceman, and Nelson were happy to meet the challenge.

Among their early audacious endeavors was the 1945 purchase from hockey pioneer Lester Patrick of the Denman Auditorium and the neighbouring site of the Denman Arena. The 1927 auditorium was in good shape, but the 10,500-seat arena, which the Patricks had built in 1911, had burned in the spectacular fire of 1936, leaving nothing but a massive concrete floor. These two enormous buildings had sat on the north side of Georgia at the foot of Denman near the entrance to Stanley Park. Hymie announced to much fanfare that he was going to build a $1,000,000 sports arena patterned after Madison Square Garden on the site of the old arena. Soon this plan expanded to include an "indoor-outdoor emporium for boxing, wrestling, roller skating, dancing, burlesque, etc." according to Hymie's press release.

Also in 1945, Singer and Aceman picked up Charlie Royal's old theatre at 142 East Hastings Street and set out to bring back vaudeville, but in its earlier and spicier form of burlesque. This particular theatre had never left the vaude tradition. After the Pantages, Charlie Royal had kept it going until he passed it to W.P. "Nick" Nichols and his "vodvil" of the '30s. Even after he and his wife were blown out of their beds by the terror bombing of 1933, Nichols kept vaudeville percolating along at the Royal, until the war. Now the theatre, renamed the State, would become the base for the newly formed entertainment company, Singer & Aceman Ltd. Singer was president; Aceman, V.P.; and they set up shop in the same office used over the years by Alex Pantages, Charlie Royal, and Nick Nichols.

The new group of showmen were going to breath life back into the old palace. Local theatre preservationist Arthur Irving remembers the place (which he refers to as "that old dump") being shut down for some months in 1945 while they kept "taking all sorts of old red-painted millwork out of there." When it reopened, it was painted a soft green with a large new streamlined neon blade sign surrounded by chaser lights reading "State" and, lower on the marquees, "The Best Show in Town." Painted across the side and visible on Hastings were the words "America's Best Show Value" and "Midnight Show Every Sunday 12-01." A one-hour show at midnight on Sunday

East Hastings Street 1948: The State with its wall sign proclaiming the Sunday "midnite show"—actually, Monday morning. VPL SPECIAL COLLECTIONS 80617.

(in reality, on Monday) was a clever way of circumventing Vancouver's no-open-on-Sunday laws.

Despite the new signage and fresh paint, Irving remembers the place was crawling with rats. He recalls "one scampering across the front of the balcony during a show!" The whole place smelled of mould and must and rose perfume—which, along with the inevitable perspiration and cigarette smoke, sounds nauseating.

Singer saw the returning servicemen wanting entertainment that was a bit raunchier than the G-rated Hayes-code films that Hollywood was putting out, and the dine-and-dance scene was already well-covered. So, in the spirit of the older Hastings Great White Way, he brought back continual live variety. There were comedians, musicians, dancers (always scantily clad), and even a chorus line—the Statettes—followed by a double film feature (typically westerns, action or crime films). If you were having a good time, you could stay seated, and it all started again.

This place was everything a returning GI could want!

The mix of straight vaudeville, more risqué burlesque, and double-feature films changed back and forth constantly at the State—all due to tangles with the law, either federal or local. In 1946, the theatre was targeted by the still-functioning Wartime Prices and Trade Board (WPTB) in Ottawa, which had a strict policy on cinema pricing. With the large staff on-and-off-stage at the State, Hymie had to charge higher than typical movie-only rates. Unlike regular movie theatres, the State had a payroll of up to 67 employees. His auditors had sent complete records showing how he'd lose $1000 every week if he had to conform to Ottawa's guidelines, but they didn't care. So, he went ahead and charged what he needed to, which resulted in a $1000 fine in April 1946. Hymie was faced with only two options. One was to ditch live entertainment and show films only for the mandated 25¢ for matinees and 40¢ for night. The other was to drop films and go all-live. *Billboard* reported April 20 1946:

> After the fine, Singer closed the house for one day and opened the next day with an all-flesh show (burly reviews) at admissions of 50 to 75 cents for matinees and $1 to $1.50 nights. WPTB has no jurisdiction over stage shows when no pictures are shown, hence Singer can thumb his nose at the board and give his competition, which he claims was responsible for pressing the board to take action in his case, a Bronx cheer.

The WPTB started to fade away soon after, and it wasn't long before double-feature films came back onto the bill. Hymie's next challenge wouldn't be from Ottawa but from the VPD Vice Squad. Constantly warned to clean up the act when it pushed the edge of allowable decency, Singer was finally charged with permitting an indecent performance. He was tried, convicted, and sentenced to three months of hard labour in Oakalla, a sentence he appealed and had reduced to a $50 fine. One high point of the trial was when stage manager Jack DuVarney testified "This show couldn't be done any cleaner if we carried a Bible in our hands ... this here is Sunday school compared with some of the shows I've worked."[3] According-ing to the *Montreal Gazette,* another bright

Lois De Fee—the act that got Hymie Singer sentenced to three months hard labour. *VANCOUVER SUN*, JUNE 29, 1946.

moment came when 24-year-old exotic dancer Dorothy Fitzimmons disappointed a packed courtroom by showing up in a smart "powder blue suit and grey squirrel coat." She'd been excused from having to wear her abbreviated fishnet stage costume and was allowed to tell the court about the art of strip-tease dancing rather than give the anticipated demonstration.

When he wasn't at the State in these years, Charlie Nelson was still the king of the Mandarin Gardens, a block over, and he was working with his pals in the other ventures too. According to Dal Richards, it was Charlie who came up with the idea to build a wall around the abandoned concrete floor of the old Denman Arena. As Hymie's grand plan for a new "Vancouver Madison Square Gardens" wasn't gaining traction, Charlie proposed turning the huge cement pad into an open-air ballroom, complete with restaurants open 24-hours. The czars christened it "The Starlit Gardens." The Dal Richards Orchestra was a regular fixture, and Dal remembers them packing in the crowds on summer nights—under the stars right there on Coal Harbour. Some people would try to listen for free just outside, but all the action was inside. The Starlit Gardens was a hit, so Charlie went out on a limb and booked Lionel Hampton and his orchestra. This would either make them a fortune if the weather cooperated, or bankrupt the consortium if it rained. As the date came closer, days of drizzle had Nelson biting his nails, but just in time the sun came out, and it turned into a beautiful warm summer night. The place was jammed, and the czars were rolling in cash.

Between the Palomar and the Mandarin, in '42 and '43, Charlie was also running other promotions around town for Foto-Nite Amateur Shows Ltd., including amateur contests in the long movie-theatre lineups. He'd have a few local young musicians entertain the lineups, and whoever got the loudest applause would win five bucks. Young June Govier played her accordion and won consistently.[4] Nelson liked her chutzpah as well as her prodigious playing, so he asked her to try out at the Mandarin. She had to run it by her parents, but Charlie assured her he'd talk with her mother and work it out. He did, and June started at the Mandarin. She remembers, "Mr. Nelson

When Hymie Singer ran into opposition for his mega-entertainment complex, he and Jack Aceman turned the old floor of the burned-down Denman Arena into the Starlit Gardens. The Mandarin may have been open 'til 3 a.m., but the Starlit was open 24 hours!
VANCOUVER SUN, JUNE 29, 1946.

June Govier plays in front of the Sandy DeSantis Orchestra at the Palomar, 1945. The most-booked act at the Palomar, she was discovered by Charlie Nelson playing for a movie theatre lineup. JUNE COARD COLLECTION.

always had a number of big men around who made sure everything ran smoothly." One of these "big men" would walk her to her car parked in the foggy darkness behind the old club on the False Creek waterfront. "I could see Mr. Nelson in the upstairs window looking to make sure I was all right." Soon June would be playing over at the Palomar as well; in fact, she became the most-booked act to ever play there. She'd also play at the State, which Nelson also ran first under Hymie Singer and later with Isy Walters. Even though June was part of the musical entertainment, elegantly dressed in evening gown, and definitely not one of the strippers, she occasionally got a heckle from "some old Chinaman in the front row who'd call out 'Take it all off!'"

Another young lady Charlie Nelson discovered one night was a teenager who asked in the early hours of the morning if she could sing "September Song." Mimi Hines had buck teeth and a killer voice. Nelson immediately hired her. Soon she was doing three shows a night at the Mandarin and another five at the State. She also had to drive across Burrard Inlet to another club Charlie had in North Vancouver—the Diamond Horseshoe (previously the old Narrows Club that Charlie's partner at the Mandarin, Jack Carveth, ran in the early '40s). One night in January 1952, Mimi was on a bill at the State called the Matzah Ball and Farfel Revue, a typical lineup of raunchy comedians, burlesque girls, and Statettes, when the place was raided by the police and everyone was hauled off to jail. Mimi remembers a Sergeant Scully saying to her upon entering the police station, "Mimi, I know you're a good girl, so you can go." Scully was a regular at the State and routinely enjoyed her performances, as well as all the others. She tells of how Peg Leg Bates, the one-legged tap dancer, was playing the Palomar and came down to catch her sing. He said, "Mimi, you gotta get outta this dump. I'll see what I can do." Peg Leg "really sold her" to Hymie Singer, moving her up to the Palomar. Of course, Singer would have been instantly aware of what was going on at the Mandarin through not only his buddy Charlie Nelson but also Sandy DeSantis, who would probably hear about new prospects from his brother Carl. A voice like Mimi's would have been talked about.

While playing the Mandarin and State, Mimi became friends with the young Sammy Davis Jr. who was in the Will Mastin Trio with his father and uncle. They were popular in Vancouver in the '40s and played here many times. Being about the same age and in similar circumstances at the Mandarin Gardens, Mimi and Sammy hit it off. She remembers his plan to leave music and become a Hollywood cowboy (a dream he one day realized). They practiced gunfight shootouts and death scenes in the middle of Pender Street in front of the Mandarin after closing, with Sammy ending melodramatically laying face down "dead" in what is now the intersection of Pender and Columbia. Their friendship started at the Mandarin but continued until his death. He told her, when they reminisced about Vancouver, that "Vancouver was the place vaudeville went to die." When asked what he meant by this—was it a slight of some sort?—Mimi explains, "No, no slight ... it's just Vancouver ran vaudeville long after anyplace else in the world" and Sammy—the vaudevillian son of a vaudevillian—recognized that.

Like the State, the Mandarin Gardens ran an adult-oriented show that included hot music, big-name talent, and pretty showgirls in pasties and headdresses. The Mandarin even matched the Statettes chorus line with their own Mandarinettes. Predictably, Charlie Nelson also faced endless warnings and scrapes with the vice squad. In August of 1952 he became the target for a consortium of church groups.

They were enraged when city council, having suspended Nelson's business licence following the conviction of two people arrested for bootlegging on the premises, allowed him to reopen. Annoyed by the attacks and furious over what he believed was ongoing police persecution, Charlie Nelson offered to pay $5000 to anyone who could prove he ever sold a bottle of liquor. Days later, council called his bluff. They voted to demolish the building housing the Mandarin, ridding the city of a place "long a target for police attacks as a trouble spot," as the *Vancouver Sun* put it. This put 25 employees (and the Mandarin Garden's resident ghost) out of work and it put Charlie out of business.

In other ways, too, 1952 was a watershed year for the czars and vaudeville in Vancouver. That year saw Aceman and Singer renovate the Denman Auditorium and reopen it as the Georgia Auditorium, now a full-fledged concert venue. Aceman and Nelson, tired of the VPD's endless hassling and not impressed by what befell the Mandarin, converted the State from burlesque to legitimate theatre. They struck a deal with Sidney Risk's Everyman Theatre Company to move in as the house repertory company and renovate the old theatre, now renamed the Avon. It opened with Shakespeare that fall. The August 28 *Sun* reported, "The new deal wraps up Nelson and Isy Walter's costly fling in the burley business and means tough times ahead for local Vaude artists." Despite a good scrubbing and fresh paint, the Avon couldn't completely shake its vaudeville past. Charlie Nelson stayed the same old operator, bellowing to director Dorothy Davies during a performance of Shakespeare, "Hey, what time does your next act go on?" Davies also recalled an audience member shouting from the balcony for her to "take it all off!" during a performance of *Macbeth.* "He went into a Charlie Nelson joint," she said, "and expected a Charlie Nelson show."

The *Sun's* suggestions that the boys had gone upmarket legit were, Shakespeare notwithstanding, premature. They had already launched their next big move: into Amato's Cave. The Walters/Nelson partnership seems to have lasted at least into this next venture. *Billboard* reported on July 19 that "the Cave Supper Club has been sold by George Amato and associates to Izzy Walters and Charlie Nelson. The new owners operate the Mandarin in Chinatown and the State Theatre, burly house."

Nelson doesn't seem to have stayed long at the Cave. He concentrated more on the Avon, stirring up lots of press, wining and dining the visiting Hollywood celebrities who were the weekly features of the stock company. The infamous January 16, 1953, *Tobacco Road* incident seemed to boost attendance, and the marquee lineup that year was impressive: it included film stars Margaret O'Brien, Joe E. Brown, and Lon Chaney Jr., to name a few. The Avon was riding high, and Charlie Nelson and Jack Aceman were enjoying the limelight. Aceman's daughter Lola recalls family dinners with the celebrities in attendance and how her mother tried to set up teenage brother Byron on a date with featured teen star Margaret O'Brien. Margaret's strict mother wouldn't have it. Despite successes in '53, by '54, attendance was sagging, so Nelson and Aceman threw everything into getting Hollywood star Miriam Hopkins to play in *The Cuckoo* in hopes of turning things around. Reported the *Sun* on October 30, 1954, "If attendance is satisfactory, plans call for an array of top Hollywood talent for the season,' says producer Jack Aceman. 'The future of legitimate theatre in Vancouver hinges on this first production' says co-producer Charles Nelson." It wasn't a success. According to people there, Hopkins made it known she was slumming, taking this job in a shabby old theatre on Hastings. The former Hollywood A-lister was intent on making everyone as miserable as she was. Lola Aceman remembers with a laugh, that Miriam was "a terrible drunk," and Jack Wasserman reported in his column of November 23: "As she was leaving town, actress Miriam Hopkins let it be known she didn't think much more of the Avon Theatre group than

The Avon Theatre's Jack Aceman (far left) and Charlie Nelson (far right) introducing Hollywood actress Teresa Wright to the epicurean delights of Chinatown. Wright was here to star in the Avon's *The Country Girl*, April 1954.
ACEMAN FAMILY COLLECTION.

they did of her. Oooo. Such things!" A few more shows followed, but a planned May 14 to 22 run of Vincent Price in *Angel Street* never came off. The Avon shut down, and in May of 1955, Jack Aceman leased it to the Canadian Legion Branch 178 as a bingo hall. Thereafter it occasionally returned to cheap B-pictures. Aceman held on to the Georgia Auditorium, which was the primary big live-concert venue until it was eclipsed by the new Queen Elizabeth in 1959. That year the auditorium was demolished, and Aceman's career in entertainment in Vancouver ended as well. He moved on to large-scale real estate developments, including the new Kingsgate Mall. In this new venture he was following in the footsteps of another czar, Hymie Singer.

By the early '50s, having left Vancouver's nightlife for several years, Hymie was in the family's development business big time. According to Jack Singer's obituary in the *Calgary Herald*, "Jack and his brother Hymie brought the strip mall concept to Alberta in the 1950s and 1960s, building malls with Safeway and banks as the anchor tenants as quickly as they could buy land and obtain financing." Hymie moved down to California, and in 1955 Jack Wasserman reported in the *Sun*, "Hy Singer, promoter extraordinaire and idea-man deluxe," was now a dog-food manufacturer in Los Angeles. In that year Hymie returned to Vancouver to promote a scheme to put up a 24–storey office building at Georgia and Granville. Hymie's bravado hadn't changed a bit, and in explaining why the scheme didn't work, he said "The $40,000,000 for the building didn't worry me. The $3,500,000 they wanted for the property didn't bother me either. But where could I get $10,000 for the deposit—IN CASH?" This kind of talk wasn't new: big plans were his stock and trade. Even in the mid-'40s, when Singer trumpeted his Denman and Georgia Street mega-complex, the *Seattle Daily Times* had wryly commented, "We'll wait and make our reservations for the world's championship fights in Vancouver until Singer quits announcing and starts building."

Among the reasons for Hymie Singer's departure from show business (and the show girls that went with it) were his marriage in 1951 and the daughter that came along in 1952. The switch from nightclub czar to respectable family man must have been a bit difficult, and by 1957, he was divorced and once more a bachelor. Along with his brother Jack, Hymie liked the celebrity life of Hollywood—he'd been in star circles since the '30s—and soon he was dating Lita Warner, daughter of Warner Bros. tycoon Sam Warner and a Ziegfeld Follies showgirl who was raised by Harry Warner.

This Hollywood romance didn't last, though, and in 1962, Hymie married a good Jewish woman, Ruth Cohn, and they lived happily ever after in the largest house in Beverly Hills—the old Tom Mix estate. Singer was still dabbling in entertainment, bankrolling the independent never-finished film *Dante's Inferno*, trying

Romance is rumored between former Vancouverite Hyman Singer, 47, Calgary real estate man, and adopted daughter of film magnate. Mr. Singer built old Palomar Club and owned State Theatre.

Reports of marriage are premature, said Lita Warner Hiatt of romance, between her and Mr. Singer. She is daughter of movie tycoon Harry Warner. Mrs. Hiatt was recently divorced.

Hymie Singer got very close to the Warner Bros. in the '50s, almost a member of the family in 1957. He'd name his development company Warner Holdings in their honour.
VANCOUVER SUN, MAY 30, 1957.

unsuccessfully with his brother Jack to take over Canadian Famous Players, and then successfully parting Francis Ford Coppola from his studios. Having lent Coppola $3 million to finish *One from the Heart*, the Singer family covered themselves in case the film bombed, which it did. Said Singer glibly in a *Variety* interview, "If *One from the Heart* doesn't pay, we will wind up with the studio." The family owns Hollywood Center Studios to this day. Although Singer obviously made good money in his investments (leaving Ruth the bulk of his $8.5 million estate when he died July 17, 1998), Ruth contributed to their lavish life too. Says Dal Richards, "It was never Hymie's money—Ruth had all the money," and he liked to splash it around. Hymie, Richards recalls, was the sort of guy you could count on to support the Variety Club while taking the most lavish hotel room he could find—and while everyone else stayed in the standard rooms. In 1977, in a grand Valentine's Day gesture, Singer famously (or perhaps infamously) bought Ruth the 301-foot *S.S. Catalina* at auction. The retired steamship was intended to be her new yacht but, after spending millions of dollars moving, mooring and patching it up, it sank off the coast of Mexico two years after Hymie's death in 1998.

While Singer was hanging with the Warner brothers and building his real estate empire from Beverly Hills, and while his brother-in-law, Jack Aceman, was segueing from theatre-owner to commercial developer, Isy Walters and Charlie Nelson were still slugging it out in the bump-and-grind world of variety entertainment. Television was making it increasingly tough to compete with live acts, just like earlier big-circuit vaudeville had been squeezed by motion pictures. This time it was worse: TV was free, and you could enjoy all the vaudeville you wanted on *Ed Sullivan* without getting a babysitter.

Charlie Nelson had bad luck to boot. He had taken over the old Narrows Supper Club and turned it into the Diamond Horseshoe, but a city works crew accidentally blew it up when they hit a gas main in November 1955. The fire destroyed the club and, yet again, Charlie was picking up the pieces to start over. By 1956, he'd convinced two backers to set up a new Mandarin Gardens at 164 East Hastings Street near Main, just a stone's throw from the old State/Avon. The new club opened April '56, promising "old-time Mandarin floorshows, with chorus line and all ..." This move to keep the new club "old-time" seems to have been out of step with the shift in public tastes, and it wasn't going to help him compete with the slicker new nightclub acts at the Cave and Penthouse and the coming onslaught of rock 'n' roll. Nelson's menu was, as well, a bit bizarre. The *Sun* reported on November 29, 1956, that it was "the only Chinatown restaurant, in any Chinatown anywhere, that features Russian style Cabbage Rolls as a house specialty."[5]

Isy Walters was faring better, running the Cave in top form with the assistance of his son Richard and very capable manager Ken Stauffer. Stauffer would end up buying the club and ride it even higher into the rock and contemporary music scene of the '60s and '70s. The Cave is legendary in Vancouver, of course, so there's no need to rattle off the endless list of headliners who played to packed houses.

No one knows what compelled Isy Walters and Charlie Nelson to join forces once again in 1958 and take over the Majestic at 20 West Hastings (formerly the second Pantages vaudeville theatre). Their avowed goal was to bring back what must be considered the last real vaudeville anywhere. (It was this bold step backwards that Sammy Davis Jr. remembered years later.) They opened in March '58 with a bill that included four imported American acts, the Carl DeSantis Orchestra and two Cinemascope movies—the whole lineup running nonstop from noon until 5 in the morning. Even in the glory years of vaudeville fifty-plus years earlier the continuous shows would end at a respectable midnight. The cost of talent on and off stage must have been astounding, especially at a time when the competition was typically a four-piece rock band or vocal with small combo. At first the novelty brought in good houses, but soon the spectacle onstage was playing to just a handful of people in the massive old theatre. By March the musician's union was calling the all-night show too rough on its members, and the writing was on the wall. A look at the *Sun*'s entertainment page of May 13 shows the Majestic headliners "Gay 90s Stars Ma & Pa O'Hagen" competing against the new drive-ins featuring *Rock All Night*, *Dragstrip Girl* and films starring Elvis Presley and Bill Haley.

In an effort to cut their considerable losses, Walters and Nelson pulled the plug on vaudeville and parted ways. Charlie Nelson limped along with the New Mandarin, shutting down, opening for a week and then closing again. The May 12, 1959, *Sun* coyly reported, "Charlie Nelson has returned from a visit with family in Edmonton which is a nice way of announcing that he has fresh money and his Mandarin Gardens will probably re-open later this week." The sun really was setting on Charlie Nelson's time in variety entertainment, and he was ready to move on. In 1960, he took over an old house at 1216 Robson and turned it into a restaurant serving corned beef sandwiches and his standby cabbage rolls. Charlie's Place was a hit, despite 18 police showing up on opening night in 6 squad cars, expecting violations. Within months, although the place was booming, they took away his licence for "operating a cabaret by permitting dancing." The neighbours' noise complaints at 4:00 a.m. weren't helping. The *Sun* reported November 18, 1960:

> Charlie Nelson's restaurant at 1216 Robson might keep some residents awake because of the noise, but it gave the city vitality and colour, lawyer G.R.B. Coultas protested. But to city prosecutor Stewart McMorran, the colour reminded him of Charlie's other place, the old Mandarin Gardens, that Nelson managed. "Colour" said McMorran, "most of it was blood that ran down the stairway." Council agreed and decided to lift Nelson's license ...

As Jack Wasserman said about the incident, referring to Charlie as Vancouver's absent-minded answer to NYC impresario Billy Rose, "It seems that somebody 'up there' doesn't like Charlie ... I think it's a darn shame."

Charlie Nelson finally left Vancouver, alone and without fanfare, with about as much in his pockets as he had when he arrived. After a stint managing a banquet room in Calgary, he quietly returned to suburban Richmond, selling mattresses and chesterfields at Discount Traders until he died at the age of 72, in April 1981. Denny Boyd, in the only tribute paid to him, said, "all he wanted was a crowd around him at four in the morning and enough in the till to stay open. But he never got the big break."

Of all the czars, only Isy stayed the old-style showman right to the end. Upon selling the Cave in '58, around the same time he was bailing from the Majestic vaudeville debacle, he converted an old Dodge dealership on Georgia near Thurlow into a glamorous new supper club called Isy's. Through the '60s, the lineups were impressive, both on the bill and outside the front door on the sidewalk. By 1970, though, the numbers just weren't what they used to be, so rather than compete with TV variety, Isy the survivor knew what would work and returned to his girlie-show roots. Recalling the State years (and his carnival days before that), he gave people what they couldn't get on TV—live girls and adult entertainment. Times had

Isy Walters, who started with Charlie Royal on Hastings Street in the '20s, ran his supper club until his death in 1976. *VANCOUVER PROVINCE.*

changed enough since the State that the police left him alone, and the newly re-named Isy's Strip City enjoyed a place in Vancouver's night scene right up until Isy's death in 1976.

By the time the wreckers finished taking down the old Pantages (a.k.a. Charlie Royal's Royal and the czars' State/Avon) on Hastings at Main, every man associated with it was long gone. Also gone were Isy's Cave and Isy's Supper Club/Strip City, Hymie's Palomar, and Charlie's Mandarin Gardens and Diamond Horseshoe. Gone too were the Denman/Georgia Auditorium, the old concrete pad where the Starlit Gardens had been, and of course the other Pantages—the Majestic, where, despite the valiant efforts of two of the czars, vaudeville came back to Vancouver . . . and finally died.

Research for this paper was helped enormously and made a great pleasure by the recollections offered up by Byron Aceman and Lola Pawer, Arthur Irving, June (Govier) Coard and Betty Brown, Andrew Martin, Dal Richards, and Drew Snider.

(ENDNOTES)

1   By 1930 Charles E. Royal had been featured in the first sound Western serial for Universal Studios. Soon he'd be writing screenplays for Edgar Rice Burroughs, turning out two *Tarzan* serials as well as pictures for Republic and Columbia. His wife and Vancouver co-star Edythe Elliott had also signed with RKO, and their old partner in Vancouver Ray Collins would soon be in the Mercury Players, costarring in *Citizen Kane* and, later, across from British Columbian Raymond Burr in the TV series, *Perry Mason*.

2   The Fillippones were the last owners of the Palomar. It was demolished in 1956 to make way for the Burrard Block where Tiffany's now stands.

3   Jack DuVarney was also MC the night of the Matzah Ball and Farfel Revue—another night everyone, including Mimi Hines, was hauled off to jail for indecency. DuVarney was even working there when the theatre was the Royal, the night of the bombing in 1933. He'd done the rounds locking up just hours before the box office and lobby were blown to smithereens. DuVarney claimed to play the Pantages the night of its opening in 1908, but there's no real evidence to support it. There was a DuVarney family connection with the Pantages/State as well: Jack's wife, Carol, ran the chorus line, even sewing the Statette's costumes.

4   The secret of June Govier's success was "Deep in The Heart of Texas". It got the crowd used to clapping in the choruses, and by the time the song ended, they were all ramped up and kept applauding.

5   They were still puzzled a few years later, noting that the Mandarin would finally have Chinese food. "Charlie Nelson opened his East Hastings cabaret and immediately discontinued sale of Chinese food 'because it was bad'. Instead he substituted Ukrainian cheese dumplings . . . Italian spaghetti and Mexican chili con carne. This week he found a new chef who can also prepare Chinese food, so he added that to the menu."

THE DANIEL JOSEPH KENNEDY STORY

JASON VANDERHILL

Whenever Vancouverites enjoy a cocktail, they have—in some measure—Daniel Joseph Kennedy[1] to thank. A pioneer of the mixed drink, his long career was kept afloat on a sea of craftily packaged booze.

Kennedy's birth predates that of the City of Vancouver's inauguration by some two dozen years. He would end up spending the last 40 years of his life in Vancouver, although barely anyone remembers him. He typically went by the name Joseph Kennedy.[2] He was born on March 1, 1862, possibly at Table Rock, Nebraska. His birth comes 10 years after the Great Irish Potato Famine, which could explain why his Irish immigrant family found themselves in the rich farmland of midwest America.[3]

At 20 years of age, Joseph Kennedy was living in St. Joseph, Missouri, working as a clerk in his father's grocery store, Thomas Kennedy & Son. One year later, he married Mary Teresa Hogan (also of Irish descent), on November 29, 1883. John Joseph Hogan, the first bishop of St. Joseph and Kansas City, officiated at what was undoubtedly a good Catholic wedding. Three years later, Mary and Joseph had their first and only child: Aileen Marie Kennedy, born on July 4, 1886, in St. Joseph, Missouri.

Within a few years Joseph branched out from Thomas Kennedy & Son. The St. Joseph city directory of 1887 lists his profession as "com'l trav": commercial traveller or travelling salesman. In 1888, he was representing the California Wine Company which was very likely the company founded in Kansas City in 1883.

The 1890s would have been a fascinating period of time to be selling spirits. Joseph Kennedy would have witnessed the height of steam-train travel, rapid industrialization, and a formative era for American branding, merchandising, and advertising. Though the California Wine Company defaulted on its debts in 1895,

Daniel J. Kennedy did not abandon his profession and he continued to seek opportunities to ply his trade in the sale of liquor.

According to the 1900 United States census, Joseph Kennedy was living a few hundred miles east of St. Joseph in the city of St. Louis. His address was 2909 South Broadway, effectively around the corner from the Anheuser-Busch headquarters, a prime location for a liquor salesman. For the 1910 US census, the family claimed Reno, Nevada, as their home, though Joseph changed his profession to "Prospector," possibly in jest. Whether or not he struck it rich in the west, adventure beckoned north, and the family moved to Canada, settling briefly in Swift Current and later in Saskatchewan's "Opportunity City," Weyburn.

By 1913, real estate rumours led to the spontaneous creation of a boomtown in Shaunavon, Saskatchewan. It seems the CPR had purchased the entire townsite, and then made public a plan to establish in Shaunavon their divisional office for traffic westbound to Lethbridge. The announcement made purchasing lots in the area extremely popular.[4] This early form of real estate speculation was a favourite technique of the CPR, a strategy that was tested repeatedly in Vancouver's own real estate history. In just eight hours on September 17, 1913, a total of 370 lots were sold, and lot number one was sold to none other than Daniel Joseph Kennedy.[5] George Limerick, a barber, had sold his position in line for $1,000 so that Joseph had first

Construction of the Kennedy Hotel 1913–14. Could that be Daniel Joseph Kennedy himself, proudly waving from the top of his hotel? PHOTO COURTESY OF GRAND COTEAU HERITAGE & CULTURAL CENTRE, SHAUNAVON, SK.

dibs on his choice of lots in this new town-to-be.[6] He proceeded to build the Kennedy Hotel and Bar in the centre of town, opening in March of 1914. His plan was to establish the finest, most advanced hotel in the region. On completion it had 75 rooms in total, with a dining room capacity for 60 guests. During construction, plans were expanded to include a billiards hall and bowling alley in the basement.

Later that same year on September 17, the *Shaunavon Standard* reported a new enterprise: Hotel Systems Ltd. "Jos. Kennedy" was president, and the object of the company was to buy, build, and operate first-class hotels throughout Western Canada. They had already acquired the site for a hotel in Drumheller and they opened their stock for sale to the public. It was an undeniably ambitious scheme, with a key part of their formula based on projected earnings from serving drinks in their hotel bars. What a blow it must have been when just one year later, the prohibition movement arrived early in Saskatchewan with proposed liquor legislation that would transfer control over the trade to the provincial government.

The *Shaunavon Standard*, May 6, 1915, published an open letter of protest to Premier Scott, signed by 16 Shaunavon businesses. The newspaper took a sympathetic view of their position, writing:

> If our local hotels are closed and the government takes over the liquor business by establishing dispensaries, or wholesale liquor houses, they will be taking the profits which rightly belongs to our businessmen if the liquor business is to be continued at all. This will reflect on every resident of the Shaunavon district. Shaunavon today has the reputation of being an exceptionally good trading point where goods are sold right, in some cases equaling Regina. Can the business men continue this low rate if they are forced to lose this money?[7]

At some point in his career as a liquor distributor, Joseph Kennedy had met with some powerful men in the brewing and distilling trade. This newspaper account from the *Shaunavon Standard* dated June 17, 1915, confirms his connections reached as far as New York, and in light of the uncertain future for a life-long liquor distributor, announces a most fortuitous political appointment:

> The Provincial Government Liquor Commission who appointed J.F. Bole as commissioner has also appointed our local hotel man Joseph Kennedy as his assistant. His duties will be a general superintendency of distribution and assistant purchasing agent.

Owing to Mr. Kennedy's previous connection with the distilling business and building of same, and has been for years associated with Strauss of New York as their European buyer, Mr. Kennedy is especially fitted for the position. The residents of Shaunavon feel that the department has done well in securing his service and it is felt that the department will be guaranteed an excellent line of goods. All purchases made by Mr. Bole will pass through the laboratory under the personal inspection of Mr. Kennedy. Mr. Bole, who has resigned his seat as member to accept the new position is a member of the Regina Trading Co., one of the largest departmental stores of the west.

"Mr. Strauss" of New York in all likelihood refers to Mr. Nathan Straus of the R.H. Macy & Company and Abraham & Straus department stores.[8] But perhaps more important now was Joseph Kennedy's newfound political influence. Saskatchewan was an early adapter of prohibition, and working from the inside, Joseph Kennedy would see firsthand how to exploit emerging market conditions.

He promptly moved to Regina in June of 1915 to take up his new position. On July 1, the provincial government closed bars and took over the wholesale liquor business. It did not take Kennedy long to make his move. Within a few weeks, the headlines of the *Shaunavon Standard* on July 22, 1915, announced, "Joseph Kennedy Forms Drug Company." The article read:

> In a letter from Joseph Kennedy from Ottawa, he states that he has organized the Druggists' Sundries Company and is now in the East purchasing machinery and transacting other business in connection with the new organization. The factory and officers will be located at Weyburn. The company has strong financial backing, Mr. Kennedy being vice-president and general manager, and a number of other parties with strong financial backing are identified with the concern.[9]

To start the Druggists' Sundries Company at a time like this might seem like a curious career change, until you realize what he was selling. Kennedy's Stomach Bitters would become one of his trademark brands. A nourishing and invigorating tonic with medicinal qualities, it also happened to fall into the realm of consumer products that could legally contain alcohol and still be purchased over the counter without regulation. By choosing a medical-sounding name for his business, he might just deflect attention from the prohibitionists and become the secret saviour to the moderationists.

By August 26, 1915, the Kennedy Hotel's bar had been converted into a short-order lunchroom. The hotel, which had been managed by Kennedy's son-in-law, Harold (Harry) Gray Eakins, carried on. A small fire struck the hotel on January 13, 1916, but quick work by the night watchman saved the structure from serious damage. Much investment had been made to guard the building against the risk of fire, but perhaps this event was an omen: leave town before it's too late. Joseph Kennedy would do just that.

His investment in Druggists' Sundries Company must have shown its potential under prohibition in Saskatchewan. Ever the prospective entrepreneur, when Kennedy heard British Columbia would be implementing its own form of prohibition starting October 1, 1917, he promptly moved to Kitsilano and established his operations in the warehouse district of Yaletown. From this date forward, he made Vancouver his home, leaving Weyburn, Shaunavon, and Regina behind. It was most fortuitous timing, as a second—this time disastrous—fire on June 4, 1918, burnt the Kennedy Hotel to the ground, wiping out half of Shaunavon's business section in the process. A great prairie hotel was lost, but opportunities beckoned west.

> Immediately after October 1 and the arrival of West Coast prohibition, advertisements for Kennedy's Stomach Bitters from the Druggists' Sundries Company Limited, Vancouver, Canada, appeared in the *Vancouver Daily World*. The fact that they were published in the *World* is somewhat ironic, as this newspaper was "for a time . . . the official organ of the Prohibition party which was an important force in British Columbia politics."[10] Kennedy's antidote to BC's dry spell was remarkably simple: fool the prohibitionists with a bold new drink masquerading as medicine! The iconography in his first ad provides a symbolic clue: this drink will provide you with the "Keys to Good Health and Long Life." (The cross-keys have deep Catholic roots, hearkening to the keys to the Kingdom of Heaven. They are also a quintessential symbol of the papacy. Later, the logo of the cross-keys would be replaced by a pair of crossed swords.)

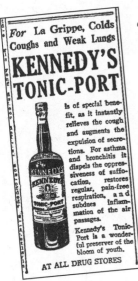

For La Grippe, Colds Coughs and Weak Lungs

KENNEDY'S TONIC-PORT

is of special bene-
fit, as it instantly
relieves the cough
and augments the
expulsion of secre-
tions. For asthma
and bronchitis it
dispels the oppres-
siveness of suffo-
cation, restores
regular, pain-free
respiration, and
subdues inflam-
mation of the air
passages.
Kennedy's Tonic-
Port is a wonder-
ful preserver of the
bloom of youth.

AT ALL DRUG STORES

Kennedy's Stomach Bitters were promoted as a powerful re-constructive tonic for all of the stomach and digestive organs. The product was "Guaranteed to contain none but the purest ingredients compounded in a scientific manner." The prescribed dosage was half a wine glass three to four times daily, before or after meals. One cannot be sure how important those instruc-tions actually were, except for the explicit use of a wine glass; they could just as well have said drink it whenever you like.

Another ad for Kennedy's Tonic-Port which appeared in the *Province* newspaper in late 1917 was seen as a cure-all for La Grippe (influenza, or the flu), colds, coughs, and weak lungs. The drink contained cinchona bark extract, a medicinal herb also known as Jesuit's bark, along with a good dosage of alcoholic wine.[11] The ad was not afraid to boast: "Kennedy's

Kennedy's Jazz Cocktails
by Druggists' Sundries
Company Ltd, Vancouver, an
advertisement that connects
drink with a glamorous
and sophisticated lifestyle.
Reproduced from the book
*Vancouver's First Century:
A City Album 1860–1960* by
Anne Kloppenborg.

Tonic-Port is a wonderful preserver of the bloom of youth." It claimed to be available at all drug stores.

Prohibition caused a shift in consumer tastes with respect to the popular beverages of the day. As liquor stocks were depleted, the quality of liquor available also deteriorated. During the 1920s, a new style of drink became *de rigueur* in clubs and speakeasies. "Cocktails" were sociable and acceptable for both men and women, even if they were served in a blind pig or an underground club. They became a staple alternative to traditional heavy liquors as they could both mask the taste of inferior ingredients and "were easier to drink quickly, an important consideration when the establishment might be raided at any moment."[12] The cocktail was also becoming increasingly glamorized in film, a trend that would continue even into the Great Depression of the 1930s, when most of the working class had to give up such frivolities.

Kennedy's Jazz: that mystic South American drink, containing a mysterious spirit of energy. *VANCOUVER DAILY WORLD, JUNE 12, 1918.*

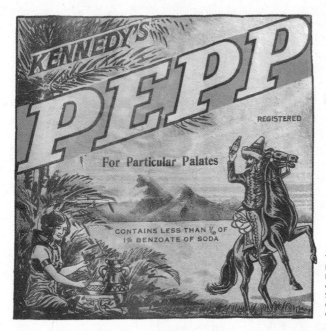

The colourful product label of Kennedy's Pepp "For Particular Palates," one of the curious concoctions of Druggists' Sundries Company Limited. COURTESY OF THE NEIL WHALEY COLLECTION.

There is very little in the way of critical or scientific writing that would help to describe the exact composition of these concoctions. Never mind actual recipes or ingredient lists—without consumer reviews or any indication of a percentage of alcohol, it's extremely hard to know what they would have tasted like. Instead, we are forced to imagine the molecular makeup of these drinks through the product advertising and, occasionally, a rare surviving bottle.

The ad for Jazz Cocktail above reveals a sophisticated early line of products from the 1917–22 era, when the company was still called Druggists' Sundries Company Limited. No longer masquerading behind bitters and medicinal tonics, this product made no apology for its makeup. The family included the Jazz Frappe, Jazz Juleps, Jazz Rickies, Jazz High Balls, Jazz Punches, and Jazz Cocktails. Best served in a cocktail glass of course. The title of the drink may even suggest that you were expected to add a little shot of something extra to give the drink its vigour.

You can see from the illustrated advert just how much electricity these beverages could create. A drink or two after the show might even lead to ballroom dancing! The ad coins the phrase "Jazz a Rickie with Me," employing the word "jazz" as a verb. Given the time period, this brand name was not only appropriate, it was also downright prophetic. To combine jazz and cocktail culture practically predicted the roaring '20s. But prediction is a fickle game, and sometimes being too far ahead of the curve can hurt you. It is hard to know how many Jazz Cocktail bottles were sold.

Kennedy's Pepp, Kennedy's
Stomach Bitters, and an imported
bottle of Vino Vermouth; these
bottles reveal a diverse variety
of branded products offered
by Joseph Kennedy.
PHOTOGRAPH BY JASON VANDERHILL;
BOTTLES COURTESY OF THE NEIL WHALEY
COLLECTION.

To the chagrin of local bottle collectors, no known examples have survived.

Another advertisement for Kennedy's Jazz Cocktail from 1918 reveals the exotic origins of this particular drink. The "ancient Indians of Brazil" are credited with finding the "Spirit of Energy" imprisoned in a mountain bush. A drink brewed with the leaves of this plant provided immediate refreshment, exhilaration, and left hunger satisfied. Text in a following ad provides fairly solid evidence it was the cocoa plant they were alluding to: "Tired from a strenuous day of cattle herding, with its lusty calls of Co-Co-Coa—mighty thirsty—the Brazilian Vaquero drinks an amazingly bracing and refreshing beverage . . . This, then, is the wonder-working substance—the secret of the stimulating, health-building properties of Jazz Cocktails. A rich, winey drink, absolutely without any aftermath, and as unique in flavor as the drink itself. Can be drunk straight or diluted with water."[13] It would seem Kennedy was experimenting with the coca leaf just as Coca-Cola had done years earlier. Thus, the source of that extra spark in the drink might actually be a narcotic.

One rare bottle that has survived is for a drink called "Kennedy's PEPP . . . for Particular Palates," evidently a variation on the same theme. The colourful illustration on the label features the same imagery seen in Kennedy's Jazz advertising, namely a South American cowboy on horseback waving a bottle in the air. A woman kneels to the left, mixing up her own concoction; she might just be interested in a drink! The label stated it "contains less than 1/10th of 1% of benzoate of soda," failing to mention anything else.

An imported bottle of Vino Vermouth, from Fratelli Cora in Torino, also bears the name of Joseph Kennedy. An ad for this product in the *Montreal Gazette* explains how the drink can be used:

> What is Genuine Italian Vermouth? An ideal beverage. It has for basis Italian White Wine, flavored with Vermouth root and a small percentage of wormwood. Taken neat as a tonic it is excellent, as an appetizer a success. Blends admirably with sparkling Londonderry water; a few slices of lemons, cracked ice—suggestion of Fernet Branca bitters, a liberal amount of Fratelli Cora Vermouth—the whole making a pure refreshing and wholesome drink called "Cocktail."[14]

Prohibition remained contentious in British Columbia throughout its lifetime. There was the initial inquiry into allegations of fraudulent ballots cast during the 1916 vote by overseas soldiers, followed by opposition from the returning veterans of the great war. There was fallout from prohibition supporters who criticized the many loopholes in the system, saying it didn't go far enough, and there was continued pressure from industrialists and moderationists alike, who insisted that changes needed to be made in the legislation.

Even Joseph Kennedy went to court to test the spirit of the prohibition laws over the sale of his tonics and bitters. Walter Chester "W.C." Findlay, the Prohibition Commissioner for British Columbia, tried to put a ban on the drinks Kennedy was producing, but the commissioner was subsequently sued for damages, and the appeal court ruled in Kennedy's favour in 1918. The powers of the commissioner were reined back, and it was clarified in court that Kennedy's drinks did not, in fact, contravene the "dry" act. It would soon come to light that W.C. Findlay had his own private liquor warehouse on Helmcken Street. He was later arrested and convicted for theft of liquor. Cracks in the prohibition act were running in all directions.

Change eventually came to BC, with the caveat that the sale of liquor must be controlled strictly by government stores. British Columbia repealed prohibition in 1921. More significantly, America was fully engaged in its own form of prohibition by 1920.

The Vancouver city directories reveal that by 1922, Druggists' Sundries Company Limited had a new president. The man now listed in charge was H.G. Eakins, and offices had moved a few doors down to 1164 Homer Street.[15] This was, of course, Harold Gray Eakins, the man who married Kennedy's daughter Aileen. He had followed his father-in-law's footsteps to Vancouver and was promptly listed with the prestigious personal address of 3362 Point Grey Road.

By 1923, the name Druggists' Sundries Company Limited had fallen out of favour. Joseph Kennedy's name instead emerges as the managing director of the

Advertisement from the *Vancouver Star*, dated June 12, 1926, showing the Joseph Kennedy Limited warehouse prominently decorated in oversized painted signage.

Duker and Shaw billboard for Silk Hat Brand Cocktails and Our Best Flour, as seen on the west side of the Gray Building. Does this ghost sign remain buried behind layers of paint and bricks? Gray Building, 1925.
CITY OF VANCOUVER ARCHIVES, CVA BUN289. PHOTOGRAPH BY WILLIAM JOHN ('W.J.') MOORE.

California Wine Company in Henderson's 1923 Greater Vancouver Directory. The revival of this name harkens back to one of Kennedy's earliest employers when he began working as a liquor salesman in Missouri. Robert A. Campbell described the California Wine Company as "an old pickle factory on False Creek" in his paper, "Liquor and Liberals: Patronage and Government Control, 1920–1928." But before long, something caused this nostalgic name choice to sour, and on March 29, 1923, the *Vancouver Daily World* announced that the California Wine Company was changing its name to Joseph Kennedy Limited.

The company address changed as well: they were now listed at 1206 Homer Street, in a building known as the Gray Block. An impressive Yaletown warehouse built in 1912 (and which still stands today), the Gray Block would be the firm's home until 1931. Throughout most of the 1920s, Joseph Kennedy's home address remained at 1119 Nelson Street, a short walk from the Gray Block in Yaletown.

If Druggists' Sundries Company Limited kept a low profile, Joseph Kennedy Ltd. did not—as evidenced by the signage on the Gray Block made up of dramatically large letters painted on all sides of the building. By the mid 1920s, the signs proudly announced to the world "Importers and Exporters Joseph Kennedy Limited," and "Home of the 'Silk Hat' Brand Cocktails." A 1926 advertisement had a few extra floors of text, trumpeting "Importers and Exporters," "Wines and Liquors," "Customs Bonded Warehouse," and "Wine Cellar" in the basement. In reality, they shared the building with Western Cloak & Suit Co. Ltd, Quality Cloak & Suit Ltd, His Masters Voice, Envelope Makers Barber Ellis Ltd, Tuckett Ltd Tobacco, and Pacific Waxed Paper in the basement.

Of all the drinks Joseph Kennedy produced, the most prominent brand name seems to be Silk Hat Cocktails. By the mid-1920s, newspaper ads for Silk Hat Cocktails appeared almost daily. The line of pre-mixed drinks included a Martini, Manhattan, Bourbon, and House of Lords Cocktail. A Martini or Manhattan bottle was priced at just $2.50, less than a bottle of whisky, which might go for $3.00 to $5.00. Eloquence and economics are used to sell drinks here, as this 1926 advertising copy states: "A 100 percent blend of choice European liquors and liqueurs. Deliciously palatable, full strength, satisfying, economical." One of their primary selling points is the price, offering the best value on the shelves:

> "Silk Hat" Cocktails are the result of many years of blending rare and delicious cocktails—they represent an expert blender's crowning success! In palatability, exhilarating and satisfying qualities, they are unsurpassed. They will appeal to both the connoisseur and the man who takes only an occasional drink. Being full strength,

"Silk Hat" Cocktails are an economical drink also; in fact, there is
no better value on the shelves of the Government Liquor Stores.

It may have seemed like the city was being supersaturated in alcohol advertising, but it is possible the target audience was not the local Vancouverite at all. With prohibition in full force in the US, Joseph Kennedy would have been unable to advertise anywhere below the border. Perhaps they were targeting the bootlegging buyer or tourist who would purchase by the caseload and export south. Their greatest competition may well have been a Canadian whisky or beer, but these bottled cocktails were produced with by-product liquors, and therefore could be produced faster and cheaper than conventional hard liquor. Thus, this campaign could be seen as an attempt to shift the taste of the buyer with stylish new drinks, all while undercutting the competition.

If you read between the lines in the *Vancouver Star* advertisement from June 12, 1926, you might begin to see a connection between Kennedy's operation and that of a local liquor legend, Henry Reifel. The top of the ad featured the BC Distillery; separated from that by a thin dividing line, Joseph Kennedy Limited fills the bottom of the page, suggesting a close relationship between the two firms. Veteran Vancouver brewer Henry Reifel had purchased the BC Distillery in New Westminster in 1924, and it would soon become clear that he also had a hand in the affairs of Joseph Kennedy Limited.

Henry (Heinrich) Reifel hailed from the German city of Speyer, not far from Heidelberg, and was just a few years younger than Joseph Kennedy. Reifel received his education in the brewing craft very early, and he was brewing beer in 1879 at just ten years of age. Like many of his generation, he was part of a diaspora of German brewers and brewing schools spread the world over. Reifel worked at the Weinhard Brewery in Portland, Oregon, in 1886, then moved to the Chicago Brewery in San Francisco in 1887.[16]

In 1888 he traveled to British Columbia, and together with his brother and Charles Miller, they started a small operation on Brewery Creek at the corner of East 11th and Westminster Avenue (now Main Street) in Vancouver. Listed in William's 1889 British Columbia Directory as the "San Francisco Brewery," they soon had a handsome new delivery wagon built by Columbia Carriage Works on Hastings Street to deliver their beer.[17]

Alas, their finances were stretched to the limit, and they were forced to relinquish control of this enterprise in March of 1889.[18] Henry sought work at the Victoria Brewery on Vancouver Island before moving on to the city of Nanaimo, another major brewing centre in the province, where he worked for eight years, assisted by his brother Conrad. Henry married, started a family, and then set his sights back on the city of Vancouver again.

In 1906, he set up a bottling plant in Vancouver. Within two years, he was establishing his own firm, the Canadian Brewing & Malting Co. Ltd. The company was incorporated on October 22, 1909, but operations had actually begun in 1908.[19] With Conrad taking charge of the Nanaimo facility, Henry was crafting his very own brewery empire from the ground up, and soon a merger was announced between Henry Reifel and the old guard of brewing in Vancouver.

On February 20, 1911, a holding company called BC Breweries was created to hold the assets of his Canadian Brewing & Malting Co. Ltd., Union Brewing Co. Ltd. in Nanaimo, and Vancouver Breweries Ltd. operated by Charles Doering and John Williams.[20] A few months later, another brewery was added to the collection, the Pilsner Brewing Co. of Cumberland. It was an exciting time to be building a brewing empire, but it was not without risk. A worldwide recession, World War I, and the prohibition movement were all serious threats to the business of alcohol, and any one of them could have put an end to Reifel's ambitions. In spite of the odds, Reifel managed to survive the BC era of prohibition and was poised to take over where he had left off through acquisition, expansion, and export.

By 1927 Joseph Kennedy had reached 65 years of age, and it seems quite plausible that he took retirement, as he is no longer listed in the directories next to Joseph Kennedy Ltd. For the years 1927 and 1928, Oakland Darius ("O.D.") Lampman's name was listed as managing Joseph Kennedy Ltd, Importers & Exporters, though it was becoming clear there were others working behind the scenes at the firm. The timing was significant, as his company name had started to take some heat in the spotlight.

In 1926, a Royal Commission on Customs and Excise was set up largely to investigate the problem of smuggling into the United States. The committee did indeed confirm that " ... widespread inefficiency and laxity was in evidence in the [Department of Customs and Excise]; liquor was smuggled into the United States where prohibition existed; stolen automobiles were smuggled into Canada; and some senior employees of the department were so delinquent in their duties that the report recommended the dismissal of nine of them . . . "[21] Prime Minister William Lyon Mackenzie King nearly lost control of Parliament as a result of the scandal, although it was not directly linked to King.

The name of Joseph Kennedy Ltd appears in the transcripts of hearings from the Royal Customs Commission.[22] Describing the findings of the Royal Customs Commission, Terence Robertson wrote in an unpublished draft of a biography on Samuel Bronfman:

The British Columbia Distillery Company Ltd. owned by the Reiffel [*sic*] brothers in Vancouver came in for particularly harsh treatment by the Commission. After pointing out that the company had made shipments consigned to W.O. Watson of Ensenada, Mexico and to J. Hamilton of San Jose, Guatamala [*sic*], the Commission said: "This Company produced fraudulent landing certificates signed by persons alleged to be a Mexican customs officer and a British Vice-Consul, neither of whom exist. None of these shipments were ever landed at their alleged destinations and it may be presumed that the goods were smuggled into the United States." [...] The criticism spilled over into a subsidiary company called Joseph Kennedy, Ltd., a name that should not be confused with the Kennedy's [*sic*] of Massachusetts. This name was borrowed from a cocktail waiter in a Vancouver bar. The company was accused of selling liquor in bottles to which forged US Revenue stamps were attached.[23]

This Robertson quotation highlights a number of significant points. First, the association with the Reifel family had emerged. When invoking Joseph Kennedy Ltd, Robertson clarifies we are *not* referring to the Kennedy family of Massachusetts. Beyond this, Daniel Joseph Kennedy—a career dealer in liquor whose entrepreneurial imagination made him a wealthy Point Grey patriarch—is relegated to the status of a cocktail waiter in a Vancouver bar. The fact that forged US Revenue stamps were attached to smuggled liquor adds to the scandal, but it was not an allegation that was unique to Joseph Kennedy Ltd. It is safe to say few—if any—exporters were paying duties on liquor during the rum-running era.

In July of 1928, further investigation followed with another Commission of Inquiry chaired by Gordon Clapp Lindsay at the Vancouver Courthouse to investigate and report on the illegal removal of alcohol in bond. A higher than normal grade of grain alcohol from the British Columbia Distillery Company, then owned by the Reifels, seems to have been purchased with side money by the Sunset Vinegar Company (later named the British Columbia Vinegar Company, Limited). The alcohol was supposedly for the production of vinegar, but this type of alcohol was not normally required in vinegar production. Barrels of said alcohol were allegedly diverted and sometimes resold to others such as the Joseph Kennedy Company for a higher price. It all seems terribly complicated and convoluted, especially when the commission's report stated that George Conrad Reifel had been the president of

Joseph Kennedy, Limited, in 1925 and 1926, and his brother Henry Frederick (Harry) Reifel was then the president of Joseph Kennedy Ltd. in 1928. Notably absent from the inquiry was Mr. Daniel Joseph Kennedy himself.

After reading the report from this commission, you might get the impression that Joseph Kennedy Limited was little more than a front or holding company used by the Reifels. To do so would be to discount the legacy of Daniel Joseph Kennedy. Remember, he had a long career in liquor distribution working for some very powerful people in New York. He had built the hotel that gave birth to the town of Shaunavon, Saskatchewan; he planned on opening a chain of fine hotels all along the West Coast; he founded his own Druggists' Sundries Company barely a month after Prohibition started in Saskatchewan, and then took this very same company to Vancouver, where he continued to hone his craft, releasing cocktail after cocktail to a very thirsty market in Canada and the US. The company was not merely a front, though it may have kept a few secrets.

The tale of Canadian alcohol finding its way down to America during prohibition has been told many times. And yes, if there was any doubt, much of the alcohol produced by Joseph Kennedy Limited was likely destined for the US market. In a three-part article called "The Reifel Story," Wendy (Fuchko) Rennison describes the time and place:

> Often referred to as "rum-running," much of the "booze" destined for faraway ports wound up in the hands of Americans who would intercept boats off Seattle, Portland and other coastal cities to buy the forbidden merchandise. As the patrol boats could not possibly be everywhere at once, it became common, if dangerous, practice.
>
> Many producers on this side of the border, among them the Reifels, had a great deal at stake and the Americans conducted the so-called "rum-running" into US ports.
>
> During the late 1920s, George C. [Reifel] became interested in an area of southwest Delta then known as Smoky Tom Island. Close to the mouth of the Fraser River, it was a virtual paradise of bird and wildlife.
>
> As a big game enthusiast, George C. travelled extensively throughout British Columbia and the Yukon on hunting trips, often taking son George [Jr.] along. He recognized the island as an ideal retreat for pursuing his hobby of hunting and preserving game birds. He realized that, with care and management, the area would remain a haven.

In 1927, George C. was in a position to buy a large parcel of land there and over the next few years, he reclaimed a significant amount of land at his own expense.[24]

This area of South Delta today is known as the George C. Reifel Migratory Bird Sanctuary, a natural wildlife oasis that is also one of the great lasting legacies of the Reifel family. Less well known, and a little further inland, closer to the US border, I found traces of the Reifel influence on a small British Columbia community called Crescent Beach.

During the 1920s, the Reifels also acquired some land in Crescent Beach, where they built a recreational summer house at the end of Sullivan Street, overlooking the waterfront. It was a perfect spot to enjoy a weekend getaway and was a popular local retreat for residents of Vancouver and the vicinity. Just a few miles from White Rock, BC, Point Roberts, Washington, and the US border, the location would have also offered strategic advantages for distributing shipments by land or water. While it is virtually undocumented, I can confirm I've spoken with a past resident of the Reifel property, the current owner of the site, and a former neighbour who lived next door, and they all recounted events from the earliest days of the town.

This postcard photograph taken in the late 1920s shows the Reifel's summer home on the waterfront of Crescent Beach. A fire that started in the Crescent Beach Dance Hall destroyed the Reifel home and two others on July 20, 1932. SURREY MUSEUM AND ARCHIVES 2013.0047.02. PHOTOGRAPH BY CHARLES EDGAR STRIDE.

The current owner told me about a dramatic fire that destroyed the Reifel house in the early 1930s and, due to the fact that a large volume of alcohol was likely stored there, it apparently burnt for days. (It did not help that Crescent Beach did not have a fire department until 1949.) Other accounts of Crescent Beach history suggest that many of the locals were involved in bootlegging during those days. And one of those residents recalls how her grandfather, then a neighbour to the Reifels, was recruited to assist with the delivery of certain goods for a Joseph Kennedy.

By the 1930s, the cocktail era had fizzled to an end. The same could be said for Joseph Kennedy Limited, the dissolution of the company occurring in 1931 without much fanfare. American Prohibition was repealed in late 1933, and the Reifels began divesting their brewing and distilling assets. Around the same time a Joseph P. Kennedy of Massachusetts began to acquire his own. Joe Kennedy's Somerset Distributors immediately took advantage of the post-Prohibition market in the US, the fortuitous timing reminiscent of Daniel Joseph Kennedy years earlier in Saskatchewan. While some have tried to associate Joseph P. Kennedy—the father of John F. Kennedy—to Joseph Kennedy Limited and the bootlegging scene, I can't help but wonder if the influence didn't run in the opposite direction. Did Joe Kennedy ever come across one of those bottles with his family name on the label, and if so, did it inspire him to get into the distribution game?

As for our man, Daniel Joseph Kennedy, he appears to have retired in near anonymity in Vancouver. For the last ten years of his life until his death on November 21, 1955, he resided at the same address as his son-in-law Harry at 3003 Point Grey Road. The view from his property would have afforded him picture-perfect sunsets across English Bay, and perhaps that was his due reward. His certificate of death makes no mention of his career in spirits. Instead, it states he was an apartment owner. Daniel Joseph Kennedy, his wife Mary Teresa Hogan, his daughter Aileen Marie Eakins, and his youngest grandson, John Joseph Eakins, are buried at Ocean View Burial Park in Burnaby.

Kennedy's career as an Irish-American liquor salesman saw him travel the continent, from small town USA to the Big Apple. He then showed his pioneering spirit, practically founding a town in Saskatchewan and dreaming of starting a line of high-quality western hotels. The man knew how to make important connections with the powerhouses of the day, from Nathan Straus to Henry Reifel. Most important, he knew how to mix and market a drink; in fact, his uncanny ability to take lemons and make lemon fizz actually solved the paradox of Prohibition for brewers. His story almost vanished through the cracks of history. Sometimes, the smallest artifacts can be gathered together to tell a story. To this sentiment, I raise a glass—to the ghost sign, the antique bottle, the city directory listing, the newspaper ad, all of which bear witness to this story, a testament to history reclaimed.

(ENDNOTES)

1   This story would have been forever lost, were it not for a devout local collector, Neil Whaley, whose initial research inspired me to tell this story. And the story could not have been told so richly without the thorough research assistance I received from: Wendy Thienes and the reference librarians at the Grand Coteau Heritage & Cultural Centre, in Shaunavon, Saskatchewan; Vicki L. Thornton, a reference librarian at the St. Joseph Public Library; and Allison Ward, a graduate student at Queens University who delved into the McMaster University Archives in Hamilton. The lowly city directory was also an invaluable aid. Tracking a common name like "Joseph Kennedy" was made easier by online repositories of census data, death certificates, newspapers, and city directories.

2   David Nasaw, *The Patriarch: The Remarkable Life and Turbulent Times of Joseph P. Kennedy* (Penguin, 2012).

3   While his death certificate in the BC Archives states 1861 and his tombstone states 1863 as his birthdate, the year 1862 was written on his marriage certificate and seems most likely.

4   Town of Shaunavon website, "History," http://www.shaunavon.com/?s-&p-55.

5   Wendy Thienes, *The Shaunavon Standard*, September 17, 2013.

6   *The Shaunavon Standard*, September 18, 1913.

7   *The Shaunavon Standard*, May 6, 1915.

8   Isidor Straus, Nathan's brother, who was a co-owner of Macy's, went down with the *Titanic* in 1912.

9   *The Shaunavon Standard*, June 17, 1915.

10   Bessie Lamb, "The Origin and Development of Vancouver Newspapers" (master's thesis, University of British Columbia), 38.

11   *Vancouver Daily World*, November 22, 1918.

12   http://en.wikipedia.org/wiki/Cocktail.

13   *The Vancouver Daily World*, June 19, 1918.

14   *The Montreal Gazette*, September 8, 1906.

15   Henderson's Greater Vancouver Directory (1922), 635.

16   http://reifeltree.tripod.com/henryanniereifel.html.

17   *Vancouver Daily World*, January 28, 1889, 2.

18   *Vancouver Daily World*, March 12, 1889, 1.

19   Bill Wilson, *Beer Barons of BC* (Lantzville: Tamahi Publications, 2011).

20   Wilson, *Beer Barons*, 59.

21   Archives Canada, CAIN No. 257782 (website), Royal Commission on Customs and Excise fonds [textual record].

22   Douglas L. Hamilton, *Sobering Dilemma: A History of Prohibition in Canada* (Ronsdale Press, 2004); Daniel Okrent, *Last Call: The Rise and Fall of Prohibition* (Scribner, 2011).

23   Terence Robertson, *Bronfman* (unpublished manuscript from the Jack McClelland fonds of the McMaster University Archives, file 10, box 18, 302–04).

24   Wendy (Fuchko) Rennison, "The Reifel Story," *This Month in Delta* magazine, Part 1: June 1983.

THE *OYABUN* AND THE *YŌJIMBŌ*: MORII ETSUJI, RIKIMATSU KINTARO AND THE BLACK DRAGON SOCIETY"

TERRY WATADA

Grandpa was dead. He had been on dialysis for about six months when his body finally gave out. In truth, he really wasn't my grandfather; he was my father's former *bosu* or boss in one of the pre–World War II logging camps on Vancouver Island. Our families were very close—well, we were more like *kerai** while he was lord and master. My father was the foreman of his camp and my mother the cook. We were the retainers. During my 1950s childhood, I was told to call him Grandpa. I took full advantage, since we didn't have any relatives in Canada.

During the war, Grandpa sponsored my family (my mother and my ten-year-old *oniisan*) to a self-sustaining camp called Minto near Lillooet. The only way a Japanese Canadian family could leave Vancouver intact was to provide for themselves. For that they needed money: $1800 in cash allowed anyone to pay for food and shelter in a so-called self-sustaining camp—a huge savings for the government. Otherwise, the father and older sons were separated from the mother, siblings, and grandparents in some cases. Such was our case—my father served on a road gang in the wilderness, while my mother and brother stayed behind in Vancouver. When the order to "evacuate" came down, my mother begged *Bosu* for help. He arranged for them to go to Minto together. He knew his obligation as their employer and lord. There were limitations to his generosity, however. His family lived in a grand cabin with electricity,

*see glossary, page 76

running water, a garden, and a white picket fence. My mother and brother were provided with a miner's shack dragged from some desolate place in the mountains. Each morning, they hauled water from some distance away. Their washroom: the outhouse in back. Light came from candles, heat from a potbelly stove.

After my family was reunited, Grandpa made it possible for all three of them to settle in Toronto. No one was allowed to go back to the West Coast until 1949. He may have felt his obligation to us as master and benefactor, but my family also knew their obligation to Grandpa as a result. Even so, I genuinely loved my grandpa; he was always kind to me.

At the funeral in the Toronto Buddhist Church, clouds of incense—the perfume of ancient temples and congested Japanese cemeteries—filled the *hondō*. My grandpa in his casket seemed at peace as I imagined the wide, toothy, and generous smile he always gave me whenever we saw each other. My aunt, Grandpa's oldest daughter and now head of the family since her mother, Grandma to me, had grown too old to care, was a too-slender yet elegant woman who was reminiscent of a mature Audrey Hepburn. She worked the crowd like the socialite she always wanted to be, until she came to settle in the reception line to greet the mourners.

As I waited to pay my respects, a grizzled old man approached Auntie, more than slightly bent, with balding head and scant grey hair. He tried to comfort her and offered an envelope. *Kōden*, I thought, so *Japanese*. She balked and demurely pushed it away, but he insisted, until she had to take it. He then bowed as best as he could and grabbed hold of his two canes to steady himself before turning away. It was Rikimatsu Kintaro, perhaps Grandpa's oldest friend and consequently my father's as well.

He hobbled down the aisle until he came to me.

"*Botchan*," he greeted. "*Remember me?*"

"*Hai, I do*," I answered in my best rudimentary Japanese.

He coughed and cleared his mucus-clogged throat as he reached into his pocket, pulling out a crumpled five-dollar-bill. "*Here, something for you.*" My father's decrepit friend pushed the tired bill into my hand.

"No, Rik-*san*," I said, switching to English. "That's not necessary." I was thirty years old for crying out loud.

He insisted with a few grunts and an extended hand.

"It's okay. I've got a job now," I said in a joking way.

But he persisted until I took the money. He nodded a satisfied nod and hobbled away, leaving me with the pathetic bill hanging from my hand. My mind flashed to my childhood.

Rikimatsu Kintaro was a scary guy to a seven-year-old or to anyone of any age for that matter. Even as a middle-aged man, his head was skull-like and thin, with wisps of grey hair sprouting on top; his face was dried out and fossilized, jagged, with gouges in his cheeks and—most disturbingly—no nose. The surviving nostrils were much wider than normal and barely supported by cartilage, callused skin and not much else. He chewed and growled words, his voice full of razor blades and dust. I never wanted to go near him, but he was my father's good friend and dinner guest from time to time. He always offered me a five-dollar bill, perhaps as a salve for his frightening presence. I was attracted by the money of course, but my mother frowned as I looked back and forth from Rik-*san* to her. I knew I shouldn't have, but he insisted, and so I snatched it, running away to his laughter. I once overheard my mother complaining to my father, "I don't want to be obligated to that man." Dad just waved her off.

When I saw Rik-*san* at the funeral shuffling away from me like a ghost blending into the smoky haze of Buddhistic incense, I realized I knew precious little about the man. What kept all these men of the *Issei* generation together: friendly, hospitable, and loyal to one another? I understood my family's obligation to Grandpa, but what was the hold that kept everyone else together? I decided to investigate, first by asking Dad.

Now, my father was generally a quiet man, with compassionate eyes for his sons and a sense of humour for his friends. When I was a kid, he often held court at a dinner table full of the aforementioned *Issei* men from his long-ago BC past with a few shots of Canadian Club whisky in him and them. The women stayed in the living room solemnly conversing until dinner. My mom prepared the rice and several Japanese dishes and had me order some Chinese food—Cantonese chow mein, barbecue pork and tofu, and maybe some sweet and sour for me.

It was soon after Grandpa's passing that I faced Dad to ask about the enigmatic Rikimatsu. We sat in the living room; Mom was in an upstairs bedroom in front of the *butsudan* offering incense while chanting for the dead. The aroma permeated and her mumbling echoed throughout the house at the same time of day, every day—my daily reminder of her religious devotion.

Normally Dad wouldn't have said anything, calling me a *baka* to end the enquiry, but he was feeling no pain that evening, anesthetized by the whisky. Alcohol swirled with the memory of lost friends, so my timing was good.

He first told me Rik-*san* was a *yōjimbō* and gangster in the infamous Black Dragon Society. Well, he sure looked the part. Surprised as I was, what my father then revealed started me on a long journey that included a little library research and interviews with the elders of my community in Toronto and in Vancouver.

RIKIMATSU KINTARO AND THE BLACK DRAGON SOCIETY

No one, not even Dad, let on what they knew about the *yōjimbō*. What they did reveal came from the drink-and-card-game sessions that Rik-*san* attended at Grandpa's house both after and, I presume, before World War II. Little did I know there was so much more to the sinister bodyguard.

First of all Rikimatsu Kintaro had two first names—probably to disguise his identity. He spoke Japanese, Chinese, and Korean. So no one knew with absolute certainty his ethnicity, where he called home, his birth date, or his true full name, but Dad did have a wonderful bit of gossip. Rik-*san* apparently was born so ugly his parents didn't want him, though they felt obligated to raise him. Years later, he was left standing at the altar since his arranged bride couldn't stand the thought of being with him for the rest of her life.

With such a body blow to his self-esteem, he became a ne'er-do-well as a gambler, jewel smuggler, and a sailor in the merchant marine. He had no education as far as I could tell (then again, my dad had only grade 6, my mom grade 8, in Japan), but he once bragged at our dinner table that he had sailed all seven seas. On one of those voyages, his ship stopped in Vancouver Harbour. He liked the look of the place so much he jumped ship.

Contrary to that story (and much more likely), elders at the Toronto Buddhist Church disclosed that Rik-*san* landed in San Francisco and became involved with the Black Dragon Society, which controlled the criminal activity in Little Tokyo. It must have seemed a natural fit.

The Society grew out of the *Yakuza* criminal organization in Japan. In 1877, the last of the *Shōgun samurai* battled the Imperial forces in the southern province of Kagoshima to protest the Meiji Restoration. Once defeated, the *samurai* became masterless and destitute wanderers, known as *rōnin*. In order to survive, they eventually turned to crime as the vast and mainly disorganized *Yakuza*. Eventually, some subset of *Yakuza* formally came together as the Dark Ocean Society, which decided to profess loyalty to the Emperor, adhering once again to their *Bushidō* roots.

From the Dark Ocean Society, many other societies based on an ultra-nationalistic fervour then came into being: the *Sokoku-kai* [Fatherland Society], the Fatherland Protection Corps, and the Black Dragon Society, to name three. The groups, though criminal in nature, were dedicated to fighting against what they considered to be the corruption and disregard of traditional Japanese values. Some even vowed to expand Japanese influence abroad and establish authoritarian rule at home.

They bullied citizens at local voting stations to cast ballots their way, they assassinated politicians who didn't cooperate (notably, Queen Min of Korea in 1895, and the prime minister of Japan in 1930), and they brought about change in other countries. All the while *Yakuza* splinter groups filled their coffers through prostitution, gambling, and alcohol while extending their reach to the West Coast of North America.

It was into this milieu in California that Rikimatsu Kintaro fell. He soon became the muscle for the Black Dragon Society in San Francisco. And as a soldier, he met Morii Etsuji, a 17-year-old prospect for the gang circa 1900. One day, the two stood before the *Oyabun* (a *Yakuza* boss or, literally and according to traditional Japanese hierarchical structure, a foster parent) at the Dragon headquarters at the corner of Laguna and Post, opposite the Northern California Buddhist Church. The office was on the fourth floor with a high ceiling and tall windows.

I imagine both Rikimatsu and Morii were intimidated by the meeting. The room was filled with tough-looking men, half-lit with a few missing digits. The *Oyabun* himself featured a long scar that started at the top of his neck, descending underneath his collar and ending in parts unknown.

It turned out to be a propitious occasion. Morii Etsuji had impressed the gang with a new initiative. Accompanied by Rik-*san*, he'd gone into the Chinatown gambling dens, risking severe beatings, torture, and maybe even death, looking for Japanese gamblers. Once he found one, he, Rikimatsu, or both pulled the target aside to convince him to return to Little Tokyo and the Black Dragon dens, in particular the *Naniwa-ya*, the *Oyabun's* personal favourite. It had been calculated that the Black Dragons were annually losing $150,000 in income up and down the west coast to the Chinatown establishments. Morii and Rik-*san* went some way to bringing back the money.

The Bay Area *Oyabun* rewarded the two for their ingenuity and diligence by giving them more and more responsibility. One such duty was guarding Black Dragon gambling dens. Both men stood watch one night when the police crashed through the door and ordered everyone to freeze. Of course no one did, and during the mêlée the young Morii stabbed a police officer to death. Rikimatsu made sure his young friend escaped.

In order to protect both men, the Bay Area *Oyabun* smuggled them away to Canada. The *Oyabun* knew the Vancouver operation had slowed to producing almost nothing. Reports had it that Shiga Mitsuzo, the local boss, had grown fat, lazy, and indifferent to his duties, content in finding pleasure for himself in wine, women, and gambling. So the Bay Area *Oyabun* thought that Morii and Rik-*san* would shake things up and he could save one or both of them from the gallows in California, killing two birds with one stone, as it were.

In the spring of 1906, the two arrived in Vancouver. They immediately went to the *Raku Raku*, a sad storefront restaurant on Gore Avenue with windows blinded by curtains and no identifying signs outside. Inside they found a deeply dark room with only one table occupied. An obese Shiga Mitsuzo and two of his thugs were playing cards (probably poker or *pokka*). It must have seemed like a gloomy wake, with shadows huddled around an aces and eights dead-man's-hand. After some discussion and a few well-placed kicks and slugs to the head, Morii, a black belt in judo, and Rik-*san* put the hapless gangsters in their place. Morii then declared he was going to oversee operations on behalf of his Bay Area *Oyabun*. The two "Pros from Dover," as a *Nisei* dubbed them, fell into their roles naturally: Morii the new young hotshot *Oyabun*, and Rikimatsu the *yōjimbō*. Shiga receded into the background. Surprisingly, he didn't mind.

OPERATIONS—SCHEMES AND SCAMS

After taking over, Morii hired a local carpenter, his name lost in the drift of time, to renovate the *Raku Raku*. He put in booths, a black-and-white checkerboard floor, and a working kitchen. Though the place was a drinking establishment with gambling in the back rooms, the *Oyabun* initially thought to make the *Raku Raku* a family place on Saturday nights. Inevitably, its gambling and then prostitution operation soon took precedence, and families went elsewhere.

The first real challenge to Morii and Rikimatsu came in late 1907. Sikh workers in Bellingham, Washington, were driven out of town by white workers who feared for their jobs and hated foreigners. The refugees headed for Canada since they claimed to be British subjects. Catalyzed by this "new" invasion, the Asiatic Exclusion League (AEL) rallied to protest the "Oriental Threat." The AEL was first formed in 1905 in San Francisco to prevent "Oriental" immigration. The Canadian sister organization came about in August 1907 under the auspices of the Vancouver Trades and Labour Council. Its aim was to "keep Orientals out of British Columbia." A month later, the AEL first laid waste to Chinatown and then headed for the Japanese section of Vancouver known simply as Powell Street.

Morii had been keeping tabs on the agitation and so made preparations. Rik-*san* too was ready. He bought a Japanese sword at a local department store. "It was so dull it couldn't cut butter," a witness claimed. But it was effective as a club.

As the rioters moved into the Japanese sector, they encountered blockades on three sides of the intersection at Westminster (Main Street today) and Powell Streets. Once stopped, a rain of bottles, bricks, stones, and lumber came down from rooftops. Rik-*san* waited, then led a charge of men from three sides, with sword raised on high. The riot was soon quelled, and the white men limped back to the union halls downtown.

Unfortunately for Rik-*san*, he was the only one arrested for his part in the riot. He was quite embarrassed as he paid the ten-dollar fine. On the other hand, Morii Etsuji had planned the defence well and proved himself a leader and protector of the community.

Returning to business, the two Black Dragons went on to establish the *Shōwa* Club, a private gambling hall, upstairs at 382 Powell Street. The same carpenter who renovated the *Raku Raku* was given the task of equipping the club with "special features." According to members of the Vancouver Buddhist Church, he did a superb job, with false walls that could hide gambling tables and significant guests who didn't want to be arrested as found-ins. The bar was hidden by a removable cover; the bottles of booze and excess money went beneath floorboards via trap doors. The carpenter also installed a signal system so a watchman sitting in a vestibule at the foot of the stairs that led to the second-floor establishment could signal upstairs. Whenever he spied the police coming to raid the place, he pushed the button to issue a warning that put everything in motion.

The Oyabun and his *yōjimbō* had learned a valuable lesson in that San Francisco Black Dragon gambling den. They were determined not to be caught unawares ever again.

Unfortunately, a problem arose. The carpenter, being proud of his work, bragged about it loudly in public. He soon became a liability, and so Rik-*san* got rid of him. Some claimed he kidnapped him on Morii's orders and placed him on a boat back to Japan. Others said he quietly beat and killed him, took his body up to the lime pits north of the city, and buried him there to get rid of the corpse. One Toronto *Nisei* swore he ran into the Carpenter (his name for him) in one of the internment camps and asked what had happened. The man said he had been deported to Japan to be punished, and it took him nearly 20 years to get back to his family in Vancouver— only to end up labelled an enemy alien and exiled again. In any case, the Carpenter's family was purportedly taken care of with money from the Black Dragon Society.

Rik-*san's* primary job was as it had been in San Francisco: go into the Chinatown clubs to spot Japanese patrons and persuade them by hook or by crook to come back to Powell Street. "You know the dealers cheat. Look at the *fan tan* dealer. Watch his hands. Don't give your money to the *Chankoro*. Come back to the *Shōwa* Club. We won't let your family suffer if you lose your savings."

What gave him away was anyone's guess; after all, he could have passed for Chinese and he could speak *Toisan*, but as my dad told it, the tongs found him out and took him out to a back alley. He was a tough guy but he was outnumbered. They overwhelmed him, beat him, and forced him to kneel before the Chinese bosses. One pulled out a knife and sliced his nose off without hesitation, without conscience. They continued to beat him afterwards. When they finished, the tong took Rik-*san* away. His broken body was later found, bleeding and unconscious, in the alley beside the Franciscan Sisters of Atonement Convent on Dunlevy Avenue. The Chinese were probably sending a message.

Nearly a year later, after Rikimatsu had recovered sufficiently, Morii *Oyabun* ordered his *yōjimbō* to approach the owner of the Murasaki Café near Main Street on Powell to extort "insurance" money, a relatively new scheme in the mid-1930s. When the owner rebuffed the *yōjimbō*, Rik-*san* came back later with several recruits from the local judo club. As spokesman, Rik-*san* demanded the money and ordered his men to break up the place and beat the owner to a pulp. The *yōjimbō*, after it was all over, supposedly laughed and said, "See, you need insurance." Rik-*san* then gave him 24 hours to get out, lock, stock, and barrel. The owner was gone in less than 12.

What the *Oyabun* wanted the place for was a mystery to Rikimatsu (and everyone else for that matter). Morii promptly turned around and gave the place to the Vancouver Buddhist Church. "What use do I have with an empty store?" he said. He told the board of directors that he bought the place from the Murasaki family so that the old man could retire. They believed him, or wanted to believe. He also paid a visit to the senior Murasaki while he was laid up in the hospital; the *Oyabun* slipped a rather large packet of money to the man's suffering wife, who sat silently and dutifully bedside.

MORII ETSUJI AND THE BLACK DRAGON SOCIETY

Everyone I talked to about the diminutive five-foot-four-inch *Oyabun* spoke in hushed and fearful tones, even my father. One senior at the Toronto church asked why I wanted to know such things. I explained that I wanted to write an article for one of the Japanese Canadian community newspapers. His face contorted with great concern and he warned me that if I did, I would receive threats, maybe even death threats (though Morii was rumoured to have died as long ago as 1970). "Who would threaten me?" I asked. All the old gang members, apparently. I had to ask, "How old are these men?"

"In their 80s."

I smirked and said, "Don't worry. I think I can outrun them."

But worried he was, as was everyone else I approached. Some didn't want to say anything for fear of reprisal. What kind of man could command so much fear—and loyalty, for that matter—after so many years and even beyond the grave? I intensified my inquiries.

Morii Etsuji was reputedly from Hiroshima, though I couldn't confirm it without making a long, expensive trip there and bothering many officials who I know didn't want to be bothered. And then there was the language and the fact that I was Canadian, a *gaijin*. In any case, I discovered during my inquiries the surprising fact that the *Oyabun* had an interest in socialism as a teenager. Owing to his youth and the times,

I reasoned it was quite possible. Everyone, according to my research among the library stacks, was reading Kōtoku Shōsui, a popular socialist, in the *Heimin Shimbun* (the *Commoner's Newspaper*). Because of his interest and natural leadership abilities, Etsuji allegedly led a student demonstration against the coming war with Russia in 1904.

The former *Shōwa* Club bartender, Akiyama Kichitaro, often told the story around the Toronto Buddhist Church of Rikimatsu sitting in the club drunk as a pious man on a bender blubbering about Morii's days as a student radical.

"The little bastard protested against the Russian war," Rik-*san* snarled. "Why should he give a damn what governments do? He probably shouted something like—'There are no distinctions of race, religion or nationality'—like his *ketsu-no ana* hero Kōtoku. 'Russia's enemy is not the Japanese people, but it's the so-called patriotism and militarism of today!'" Rik-*san* mocked.

Akiyama swore the *yōjimbō* faded at that point: either the alcohol had conquered his consciousness or he realized that he had revealed too much.

Whatever Morii shouted in the demo, it ended badly. The protest erupted into violence when the police overreacted. Morii barely escaped the ensuing riot. Having become a hunted man, he turned to his father, Morii Yoshitaro.

Rikimatsu held Yoshitaro in high esteem, describing his friend's father as a man of compassion. Yoshitaro called in many favours and managed to enrol his son in the Japanese government's *shosei* (student) program. Etsuji soon found himself on a boat headed for the USA to study at the newly established University of Portland. He was accompanied by Matsuoka Yōsuke, a diplomat's son and future negotiator for the Axis Alliance on Japan's behalf.

There are other—less romantic—versions of the story. A former Powell Street baker still living in Vancouver claimed the Morii family were impoverished farmers

Black Dragon Clipping.
VANCOUVER SUN, NOVEMBER 13, 1942.

under the control of the Matsuoka clan. They were *kerai* under the Lord and Master Matsuoka. When a scandal broke out about the patriarch, the loyal Yoshitaro took the blame. As a reward, the lord sent Etsuji to America for an education.

And then there was the gambling-den story. Around the Vancouver community, Etsuji was said to have been a Black Dragon operative in Japan all along. Gossip held that he was a watchman for a Dragon gambling den in Hiroshima and not Northern California when the police staged a raid. In the mêlée, Etsuji grappled with a police officer who wanted to arrest him as a found-in. The teenager fought back, and when the dust settled, the teenager was standing over the constable with a bloody knife in his hand. Etsuji had to run, so his Black Dragon *Oyabun* sent him to the society's operations in San Francisco. The story was all conjecture but it does indicate all the contradictions and mysteries surrounding the enigmatic Morii.

In all likelihood, Etsuji attended the University of Portland under Matsuoka's sponsorship. Unfortunately, the young man was not one for scholarly pursuits and soon fell in with a student men's club turned political called the *Seinen Kai*, which took him to San Francisco, the group's headquarters. The group's avowed purpose was to protect Japanese citizens from any government oppression, American or Japanese. In his best-known scheme, Etsuji allegedly blackmailed the consul general of Japan to help a Japanese youth get out of jail. The young perpetrator had hit a police officer and so landed in custody. Etsuji simply started a rumour that the consul liked little boys. That did the trick; gossip was a powerful tool.

Rikimatsu, in his cynicism, was once overheard saying his friend did not do it for money. He didn't want property. He didn't want to be rewarded with position. He just wanted the family to be obligated to him. A lesson for the future, no doubt.

The blackmail brought Morii to the attention of the Black Dragon Society, which operated extensively in the Bay Area at the time. The Dragons did not like the *Seinen Kai*—too disloyal to the Emperor—and so decided to take in promising recruits from the organization. It was believed that giving them money and status would induce them to adhere to Black Dragon principles. The potential members really had no choice. Join—or get beaten to a pulp and then suffer deportation.

Morii Etsuji as it turned out was not so much a man of principle as he was a pragmatist. He knew he would be on the next boat to Japan if he didn't cooperate. What may have appealed to him, given his socialist roots, was the main tenet of the Black Dragons: to take care of the Japanese community and citizens of their constituency. So he became a member of the Black Dragon Society.

The short young man quickly excelled in the organization. Besides his extortion schemes, he came up with the Chinatown gambling den idea. The police raid triggered his flight to Vancouver.

The story of Shiga Mitsuzo, the Vancouver *Oyabun*, did not end with the arrival of Morii and Rikimatsu, the Pros from Dover. If Morii's origins were a mystery, then Shiga's rivalled the Pyramids of Giza. A short, squat man who didn't wear his excesses well, Shiga Mitsuzo was a professional gambler. His age, what province of Japan he came from, or the events of his formative years were anyone's guess. There weren't even any rumours. Perhaps there were good reasons for that.

What is known is that he grew to like the upstart Morii. He saw great value in a new *Oyabun*, young and brash though he may be. Shiga *Oyabun* hated the community obligations that were his duty as head of the Black Dragon Society; he preferred the racetrack or the card games played after dark. His young charge—the new, public *Oyabun* (under him of course)—gradually took over the mundane public appearances, while he pursued his vices.

Morii for his part loved showing up at the Buddhist Church bazaar, the summer *Obon* festival and other community events. He greeted the people as they paid him tribute. In turn, he issued orders for the betterment of the people. He bestowed favours in exchange for an obligation to him. Thus he became the face of the organization and came to be known as the Vancouver *Oyabun*.

Morii Etsuji.
PHOTO COURTESY OF THE NIKKEI NATIONAL MUSEUM & CULTURAL CENTRE, NNM 2011.64.1.29.

What the young *Oyabun* didn't appreciate was Shiga's disregard of the Black Dragon mandate to take care of the Japanese in his charge. But Morii's sense of obligation was still to his sponsor and *bosu* and so he cooperated. A community group once asked permission of Morii to stage a charity concert by bringing a well-known singer from Japan. Morii in turn asked his boss. Shiga *Oyabun* granted his blessing as long as he got his cut (as much as 20 percent I was told). When Morii complained that it was for charity, Shiga said he didn't care what it was for, he just wanted the money. "It's your fatal flaw," Shiga observed, "and it'll be your downfall." Charity may have been Morii's weakness, but he held to the two paradoxical sides of his character until World War II changed him.

OPERATIONS—SCHEMES AND SCAMS

After arriving and in·order to solidify his position, Morii Etsuji renovated the *Raku Raku* and declared it open for business. Once the place moved into prostitution, he moved the operation to the second floor of 362 Alexander Street, in the Klondike-era red light district, and renamed it the *Nippon* Club. He brought in women from Japan through his Black Dragon connections in San Francisco. He took their passports to ensure cooperation and threatened to turn them over to the RCMP if they proved uncooperative. He could also send them back to Japan for Black Dragon punishment. They worked for him in various capacities: as waitresses, hostesses, and prostitutes or "wives," as my father called them. After a while, the *Oyabun* came up with a scheme to make the business more cost-effective.

He convinced certain of the wealthy to sponsor a woman by paying for her papers, travel, and living expenses once she landed. She in turn would work at the club while catering to her sponsor's every wish and whim. Morii made all the connections and made sure the woman was "friendly" to the patron.

I learned the nitty-gritty of the operation when I overheard my parents talking about Grandpa, my dad's former boss, begging forgiveness of his wife while on his deathbed. I later asked my mother for details, but she rebuffed me as usual. It took some time, but I finally caught my father in an amenable mood again, and he told me the story. One day, sometime in the 1930s, his best friend, the lumber company's timekeeper and accountant, came to him as foreman about a mystery: $100,000 was missing. That was a huge amount of money. So they investigated. They eventually found out that the boss, my grandpa, had emptied the account to pay Morii for ten "mistresses" over the years. Ten! The man was stronger than I thought.

Wives, apparently, tolerated adultery as long as no scandal erupted. But such was not the case with Grandpa. Many days he would be seen coming home in the afternoon drunk as a whisky priest, pontificating to the heavens while stumbling over street debris. The neighbours smiled knowingly; Grandma, however, was not amused and so grabbed him by the hair and dragged him to the middle of the street where she kicked, spat at, and beat him where he lay. He did not fight back, probably feeling he deserved the humiliation. There was no telling if she ever forgave him, deathbed repentance or not.

At least, I finally learned the nature of Grandpa's connection to Morii and Rikimatsu—and, by extension, my father's, though he did not indulge in the practice. It was not for him: too expensive, embarrassing, and morally reprehensible.

Morii himself did not "touch" any of these women, according to all reports. He was just their boss and, in fact, a devoted husband. In 1910, he left for Japan and came back a couple of months later sporting a bride on his arm. Morii-*no okusan* was tall, a good six inches taller than her husband and even taller with high heels. She was deemed a handsome woman. They must have been quite a sight walking down Powell Street on a weekend shopping excursion. It was rumoured her maiden name was Matsuoka, the same as Morii's family sponsor. Her imperious air and haughty demeanour added credence to the rumour.

View of 300 block of Powell Street looking west. Morii Etsuji set up the Shōwa Club at 382 Powell Street.
PHOTOGRAPH COURTESY OF JAPANESE CANADIAN CULTURAL CENTRE.

The 1907 Riots loomed largely in Morii's legend. He proved his leadership skills that day. He recruited members of various judo clubs in the area (he was a first *dan* black belt at the time). He called together all the available workers in the area and devised a plan to trap the oncoming mob at the intersection of Westminster and Powell. He stood on a building-roof vantage point ready to signal the men gathered on the surrounding rooftops to begin the attack. Rik-*san* was placed in charge of the ground troops. Once the mêlée began, the mob had no idea what hit them and were soon vanquished.

Afterwards, he set up patrols to make sure the streets were safe, especially at night. Of course, such protection came at a price. Even if no further incidents occurred in the following months, Morii still demanded that the "insurance" continue and did so for many years.

The *Oyabun* expanded his empire during the ten years after World War I by establishing the Shōwa Club. In a self-published autobiography, an Issei described three social clubs in the Powell Street area: the *Toyo*, *Momiji*, and *Shintani* Clubs. Each was a gathering spot for working men who could talk, drink, play some pool, and gamble in the back rooms. By means foul or fair, Morii steadily acquired the three places. He closed down two and then converted the *Momiji* (the largest) into what would become the Shōwa Club (commemorating the new Emperor Hirohito). As stated earlier, the Carpenter was hired to perform his magic. The place opened in 1926 in the 300 block of Powell Street.

By 1925, the *Oyabun* had successfully consolidated his power and controlled all the illegal and some legal activities in the Powell Street area, using recruits from the judo clubs as enforcers. He actually built a dormitory for Japanese immigrants within the *Nippon* Club building and even installed an English-language school there. He paid off the police and RCMP with "boxes of chocolates" (chocolate boxes full of money). And he established the *Nihon Jinkai*, the Japanese Businessmen's Association—all in an effort to "protect" his constituents, the Japanese in Canada.

Thus his activities became common knowledge, although he was very careful to cover his tracks. Nothing could ever be proved against him by the authorities. Until, that is, a 17-year-old boy confronted him about his father's gambling debts.

The teenager faced the *Oyabun* in the *Nippon* Club office upstairs at the back of the building at 362 Alexander Street, from where he also controlled his *Nihon Jinkai*. Other than a desk and a couple of chairs, the room was bare. Only a huge *Hinomaru* decorated the walls. The boy was there for one reason only: to get his father's debt forgiven. Harsh words were exchanged, and the boy took flight, with Morii giving chase. The *Oyabun* caught up to the boy on the street just a short distance away from his office building, and a fight ensued. Morii with his judo expertise flipped the boy, who consequently broke his neck upon landing. He died instantly.

Morii was arrested and charged with murder. Witnesses were found, and the trial was set. Only trouble was, the principal witness disappeared by the trial date. Perhaps he was on a boat to Japan; perhaps he was buried in the lime pits to the north of the city. No one ever knew. It is a matter of public record that Morii was convicted of manslaughter and put on a year's probation. He killed a boy in broad daylight and beat the rap.

The Friday, November 13, 1942, edition of the *Vancouver Sun* characterized Morii Etsuji as the "Al Capone of the Japanese community," and indeed, by that point, he and Rikimatsu Kintaro controlled the Powell Street area and had prospered until the outbreak of World War II. Their influence spread throughout the Japanese communities across the province. The *Nihon Jinkai*, representing more than 20 Japanese businesses, proved an excellent vehicle for control. Even with war, Morii's power was not quelled.

For some unknown reason, the Federal Government appointed the *Oyabun* chair of the Japanese Liaison Committee in March 1942. This organization acted as liaison between the BC Security Commission and the Japanese communities in BC. The appointment was rather curious, since Morii was suspected of supporting Japan's interests in China, one of Canada's allies. He allegedly led funding drives for clothing and food packages for Japanese soldiers. And then there was the manslaughter conviction, which must have been difficult to ignore. Frederick J. Mead, head of the BC Security Commission, dismissed the man's unsavoury past by calling it "inconsequential." He also defended Morii's appointment by stating that the *Oyabun* was a "prominent member of the community."

Reaction from BC politicians, especially at Vancouver City Hall, must have been swift and vociferous. Alderman Halford Wilson, known for his vitriolic attacks against the Japanese and Japanese Canadians in BC, could be heard railing long and hard in council meetings against the appointment. It is interesting to note that an unconfirmed rumour persists to this day about the two men. The *Oyabun* and the racist councilman allegedly made a deal of some kind before Pearl Harbor. Wilson led a raid on the Canadian Japanese Association offices (a Morii-led organization), looking for contraband. Despite finding nothing, the raid enhanced Wilson's reputation as a defender of the white population and it enabled Morii to throw a scare into the *Nisei* upstarts who were beginning to take over what was also known as the Japanese Businessmen's Association (the *Nihon Jinkai*).

Morii and his men excelled in their roles within the commission by carrying through (often using brutality to gain cooperation) on the promise to round up as many national Japanese as possible, including Rik-*san*. The *Oyabun* betrayed his own *yōjimbō* to get an ideal situation for himself in the evacuation. Sometime later, Morii arranged entrance for his former friend to Tashme, an internment camp set up specifically for Morii's men. The act did not quell Rikimatsu's bitterness over the betrayal.

Of course, the Japanese Liaison Committee under Morii's leadership became rife with corruption. Many approached the *Oyabun* either to get a deferment of evacuation or special dispensation to evacuate as a family group. Evacuees recall that a likely candidate had first to pay a bribe (about $50) to a key Morii gang member just to gain an audience with the chairman. The supplicant then might be granted a request if he donated $300 or more to a charity fund for families in trouble. Not many could afford such exorbitant prices.

Again, the *Oyabun* proved himself fickle in his pronouncements and behaviour. To some he granted the request without a bribe. Others, he rejected outright. The two sides of his personality were on full display during this period.

His methods for expediting the evacuation proved too slow for the Security Commission, and so it closed down Morii's operations within a few months. For his efforts, however, Morii Etsuji was given Minto, a self-sustaining camp near Lillooet, the place my family went as arranged by Grandpa. The *Oyabun* didn't go to Tashme with his men, probably because he saw the writing on the wall; he knew his gangster days were over.

Morii, his wife, and his handpicked allies settled into cabins with running water, electricity, and indoor plumbing. He even brought an employee, one of his hostesses. He must have pitied her for some unknown reason. My father told me she could be heard constantly weeping in her cabin. She never stepped outside.

Minto, an abandoned mining town, soon came alive with a revived hotel, a general store, and a schoolhouse. For some reason, Morii became religious in camp and built a miniature shrine. As the story went, after the funeral of a Japanese worker, a mysterious fireball—a *hinotama*—rose in the dark, flew across the sky and fell on Morii's roof, setting the cabin ablaze. The spirit of the man appeared before Morii as a flaming demon. The *Oyabun* barely escaped with his life. Unfortunately, his charity-case employee did not. Some claim she committed suicide, since she had plenty of time to get out. Once safe and recovered from his ordeal, the *Oyabun* turned to religion.

After the war and the West Coast restriction was lifted, Morii returned to Vancouver. A decade later when his wife died circa 1960, he took her ashes to Japan. He lived there in the land of his birth and ancestors, no longer involved with the Black Dragons, until his death around 1970.

Rik-*san* migrated to Toronto, where he looked up his old friends (like my grandpa and father) and pursued his vices in Chinatown until his own death in the 1980s. I, of course, went to the funeral. He didn't look menacing in his coffin. Perhaps, like my grandpa, he was at peace with himself. Finally, after so many tumultuous years as a gangster and gambler, Rikimatsu Kintaro could rest for all eternity.

My aunt presided. She later told me that Rik-*san's* envelope at Grandpa's funeral contained $1000 and a last request. He asked my aunt to use the money to pay for his funeral. She resisted but soon relented, feeling some kind of obligation because of her father. Obligation. Such a Japanese and Japanese Canadian trait.

What surprised me most was an elderly *Nisei* who gave the eulogy. He stated that Rik-*san* "saved his life." Apparently, Rik-*san* was in a basement gambling den in Toronto's Chinatown back in the 1950s when he spied a young man who clearly was out of his depth. He also knew his family. He grabbed the young man, whom he considered to be just a boy, by the scruff of the neck and pulled him out of the place.

Once outside, Rikimatsu scolded the boy for being in such a place. The *Nisei* said as an explanation, "I got no job, no wife, no future. So why shouldn't I gamble?"

Rik-*san* harrumphed and told the boy to go home. The former *yōjimbō* looked fearsome enough to ensure the boy's cooperation. He went home with his tail between his legs. In the next few weeks, he got word that a job was waiting for him in a garment factory. Shortly thereafter, he met a single *Nisei* gal from a reputable family, arranged through Rikimatsu with the girl's father's permission. They dated and eventually married. The man now had a future.

At the funeral, the *Nisei* man bid farewell to his benefactor and expressed his undying gratitude. "I owe him my life," he said, with tears and a great deal of affection. I finally understood: obligation inspires loyalty—loyalty to the end, in Rikimatsu's case. I stood and marvelled at the conflicting sides of not only my father's friend and the whole Black Dragon Society but also of the Japanese Canadian pioneer generation.

GLOSSARY

Baka	idiot
Botchan	term of affection for a boy
Bushidō	way of the samurai, loyalty
Butsudan	family altar
Chankoro	the Chinese (pejorative)
Dan	· marital arts rank
Gaijin	foreigner
Hai	yes
Hinomaru	Japanese flag
Hinotama	fire ball, said to be the souls of the dead
Hondō	main hall of a temple
Issei	first generation of Japanese Canadians
Kerai	retainers, servants
Kōden	funeral money given to help defray costs
Naniwa	former name of Osaka, Japan
Nisei	second generation of Japanese Canadians
Obon	Buddhist festival of the dead
Okusan	wife
Oniisan	oldest brother
Oyabun	boss
Raku Raku	easy, comfortable
Rōnin	masterless samurai
Seinen kai	young men's club
Self Sustaining camp	camp for evacuees with $1800 to fend for themselves as a family
Shōgun	general
Shosei	student
Shōwa era	1926–1989
Toisan	Chinese dialect common to early immigrants to North America
Yōjimbō	bodyguard

1   ' "The *Oyabun* and the *Yōjimbō*" is dedicated to the memory of my loving father, Matsujiro Watada, and to Rikimatsu, who scared the living Buddhist out of me.

2   Despite his laziness, Shiga did get one thing right—the alcohol. The Alien Labour Act of 1897 prevented Japanese from obtaining licences to buy and sell booze to the public. So Shiga, adhering to Black Dragon methodology, "persuaded" nearby farmers to set up stills and breweries to provide alcohol for his gambling operations.

THE EYES OF LUCILLE MARS

JAMES C. JOHNSTONE

I am what is called a "house historian." What interests me is not just the bricks and mortar (although I'm especially keen on bricks). It's the people who made those houses their homes. There are close to 300 houses in the old East End that I have studied. I rely heavily on the old, crumbling city directories at the City of Vancouver Archives to catch a glimpse of the people who made up a neighbourhood. From time to time and through a combination of hard digging and sheer luck I have been able to track down descendants of the people who lived there. Much more rarely, I get to meet someone who knew the oldest neighbourhood in Vancouver when it was still young. When that happens, I have an opportunity to see these houses, homes, and little corner shops as a threaded pattern of relationships. I am fortunate to have had the chance to see the East End through the eyes of Lucille Mars.

The old East End—which includes everything from Clark Drive west to China-town and from the Waterfront south to the rail yards—has been a story of succes-sions. From early on, one wave of immigrants replaced the last. The first residents of the nineteenth century neighbourhood were mostly of British heritage. They were replaced by newcomers from Italy, Norway, Sweden, and Finland; Jews fleeing pogroms and persecution in Eastern Europe; refugees piling in from revolution-torn Russia and the fragmenting husk of the Austro-Hungarian Empire. There were also many arrivals from China and Japan, as well as Blacks from the United States who came looking for a better life. There were even a number of Christian Arab families fleeing sectarian strife in the Ottoman Empire who settled in what was then Vancouver's affordable, working-class East End. For decades this was a changing patchwork of ethnic enclaves. Prior and Union Streets were largely Italian. Sections of East Georgia were at times predominantly Jewish. Vancouver's first Little Italy, Japan-town, Chinatown, and the largely Black area known as Hogan's Alley were all part of Vancouver's East End. All this, crammed into an area less than a square kilometre.

There were lots of people, and they were living cheek-by-jowl. The few row houses in the city that survive from that time are to be found in Strathcona, most of them on Hawks Avenue. They all date from the first decade of the last century, a time when Vancouver was undergoing a surge in immigration and a building boom to match. The pace of construction of single-family dwellings could not keep up with the flood of newcomers. Row houses, ranging anywhere from six to nine units built over two narrow East End lots, were not only an affordable housing option for large numbers of newly arrived immigrants; they also provided maximum rent return to landlords. Units that today house as few as one or two people had, at the time of the 1911 census, housed as many as nine, including boarders. For the first ten years or so after the row houses were built, turnover was rapid. In most cases, the names of the occupants of these units changed from year to year.

Much of the story of the neighbourhood, however, is undocumented. Poor immigrants are rarely the subject of photo studies and they don't typically leave behind a family archive. Precious little of this rich heritage is represented in the visual record housed at the City of Vancouver Archives. The photos that do exist, outside the small number of images of private homes, churches, and commercial buildings, are often crowd shots, labour demonstrations, riots, or line-ups for soup kitchens, and were more often the product of outside social commentary than any insider's attempt to document the history of their neighbourhood. The names of the potato-doling clergy and the police detectives are recorded, but the people in the background are just that, nameless recipients of a churchman's charity or a policeman's justice.

My neighbour Lucille Mars can still see it differently. I first met Lucille when I lived on the 1000 block of Odlum Drive in Grandview, where my adventure as a house history researcher began. She and her partner Bill Bain—a retired founding owner of Black Top Cabs—lived across the street from me. But it was after moving to Strathcona that I began to see her more regularly. I would often find her with Bill sitting out in front of the Union Market holding court with a number of our neighbours. Every so often I would join the throng and listen in as Lucille regaled us all with stories from her childhood in the East End. When she found out that I lived in a row house around the corner, she said that she knew it and that a childhood friend, an Italian immigrant named Giovannina Di Nicola, had lived in the very unit where my partner and I now lived. We all listened, riveted as Lucille made our neighbourhood come alive. Every house in the immediate neighbourhood held a memory and had a story. During her childhood and youth in the East End, Lucille had hobnobbed with hoboes and bootleggers, and played in Hogan's Alley. I had just started to work seriously as a house historian, and to know that some of the people I had come across in my research of houses in my neighbourhood had been Lucille's friends, or at least people she knew, made my head reel.

Over the following years I made it a point to get together and spend time with Lucille and take as many notes as I could from her recollections of the neighbourhood. The first time we got together, Lucille pulled out a box of old pictures and

Giovannina Di Nicola and her husband in their Sunday best.

produced a photograph of her friend Giovannina, the woman who had lived in my house from 1923 to 1932. It is a formal studio photograph. Giovannina and her husband pose impassive in their Sunday best. Giovannina sits cradling her baby as her husband stands stiffly beside her. This was the first of many photos Lucille allowed me to borrow and scan. Over a number of visits, piece by piece, the jigsaw puzzle of Lucille's fascinating life began to come together. The pieces were not shared in any particular order. Some parts of the puzzle were missing, some likely withheld. But her stories brought the ghosts of my East End neighbourhood back to life.

Lucille "Dinka" Mars was born in Vancouver on November 29, 1920. She was one of four children—three daughters and a son—born to Katie Fedychyn. Katie was born Karolina Bembin on January 22, 1875, in Washatina in Galicia, the largely Polish and Ukrainian part of what was still then the Austro-Hungarian Empire. In 1912 Katie followed her husband to Canada, arriving on one of the ships that took on survivors from the sinking of the *Titanic*. When she first reached Vancouver she was too poor to rent in a proper house, so Katie found a home for herself in a squatter community on the shores of Burrard Inlet. She eked out a living mending and selling burlap sacks for coal and wheat and doing other odd jobs. Eventually Katie was able to move into a house at 810 Powell Street, which is where the archival records provide a first glimpse of Lucille's father. Katie's husband, Fred Fedychyn, was born in Poland on June 17, 1870. He came to Canada ahead of Katie in 1909 and to Vancouver in 1912, where he worked as a general labourer and handyman. Fedychyn appears in the city directories in 1919, listed as a labourer living at 810 Powell. The Powell Street house is also where Lucille was born. Katie continued to work sewing sacks, and these formed the mattress on which Lucille slept from infancy. Lucille recalls even now how she loved the scent of new burlap.

When Lucille was three years old, the family moved from Powell Street to 793 East Georgia. The Fedychyns now lived in a larger house, nicely planted on the southeast corner of the block. The house no longer stands, nor does the rest of the block, come to that. (It was all demolished in a frenzy of urban renewal in the 1960s and converted into "New MacLean Park.") While Fred took jobs around town, Katie Fedychyn took in and looked after boarders to make ends meet and dabbled in bootlegging to earn some extra money.

Across the street from the Fedychyn home, at 782 East Georgia, a Jewish merchant named Max Charkow ran the small New Century Grocery. Lucille recalls that they sold all kinds of food, including pickled herring by the barrel and apples by the crate. One day, when Mr. Charkow was in the back of the store, Lucille climbed up on to an apple box beside the herring barrel and attempted to reach for an onion in among the pickled fish. Lucille lost her balance and fell headfirst into the brine.

303 Barnard (later Union) Street. *PROVINCE*, SATURDAY, OCTOBER 28, 1905, (PAGE 13, HANDSOME EAST END RESIDENCES).

She would have drowned that day had not a customer come in and fished her, flailing, from the barrel.

By 1926, the Fedychyn family had moved a block further south, to a house at 830 Union Street. This was a half-dozen doors down from the Union Market. Fred continued to work as a labourer, while Katie looked after boarders. Lucille recalls that the roomers could get rowdy at times. They would sometimes get drunk and toss Lucille around like a toy.

Lucille had a friend named Mary Glowski who lived in a house at 532 Keefer Street between Princess and Jackson. Mary's dad Steve worked as a janitor at the Empire Beer Parlour at 76 East Hastings. Lucille and Mary made pocket money by running errands. The women who would answer the door of 305 Union at Gore were special clients for Lucille and Mary, sending the girls to the butcher shop and drug store for orders. Their residence, a large house on the northeast corner of the intersection, was for many years considered—as Lucille puts it—the "biggest whorehouse in the East End."

Kitty-corner to where the brothel once stood is now a mostly unused park at the east end of the Georgia Viaduct. Through the 1920s, '30s, '40s and '50s, this block, with its T-shaped alley lined with ramshackle apartments, lane house, and stables, formed the core of Hogan's Alley. This was where much of Vancouver's Black community lived. Depending on who you were and how you looked at it, Hogan's Alley was either the most exciting part of town or the most disreputable. Its character was so lurid that in 1930, Union Street east of Vernon to Boundary Road was renamed "Adanac" ("Canada" spelled backward) so the good folk who lived on that section of the street weren't lumped together with the drinking, gambling, prostitution, and other illegal goings-on in and around Hogan's Alley. That notorious stretch between Gore Avenue and Main Street, however, was one of Lucille's playgrounds.

Another popular recreation ground for the neighbourhood children was a small ravine about where Union Street meets Hawks. A stream ran through the shallow gully all the way to a chain of dank pools that were the last vestiges of False Creek's

Rev. Andrew Roddan of First United Church supervising the distribution of food to homeless men at the city dump in September 1931. CITY OF VANCOUVER ARCHIVES, RE N4.1. PHOTOGAPH BY MOORE CO.

eastern mudflats. Before World War I the Creek stretched as far to the east as Clark. Then everything was reclaimed and filled in for the railway yards and warehouses. The puddles and sloughs left behind were, for many years, a favourite place for East End kids to go swimming and rafting. Lucille used to explore and play in this area as well.

The Great Depression that ravaged the Canadian economy changed that landscape. The city's more forgiving weather drew thousands of unemployed workers from all over the country. In the East End alone there were three so-called "hobo jungles;" the largest was on the edge of the sloughs and ponds. It stood at the site of the old garbage dump, now the Strathcona Community Gardens, south of Prior

Three unemployed men of the "jungle" at the City dump, September 1931.
CITY OF VANCOUVER ARCHIVES, CVA RE N8.2. PHOTOGRAPH BY W.J. MOORE.

Street. It was there that Lucille met a man who introduced himself to her as Tom Tinker. Tom had made a home for himself in the bottom of a big old tree trunk among the bushes at the foot of Raymur Street, near Venables. Apparently Tom was hiding out from the law. His story was that he was a former RCMP constable and that he had been accused of killing someone. Tom squatted in the old tree stump house for a number of years and was eventually given a job looking after the dump sometime in the late 1920s or early '30s. Tom survived in part on a diet of milk, which Lucille would pick up for him from the store on the corner of Campbell and Georgia.

Tom wasn't the only hobo that Lucille befriended. She was always taking hungry homeless men back to her mother's boarding house, where her mother would find something to feed them. No one was ever turned away. It was in this way that Lucille came to recognize the faces of the army of unemployed who hovered on the edge of her neighbourhood.

At one of our meetings Lucille showed me a photo taken during the Depression. This image, labelled "Three unemployed men of the 'jungle' at the City dump," is one of many taken during a visit to the jungle by Rev. Andrew Roddan of First United Church, a man described as "The East End's very own Apostle to the Poor." It is one of the most compelling and widely reproduced images in the City of Vancouver Archives collection. Two of the men engage the camera face on, while another man stares off into the distance. "That man on the right," Lucille said, "that's Mr. Tarashko. At one time, he and these other men were my mother's boarders. The man with the crutches was a Swede." The well-dressed Swede is missing his right leg, perhaps from a logging or mill accident, perhaps from "riding the rods." How did these men end up in the hobo jungle? Little is known of them, but at least now they are slightly less anonymous.

Behind Lucille's house on Union Street was a small a junkyard run by a family friend, a Polish-born dealer named John Lesik. He rented out the shed on the lane and operated his business from there. It was in that same back yard Lucille learned how to make a proper fist and how to fight. She got expert instruction from local boxing legend Jimmy McLarnin who used to spar there with Lucille's elder brother, Stephen. McLarnin, who carried a string of promotional nicknames like "The Baby-Faced Assassin" and "The Beltin' Celt," would become two-time welterweight world champion in the 1930s and later an International Boxing Hall of Fame inductee.

There were people who lived in the neighbourhood and others who passed through it, many of them at work. Although there were corner grocery stores on every block, fresh vegetables were often sold door to door off the back of horse drawn carts brought into town by Chinese farmers. Likewise heating fuel came off the back of a cart and not through a pipe or along a wire. Many of the houses in the East End in these years were heated by stoves. Some burned wood, many burned coal, others burned sawdust. There were a number of coal and wood yards in the neighbourhood, some along Main Street. One of the largest, at 569 East Georgia near Princess, belonged to H.J. Smith. They would deliver loads of fuel to homes as needed. Many of the old houses were equipped with coal- or wood-chutes down which the deliverymen would dump the week's supply into an unfinished basement. There was a coal deliveryman from Montreal, named Fred Jerry. He was another resident of Union Street, between Gore and Dunlevy. He would drive his coal laden wagon through the neighbourhood shouting out *"Coaal! Coaal!"* Housewives would flag him down as needed. Lucille used to delight in running after him and mimicking his call *"Coaal! Coaal!"* "What do you eat for breakfast? *Coaal! Coaal*! What does your wife eat for breakfast? *Coaaal! Coaal!*" He must not have minded this attention as one day Fred gave Lucille a pony. She kept it in a horse-barn in the alley between Georgia and Union between Princess and Jackson. It was one of many stables in the neighbourhood. Lucille would make money giving neighbourhood kids pony rides around the

Boxing champion and Strathcona boy Jimmy McLarnin (right) out for a run with his brother Bob, 1930.
CITY OF VANCOUVER ARCHIVES, CVA PORT P1366. PHOTOGRAPH BY STUART THOMSON.

block for a penny a go. One day the big draft horse that pulled Fred's coal wagon pushed the pony while Lucille was grooming her and almost crushed the girl against the manger. With that close call, Lucille's visits to the stables came to an end.

The radius of Lucille Mars's East End included Chinatown and the Hastings Street Great White Way. Like so many other East End children, Lucille liked to go to the theatre at 142 East Hastings close to Main Street. Originally called the Pantages Theatre, it was the State in the 1930s, but for locals like Lucille, the Pantages name stuck. It was the practice among an army of East End kids to sneak in the back door without paying. (I have heard this same story so many times before from other Strathcona old-timers, it is a wonder a guard wasn't posted at that back door.) Sometimes, Lucille would sneak upstairs and play in an area next to the offices of W.P. "Nick" Nichols, the owner. There was a huge table and mirror in the space. Lucille would tap dance on the table and watch herself in the mirror. One day she was caught in the act by Nichols, who was an old vaudeville showman. When she apologized, Nichols said, "Don't say sorry. We should have you downstairs on the stage." Lucille loved to tap dance and do acrobatics. She was self-taught. Too poor to buy proper taps, Lucille improvised, taping pennies to the bottoms of her shoes. As a child she used to busk outside of the Union Market, playing her mouth organ and sometimes tap dancing for coins from her neighbours. As she got older, though, she was more reluctant to perform. When pressed, Lucille refused. People thought that most dancers were "whores," explained Lucille, and she didn't want that reputation.

Nick Nichols wasn't the only one who recognized and appreciated Lucille's talents as a performer. Sometime around 1937 Lucille met Hymie and Jack Singer, two brothers who were making their way in the entertainment business. Hymie had recently opened the glitzy Palomar nightclub on Georgia Street, and Jack was visiting from Calgary. They tried their best to convince Lucille to come with them to Hollywood where, they promised, they would "make her a star." The Singer brothers did go on to Hollywood, where Jack in particular made it big in the film industry. But that was a long way down the road. Who knows what Lucille's life would have been like if she had said yes in 1937?

Another cultural stop in the old downtown was the Carnegie Library at Main and Hastings. For many years this landmark East End building housed Vancouver's civic museum. Its most famous attraction was the mummy of an Egyptian boy named Panechates. It is a bizarre but somehow fitting juxtaposition: the city's East End with its League of Nations diversity was also home to a 2,000-year-old mummy, something with which the locals would have had considerable familiarity. What fascinated Lucille most about the building, however, was a haunting framed painted reproduction of *Veronica's Veil*. The imprint of Jesus's face was painted in a way that, depending on

Lucille and her mother, Katie, with the family dog behind their house at 830 Union. PHOTO COURTESY OF LUCILLE MARS.

This family portrait was taken the day of the wedding. Lucille, fourth from the left, stands beside her sister Annie. The tall man on the right is Annie's Saskatchewan-born husband, George Stanley Shillington. The man standing behind Anton is junkman, John Lesik. PHOTO COURTESY OF LUCILLE MARS.

the way you approached the picture, Jesus's eyes would seem to open. This image made a lasting impression on Lucille.

The Great Depression was the heyday of the con artist. Desperate times called for desperate measures. Lucille's good looks and her outgoing personality caught the attention of one local swindler. Lucille recalls a rich man who owned a butcher shop in the neighbourhood, who, with another friend, planned to buy the old Grandview Methodist Church at Venables and Victoria. Their idea was to set Lucille up to preach like the famed Canadian-born, Los Angeles-based evangelist Aimee Semple McPherson. Their aim, of course, was to scam people into handing over their money. Lucille didn't go for it. She didn't like bullshitting people.

On April 15, 1937, Lucille's father Fred Fedychyn passed away in Lucille's arms at 830 Union. He died from cancer. He had been a heavy smoker and had not been well for quite some time. Lucille had been holding Fred's head to give him a spoonful of medicine from another local institution—Buckshon's Drug Store—when he took three gasps and died. He was 66. Lucille cut some of his curly black hair off and kept it as a memento.

One day Lucille was sitting on the front porch of her house when a man who had been standing down the road in front of the Matsubayashi's store at 810 Union

Lucille and Caroline in front of their Woodland Drive home in 1945. PHOTO COURTESY OF LUCILLE MARS.

Street sauntered over. The man's name was Florin "Frank" Lucinic. Lucille thinks that he was probably from Austria, from the same region as her mother. He told Lucille that he had met Katie in 1919 and that his own mother had platinum hair like Lucille's. With a heavy eastern European accent he told Lucille, "You are my job. And," he said, indicating another young woman with platinum blond hair who had just exited the confectionery, "there's my other job." That is how, in the space of one minute, Lucille met her birth father, realized that Fred Fedychyn was not her biological father, and discovered that she had a half-sister, Catherine Lasky.

There were other developments on the domestic front as well. On February 19, 1938, Lucille's mother, Katie, remarried. Her groom was a friend and former boarder, Anton Eletz, a 54-year-old immigrant from Grodno, Poland, now Belarus. The service took place at Holy Trinity Russian Church on Campbell Avenue, when it was still in the very early stages of construction.

With her mother looked after, Lucille felt able to get married herself. She did so in 1941, at 21 years of age. She married a carpenter from Pretoria, South Africa, named John Delfos and moved to a house at 1820 Woodland Drive in Grandview. Lucille and John had a daughter, Caroline.

The marriage, ultimately, was not a happy one. Lucille felt Delfos was dishonest and was uneasy about the reasons he gave for his flight from South Africa to Canada. When Caroline was three years old, Lucille left John and moved back to 830 Union Street, hoping to get a divorce. John refused.

Lucille's new stepfather was a good friend of archpriest Alexander Kiziun of Holy Trinity Church. Eletz donated and loaned considerable sums toward the building of the new church and—according to Lucille—helped raise the money to pay for the church's bell. Kiziun, a carpenter, was largely responsible for the actual construction of the church. The archpriest would often come over to the house, where he would enjoy more than a few drinks with Anton. In the late 1940s, however, when Eletz was very ill and dying, the church did not come to the family's assistance. Eletz worried about family finances and approached archpriest Kiziun for money he had loaned him. For whatever reason, Kiziun did not comply. Lucille was outraged and stormed over to the church to confront the priest. She found him working on the roof. Lucille shouted up at Father Kiziun, accusing him of taking money from poor people who needed it, Lucille remembers, before wheeling around, raising a finger and wagging it as she left with her parting shot: "One day, you are going to fall off that roof!" Anton Eletz died at home at 830 Union Street on February 23, 1950. Lucille is listed on the death certificate as the informant. Father Kiziun died three years later, not from the predicted precipitous fall, but from advanced heart disease. Lucille's mother, Katie Eletz, also died in 1953. Lucille continued to live in the family home on Union until 1958.

During this period, Lucille's East End neighbourhood was undergoing some profound changes. The demographic mix of the neighbourhood drastically changed with the expulsion of the Japanese community in 1942 and the outmigration of the neighbourhood's Jewish community later on. By the mid-1950s it was being shaken up again as large numbers of Italian families vacated Strathcona and headed east to Grandview-Woodlands and Renfrew. The Italian homes were now being occupied by newly reunited Chinese families made whole through the repeal of Canada's

Chinese Exclusion Act. Even as these changes were underway, plans were afoot to transform Strathcona from the ground up. The city was expropriating houses for a comprehensive demolition program that would make way for a freeway and modern high-rise apartment blocks. Over the next two decades large swathes of Lucille's neighbourhood were bulldozed. Hogan's Alley was wiped clean off the map, as were the 300 blocks from Pender all the way south to Union Street. The large brothel at Union and Gore Avenue disappeared at this time. So did Lucille's childhood home on the southeast corner of Georgia and Hawks Avenue. Lucille's long-time home at 830 Union and the Union Market where she had busked with her harmonica were slated for demolition, along with all the houses between Prior and Union Streets, for the planned freeway extension. These buildings were saved through the concerted efforts of East Enders, led by the likes of Mary Lee Chan and the members of the Strathcona Property Owners and Tenants Association.

During Lucille's sunset years she found happiness and stability in her relationship with her common-law spouse Bill Bain. The story of how Bill had a crush on Lucille in his early years and how they met and got together in the 1990s was the subject of a feature article in the November 5, 2000, *Vancouver Sun* entitled "Lucille Mars: She's Some Dame." A number of other interviews with Lisa Smedman have also been published in the *Vancouver Courier*. Bill Bain passed away on January 28, 2008, at the age of 85. Lucille now lives alone with her memories in the house they shared on Odlum Drive. Though her sight is fading, she is still as lithe and flexible as the tap-dancing teenager who watched herself in a mirror upstairs at the State Theatre many decades ago.

L.D. TAYLOR AND
THE LENNIE COMMISSION
EVE LAZARUS

L ouis Denison Taylor sat at the back of the packed room. If it wasn't for his trademark red tie and owlish glasses, he would have looked like any other small, balding, septuagenarian—hardly the main event. But now entrenched in his seventh non-consecutive year as the city's chief executive, Mayor Taylor, or L.D. as he was known to almost everybody, was as much a symbol of Vancouver as Stanley Park.

When L.D. walked down East Hastings Street, people crossed the road to shake his hand. He was a man of the people, the labourers, the longshoremen, the cannery workers, and the loggers. Today the small room was filled with the mostly working-class men and women who had elected L.D. and were eager to see him defend his controversial "open town policy." For years, L.D. had insisted that in a port city such as Vancouver, a certain number of bootleggers, brothels, and gambling joints were to be expected—and who were they really hurting, anyway?

The opening act of the Lennie Commission kicked off on April 30, 1928. Named after Robert S. Lennie, the Vancouver barrister who presided over it, the Lennie Commission was the first official clash between police and the legal system, but it wasn't the first time corruption and bribery had been investigated in the Vancouver Police Department. During the

The Lennie Commission was named after
Vancouver barrister, Robert S. Lennie.
CITY OF VANCOUVER ARCHIVES, CVA 371-1683.
PHOTOGRAPH BY J.S. MATTHEWS.

city's first 40 years, dust had barely gathered on the top cop's portrait before another one was hammered into place. This time though, the city's elite were planning to lay the blame for the corruption, uncontrolled vice, and the demoralization of the police force right at L.D.'s door.

Those determined enough to claim a seat at the inquiry were promised a rollicking ride, one that took them behind the daily headlines and showed them all the dirty laundry of the VPD. Through the course of the Lennie Commission, they would see cop pitted against crook and cop pitted against cop, as everyone from the beat cops to the chief of police and the mayor himself shared the spotlight with a litany of gangsters including Joe Celona, the King of the Bawdy Houses, and Shue Moy, the King of the Gamblers.

The commission provided a podium for lawyers with political aspirations such as the flamboyant Gerry McGeer, who represented Alderman Thomas Fletcher, the police commissioner who had set the wheels in motion.

Fletcher was hardly squeaky clean himself. He had been caught selling stocks and bonds to members of the very police force that he helped oversee.[1] He claimed that members of the constabulary regularly took bribes to look the other way, reduce charges and ignore gambling, prostitution, and bootlegging. Underworld figures not only reached deep inside the police force, charged Fletcher, but their influence also spread all the way to City Hall.

The first witness didn't disappoint the crowds in the courtroom, who were primed for outrages. Detective Roderick McLeod, a 19-year veteran of the Vancouver Police Department, set the tone for the 98 witnesses that would follow. The crowd leaned forward in their seats as he told the commission that gambling was out of control and the gambling dens were a "refuge for crooks and vagrants." McLeod, a strapping six-foot-tall highlander, sat back comfortably in the witness chair and told the Commission that just a year earlier, he had submitted a report to Chief Constable Henry Long listing the addresses of several illegal gambling joints. McLeod said that instead of getting a pat on the back, he was hauled onto the chief's carpet and told that his report had caused Long's boss, the mayor, "much worry." Instead of being told to "go out with an axe" and wreck these places as they would have done in the near past, Chief Long told him that he was to leave alone two of the gambling places in Chinatown because they were operated by a Chinese businessman who had helped get the mayor elected.[2]

McLeod's testimony was just one of dozens to come that painted a picture of a demoralized, understaffed, and underpaid police force charged with serving and protecting a city in which gambling, prostitution, and bootlegging ran unchecked. Nine officers in rank ranging from beat cops right up to the deputy chief gave accounts of trying to close down the crime dens only to be told to back off—that the mayor wanted them left alone.

L.D. sat in the audience, content to let his lawyer, Alex Henderson, square off against Gerry McGeer. He didn't have to wait long. The first major dust-up came on the second day of the hearings. McGeer demanded that the mayor should be charged with allowing gambling and brothels to flourish and with instructing police officers to refrain from carrying out their duties.

Police witnesses followed. They told of being handed lists of gambling joints and disorderly houses that were to be left alone, and of how their efforts to shut down vice and prosecute the criminals were thwarted by their bosses.

Some of the most damning evidence came from Detective Joe Ricci. During his 16-year career with the force he had worked on the anti-gambling and Chinatown Drug Squad, the Dry Squad, and the Morality Squad. Ricci said that detectives were merely a collection agency for the city. They were told to go from place to place, make the odd raid, and arrest the prostitutes from time to time, only to see them released a short time later. As proof of the thriving trade in sex in the East End, Ricci reeled off the addresses of a dozen brothels operating on Union, Keefer, Prior, East Hastings, and Alexander Streets.[3]

Police still faced the same conflict of interest that dated back to the formation of the department four decades earlier. Fines from vice brought the city substantial revenues, and gambling in particular was a cash cow for the department.

In 1928 City Hall was on Main Street just off East Hastings Street and a block from Chinatown. CITY OF VANCOUVER ARCHIVES, CVA CITY N12; 1928. PHOTOGRAPH BY J.S. MATTHEWS.

Many people following the Lennie Commission could still remember the Vancouver that had sprung up in the 1880s, populated by railway tycoons, speculators, and grifters, all wanting to forge a destiny in a city where wealth, influence, and official corruption went mostly unchallenged. But by the 1920s, a new breed of entrepreneur had emerged. Men like Joseph Kennedy were redefining the "legitimate" face of the liquor business, while others were making fortunes running booze down the coast to thirsty Americans still in the full swing of US prohibition. In 1928, brothers George and Harry Reifel were using some of the proceeds from their rum-running enterprise to build mansions on Millionaire's Row on Southwest Marine Drive. In

this moneyed enclave they were neighbours to George Kidd, head of BC Electric Railway, Philip Rogers, son of sugar
baron B.T. Rogers, and William Malkin—the wholesale grocer who would
use the issue of police corruption to
wrestle the mayor's job away from L.D.
in the fall of 1928.[4]

L.D. was no stranger to scandal.
He had stepped off a train from Chicago
in 1896, running from accusations that
ranged from breach of trust to embez-
zlement. Customers charged that L.D.,
a partner in a Chicago bank, had ac-
cepted their deposits even after he knew
the bank was insolvent.[5] Vancouver, a
frontier town being literally rebuilt from
its ashes after the Great Fire of 1886,
must have looked like a safe refuge for
the American.

L.D. spent the next decade bounc-
ing from job to job. He tried his hand at
gold mining, found work with the CPR,
and for a time, ran the circulation de-

Mayor L.D. Taylor kicks back at his home in Granville
Mansions at Granville and Robson Streets, ca. 1927.
VANCOUVER PUBLIC LIBRARY, ACCESSION #6464.

partment of the *Province*. In 1905 he bought the *Daily World* newspaper, and with the
help of Alice Berry, his business manager and later his second wife, in 1912 put up
the tallest building in the British Empire. L.D. almost pulled it off. Now known
as the Sun Tower, the building remains a landmark in the city; unfortunately for
L.D., it also bankrupted him. It did not, however, still his passion for politics. He
was elected mayor first in 1910 and then five times more to 1928. Despite his shaky
start in business and the ups and downs of Vancouver's boom and bust years, L.D
was a popular mayor. He supported the progressive idea of an eight-hour work day,
universal suffrage for women, property taxation based on land, city planning, and
regional cooperation.

By 1928, Vancouver was the third largest city in Canada and growing in
importance in international trade, but L.D.'s city still clung to its milltown origins.
Policing was caught between those who tolerated limited vice and a growing
movement demanding moral reform. At the same time there were a number of

conflicts within the Vancouver Police Department. Officers were paid 20 percent less than their counterparts in other Canadian cities, and the VPD was severely understaffed. As L.D. pointed out in his testimony, when he was first elected mayor in 1910, the city had 50 more policemen than it did in 1928, yet the population had grown from 106,000 to 153,000 in that time. Methods of policing had also evolved. Veteran detectives who once solved problems with axes and guns had trouble adjusting to post-frontier legal niceties such as warrants and real evidence.

L.D. blamed the demoralization of the VPD on what he called "the traitors in the police force" who he believed were undermining the chief. He singled out Inspector John Jewitt and Detectives MacLeod and Ricci. He said they were passed over for promotion, and instead of working together, they were lying down on the job.[6] There may have been some truth to this. Certainly the police department was a mess, with factional in-fighting and jealousy among the rank and file.

If there was any doubt left as to the extent of the demoralization, it was quickly put to rest as officer after officer pointed fingers at each other and at their superiors, and Chief Long wasted no time throwing his own boss under the streetcar.

"I might say the Mayor declared to me he had been elected by a majority of 8,000 and his policy was certainly not to run a closed town," said Long. "The underworld must have known of that because gambling spread very extensively . . . I told the mayor there was too much gambling going on in the City and I could hardly handle it and he said 'never mind the gambling, get after the major crimes.'"[7]

His testimony didn't help his case, and Chief Long came out looking like an ineffectual police chief who was seen to do the mayor's bidding.

The department that felt the most heat from the Lennie Commission was the eight-man Morality Squad and Dry Squad, part of the Criminal Investigation Department (CID). Viewed as the elite branch of the police, they worked in pairs and reported to Detective Sergeant George McLaughlin, who reported to Inspector John Jackson. While McLaughlin was described by his superiors as a "good and efficient officer," it was noted that between 1914 and 1928, McLaughlin had been investigated on four separate occasions for taking bribes. He was exonerated every time. "These things are coming all the time," he said. "If we were getting the money we're supposed to be making I needn't be working from 9:00 a.m. to midnight and taking abuse for it."

McLaughin was less than complimentary about his boss. He testified that while Long was "a good, decent, fellow," he said the chief didn't "have enough iron in him."[8]

McLaughlin was hardly finished. He accused Alderman Fletcher of having an affair, and at one point the two nearly came to blows when Fletcher stepped off the stand and crossing to McLaughlin said, "You're a dirty cur."[9]

Ricci, on the other hand, blamed McLaughlin for the mess. He testified that operators of disorderly houses told him they paid protection money, and he said that McLaughlin had told him to lay off Celona's Union Street brothel.[10]

As the 1920s drew to a close, Vancouver was still a city with a social order carved out along strict class and race lines. The city was overwhelmingly white, run mostly by Scots, and marked by pockets of colour—mostly in the East End.

Racism infected all levels of Vancouver's society. The city's sizeable Chinese population was not eligible for Canadian citizenship, and as such could not vote or hold office. They were barred from working in professions such as law and medicine, forced to pay special taxes and were regularly barred from restaurants and bars. One popular restaurant of the day was called the White Lunch, and it hired and served only white people. In 1925 the Kanadian Knights of the Ku Klux Klan set up their Canadian headquarters in a Shaughnessy mansion (now Canuck Place, a children's hospice).

Not surprising, then, that the Chinese would stick to Chinatown, but it was viewed by outsiders as a place of immorality and sin where gambling and prostitution thrived, and where white women were corrupted by drugs.

The Chinese enclave was, without a doubt, a good place to find a game of chance. Games such as mah-jong, pai-gow, chuck-a-luck, and fan tan were hugely popular in Chinatown, and lots of small operators ran illegal slot machines and punch boards that awarded small prizes or cash.

Efforts to stamp out vice had failed miserably in the past and only served to spread gambling and prostitution all through the city. The general sentiment was that opium-addicted Chinese men had a predilection for gambling. L.D. and others wanted to restrict gambling and prostitution to the East End and Chinatown.

Deputy Chief Daniel Leatherdale, a 31-year VPD veteran, testified that he didn't see gambling in Chinatown as a serious problem. He told the Commission that conditions in Chinatown hadn't changed much in the 1920s, perhaps not even over 30 years. The main difference was that whereas the Chinese had once installed iron doors with electronically controlled door locks, now gambling was carried on quite openly. When police entered the premises, they were generally ignored.

McGeer asked Leatherdale how difficult it was for police to close gambling joints.

"One would have to keep after them all the time, they are like smouldering fires," said the deputy chief, adding that it was possible. He himself had closed down 20 of them when the two senior VPD officers—Inspector Jackson and Detective Sergeant McLaughlin—who allegedly protected them were off on vacation.[11]

Allegations of graft was one thing; receipts and invoices showing pay-offs were quite another. Several Chinese gambling proprietors produced accounting books showing that they paid between $50 and $225 a month for police protection against raids, and additional expenses went to police court disbursements and other court costs.

A drug dealer named Ah Joe said he had paid out bribes to police to have his charges reduced. Joe Wing testified that he paid $400 to Inspector Jackson in $100 bills to protect two gambling houses on Carrall and on Main. Georgie Chow said that for two years, he paid $50 a month to McLaughlin and Jackson to protect his gambling operations from the police, and in 1926 he gave a $360 diamond ring to McLaughlin.[12]

But while the Chinese believed their bribe money caused police to look the other way, authorities were delighted with the steady flow of cash from crime to cop shop.

One of the most bizarre things to come out of the Lennie Commission was the discovery of a "bribe book." The official attitude towards graft was so lackadaisical that in 1921 then-Chief Constable James Anderson established an Entertainment Fund with the unanimous blessing of Mayor R.H. Gale and the police commissioners. The fund, which started that year with a $250 bribe given to Inspector John Jewitt, was set up through a special resolution of the board to establish a way of dealing with the money police received as payoffs. A "bribe book" was opened by Frank Amor, secretary to the chief of police. The idea was that they would use the extra cash to entertain police officials visiting from out of town.

Amor said there had been two banquets paid for from the fund. The backhanders had also bought Christmas presents for telephone operators and a wreath on the coffin of former Mayor James Findlay. The current balance, said Amor, was $1,082.[13]

Lennie was outraged, saying that by accepting the money, it was natural that the Chinese would conclude that they had paid a bribe to protect their gambling houses from raids.

"How can anyone countenance a fund of this kind?" Lennie wrote in his report.[14]

The Entertainment Fund wasn't the only systematic abuse in the department. The provincial government charged the City of Vancouver $1 a day for every prisoner that was sent to Oakalla Prison Farm in Burnaby. As VPD officer James Clark Proudlock testified, "The system under which the police work is to blame and not the police for existing conditions," he said. "It is difficult to say whether the police corrupts the city or the city corrupts the police or the provincial government corrupts both by taxing the city $1 a day for prisoners sent to Oakalla."

Proudlock told the Commission that if orders had been given to get the criminals off the streets, the city would have been forced to pay hundreds of dollars a day for their upkeep at Oakalla. The system, he said, was counterproductive and drove the city to work in collusion with the underworld.

"Look at the number of blind pigs, gambling joints, brothels, etc., which have been running," Proudlock said. "These places have been taken before the court, fined and allowed to open up immediately after. All this comes back to the system of driving criminals and other vicious people on careers of crime. How all the police have not been mixed up in corrupt practice is a mystery to me."

When Georgie Chow was asked why he was testifying against the police whom he purportedly paid for protection, revenge, he said, was the reason. His gambling house at 60 West Cordova was closed, while that of his competitor Shue Moy at nearby 54 West Cordova was allowed to stay open. Chow said when he went to Inspector John Jackson to complain, he was told that Shue Moy "is a good friend to the mayor. He can do anything he wants."[15]

It didn't help L.D. when Shue Moy took the stand. Yes, he said, the mayor and he were friends. Moy, who was described by a reporter as a man in his mid-fifties and of medium height and weight, was "quiet and composed."

"His features reveal native intelligence and the proverbial inscrutability of the Oriental," noted the reporter in language that would have been familiar to 1920s readers. Moy admitted visiting the mayor "once in a while," perhaps once every two or three weeks. He told the Commissioner that he and the mayor never talked about gambling.[16]

Moy, also known as the Potato King because he owned the largest potato farm in Canada, had financed part of L.D.'s newspaper the *Critic* and contributed to the mayor's first election campaign. L.D. had been seen socializing with both Moy and bawdy-house operator Joe Celona on different occasions. Several witnesses testified that they had seen the mayor at Celona's fancy Shaughnessy digs.

L.D. admitted that he'd attended part of a celebration at Celona's Angus Drive home the previous New Year's Eve, but said that it was only for a glass of champagne. He didn't know that Celona was in any other business besides running a cigar shop. He must have been the only person in Vancouver who did not.[17]

But if L.D. was corrupt, it wasn't showing up in his possessions. Lennie and Celona lived in tony Shaughnessy, and McGeer had a stately home on the exclusive stretch of Belmont Avenue in Point Grey; L.D lived in a second-floor walk-up at the Granville Mansions on Granville at Robson, where he'd been a resident since 1909.

Lennie was more suspicious about McLaughlin and Jackson, and put their finances under the spotlight.

Jackson testified that he had made "a good many thousands" speculating in real estate some years ago and had made a "chunk of money" in Tijuana. He said he had bought a lot at Campbell Avenue and East Hastings Street for $885 and owned three cars at different times, and held a $700 interest in a gold mine. The Jacksons' bank account showed a healthy $16,870 balance and only $500 in withdrawals since 1923.

McLaughlin testified that he had between $300 and $400 in the bank, and had made several good investments. He owned a home worth about $3,500 on Wolfe

Avenue in Vancouver. Asked about his vacations, he said that in 1926 he took a trip to Tahiti and paid for it by working at the races, where he made $350. Before that he went to "the Old Country," and the trip cost $1,500. Keeping in mind the low pay of the VPD, these were exceptional sums.

In the end, the Lennie Commission accomplished little. The overall impression of the police force was one of incompetency and corruption, ruled over by a civic administration that was soft on crime.

Lennie's report exonerated the police and the mayor from any charges of corruption, declaring that while he heard evidence from "people of the underworld, criminals many of them," he gave little credence to their testimony. He did, however, rely heavily on his observations of the witnesses, the nature of the charge, and the bank accounts of Jackson, McLaughlin, and their wives. Then he came to the startling conclusion that none of the bribes had reached any members of the police force except by way of the VPD's official Entertainment Fund.

Detective Sergeant George McLaughlin and his wife enjoying retirement at their home at 1938 Wolfe Avenue in Vancouver. CITY OF VANCOUVER ARCHIVES. CVA 99-3467. PHOTOGRAPH BY STUART THOMSON.

Lennie was clearly unimpressed with Chief Long's leadership, but stopped short of accusing him of corruption, concluding that L.D.'s open-town policy was the root of the problem. It was this policy and the morally weak leadership that was the cause of the demoralization and inefficiency of the force and which led to a casual enforcement of laws against drinking, gambling, and prostitution. He added that there were other contributing factors, including an undermanned department forced to cope with the increased population of the city and paid salaries that were significantly less than those of police forces with similar living conditions.

Lennie recommended changes be made to the membership of the Board of Police Commissioners so that it consist of a judge of the Supreme Court, the police magistrate, the mayor, and at least two outstanding citizens who held elected positions.[18]

If the public was expecting a clean sweep of the police department, they were to be severely disappointed. Inspector Jackson was pensioned off, and after being verbally spanked for double-dipping at the race track while on the city payroll, Detective Sergeant McLaughlin was allowed to take early retirement.

Chief Long was brought back from suspension, demoted to inspector, and remained with the police department. He was replaced by W.J. Bingham, who immediately set about cleaning house by abolishing the squad system and centralizing morality, gambling, liquor, and narcotics within the CID. His reign, like that of his predecessor, was short.

Although L.D. was fully exonerated of a crime, the stench of police corruption resulted in his loss of the next election to William Malkin. While L.D. was down, however, he was definitely not out. As his biographer, Daniel Francis, notes, in the end, the surprise was not that L.D. lost in 1929, but that he came so close to winning.[19] By 1931 he was re-elected to the mayor's office, and Malkin was back selling groceries.

(ENDNOTES)

1   *Province*, July 28, 1928.

2   Detective Roderick McLeod, testimony, Lennie Commission, May 1, 1928.

3   Detective Joe Ricci, testimony, Lennie Commission, June 6, 1928.

4   Eve Lazarus, *At Home with History: The Untold Secrets of Greater Vancouver's Heritage Homes* (Vancouver: Anvil Press, 2007), 29.

5   Daniel Francis, *L.D.: Mayor Louis Taylor and the Rise of Vancouver* (Vancouver: Arsenal Pulp Press, 2004).

6   Mayor L.D. Taylor, testimony, Lennie Commission, June 19, 1928.

7   Lennie Report, August 23, 1928, 17.

8   Detective Sergeant George McLaughlin, testimony, Lennie Commission, June 12, 1928.

9   *Vancouver Sun*, July 3, 1928.

10   Detective Joe Ricci, testimony, Lennie Commission, June 23, 1928.

11   Deputy Chief Daniel Leatherdale, testimony, Lennie Commission, May 14, 1928.

12   Ah Joe, Joe Wing, Georgie Chow testimony, Lennie Commission, May 15, 16, and 19, 1928.

13   *Vancouver Sun*, May 30,1928.

14   *Lennie Report*, August 23, 1928, 10

15   Georgie Chow, testimony, Lennie Commission, May 19, 1928.

16   Shue Moy, testimony, Lennie Commission, July 4, 1928.

17   *Vancouver Sun*, May 25, 1928.

18   *Lennie Report*, August 23, 1928, 26.

19   Francis, *L.D.*, 158.

WHERE MEN LIVE ON HOPE: VANCOUVER'S HOBO JUNGLES OF 1931

STEVIE WILSON

A Hobo is one who travels in search of work, the migratory worker who must go about to find employment ... The tramp is one who travels but does not work, and a bum is a man who stays in one place but does not work. Between these grades there is a great gulf of social distinction. Don't get tramps and hobos mixed.

—Nicholas Klein, of Chicago's Hobo College

The spring of 1931 saw the return of the damp, dewy conditions Vancouverites know so well. The changing seasons, in earlier years, had ushered in a prosperous working climate. This spring, however, there was no business as usual. The workers of Vancouver were still reeling from the effects of the stock market collapse two years earlier. The Wall Street Crash and the subsequent economic depression that set in afterwards signalled a new era for the city's industries. They were now marked by a dire lack of employment and a sense of defeat across all levels of production. Workers across Vancouver, and indeed across the country, were struggling without jobs and without the means to regain their ability to sustain themselves. However, it was Vancouver's location as a port city and its reputation as an employment centre that presented a unique and specific challenge for the Terminal City: it attracted thousands of transient unemployed with nowhere to work and an inadequate relief system to aid them.

Prior to the economic crisis, Vancouver was acknowledged across North America as a city with limitless potential, situated at the terminus of both the Canadian Pacific Railway (CPR) and the Canadian National Railway (CNR). The burgeoning city was surrounded by rich primary resources, including forests, fisheries, and mineral wealth. Additionally, it was growing fat on the handling of bulk products from eastern provinces. Settlement in Vancouver had been on the rise since its incorporation in 1886. The CPR's arrival two years earlier guaranteed the city's success with a more direct connection to the rest of the country and waves of tourists and travellers who fostered the city's growth. Connections to trade routes south of the border further bolstered Vancouver as a prime site for investment in both industry and real estate. All of this meant that Vancouver had a substantial working-class population, one that mostly enjoyed adequate housing, the means to support their families, and growing employment opportunities. Apart from the two-year economic depression of 1913, waged work for Vancouverites and migrant seasonal workers had generally been available to those wishing to find it.

In the two years following the crash of 1929, this all changed. The size and scope of Vancouver's homeless community expanded dramatically. Residents were holding onto their homes, desperately afraid of foreclosures. Unemployed from other parts of the country were drawn to Vancouver because of its temperate climate and

The hobo jungle at the Harbour Board near the site of the old Hastings Mill, with views of the nearby American Can Company. CITY OF VANCOUVER ARCHIVES, CVA AM54-S4-: RE N10.02. PHOTOGRAPH BY COL. R.D. WILLIAMS.

the (fading) promise of winter employment. It was estimated that in 1929–30 alone up to 75 transient unemployed, or "box-car tourists," were arriving in Vancouver daily, often from the prairies. As early as 1930, the City's relief officer observed that there were no fewer than 10,000 individuals unemployed in the city, many of whom were non-residents. Worsening economic conditions squeezed an already stressed civic relief infrastruc-ture. There were measures in place to deal with modest *local* relief demands, but there now was a strong political and social emphasis on the dangers of *transient* unemployed. With residents already reeling from the effects of the crash, the additional demands of non-Vancouverites were viewed not only as a financial burden, but also a risk to the status quo.[1] City Hall was wholly unprepared to handle these developments. Indeed, no level of government, from municipal to federal, had in place adequate policies or the authority to take action in the face of this tide of unemployment and dislocation.

In March 1931 the City Relief Department opted to reduce services for single men on the grounds that they did not have families to provide for and were therefore capable of sustaining themselves on a low income. Social welfare as we understand it today was not available or even thought of yet, and this targeted measure further alienated the growing number of (generally able-bodied) unemployed, which in turn contributed to a culture of disillusionment. The City's leading relief officer, H.W. Cooper, denied relief to 2,500 transient single men who had previously relied on the City's bed and meal tickets for daily sustenance. Perhaps Cooper hoped that this would encourage the transient unemployed to leave town; he worriedly observed that 50 percent of those cut off remained in the city.

One of the greatest obstacles facing the unemployed during this period was governmental confusion as to who was in charge as regards relief. The municipalities lacked the funding or well-defined authority to create jobs or extend assistance. It was clear in 1931 that cities could not weather another year of relief funding on their own and were now looking to the Province to offer support. Meanwhile, the provincial administration looked to the Dominion government for a response.

Jungleers sent to the provincial relief camps were often skilled tradesmen, as evidenced by this shack constructed at the jungle near the Harbour Board. CITY OF VANCOUVER ARCHIVES, CVA AM54-S4-- RE N10.06. PHOTOGRAPH BY COL. R.D. WILLIAMS.

Premier S.F. Tolmie, in an announcement to municipal representatives, stated that the Dominion government must make its policy on relief funding clear before municipalities could begin calculating their own share.[2] This logjam seemed unlikely to budge.

While governments bickered, the city's new homeless population came up with their own solutions. Squatter communities had existed in Vancouver well before the crash, and now new shantytowns were springing up. These "hobo jungles," as the press and the public referred to them, were distinct from the other shantytowns due to their high population of non-Vancouverites. The steep rise in displaced workers and unemployed coupled with the policy changes and inadequacies at the Relief Department meant more and more men were forced to find shelter anywhere they could. An alarmed city council warned Prime Minister R.B. Bennett "the situation in Vancouver is beyond our control."

By the summer of 1931 there were several distinct jungles within Vancouver's city limits, comprised of "dilapidated shacks, lean-tos, and other knocked-together shelters."[3] Men had gathered at the False Creek Flats, the city dump between Campbell and Heatley Avenues in Strathcona, underneath the original Georgia Viaduct, and at the old Hastings Mill site at the foot of Dunlevy. These small shelters, fashioned from scavenged lumber, abandoned automobile chassis, and assorted city wreckage, were the only refuge for the overflow of men staying in the many flophouses, hotels, and other local sites previously accustomed to the seasonal unemployment of the resource industries. The jungle shacks were typically built for long-term stays, and some even featured corrugated iron structures and tar-papered roofs for rain protection. W.J. Moore, a photographer who documented the sites on behalf of the Rev. Andrew Roddan of the First United Church on Gore Avenue, described the jungles as "a collection of nondescript habitations made out of anything which could be begged, borrowed or stolen, to be hung together some way to afford shelter from the elements to a large number of unemployed men; men from everywhere, all sorts of ages, education, characters, attainments, and which a common want and some misery had banded together in larger or smaller groups for mutual help."[4] The public and police afforded these men some sympathy, at least in the jungles' early stages. The *Vancouver Sun* observed in July that "the Jungle City is not a place to be feared [...] it is a place that should be visited by every thinking person who has a sympathetic understanding of humanity and wishes to know how 'the other half of the world lives.'"[5]

Surveys conducted mid-summer suggest that an average of 150 men lived in the shelters built along the Burrard Inlet; that number would later rise. Approximately 200 men lived near the CNR rail terminal on the False Creek Flats; another 250 lived under the Georgia Viaduct. The most heavily populated jungle at this time was near the city dump off Prior Street, which housed approximately 450 unemployed. The majority of men at this camp were of Finnish, Swedish, and Norwegian nationalities and had been drawn to BC by its forests and fisheries. However, there was not an intentional racial segregation between sites, save for the large Chinese and Japanese demographics in certain areas in Strathcona, where these communities were historically more concentrated. Later, other jungle sites included Vanier Park on the south side of English Bay and Stanley Park, which has a long history of squatting communities and was of particular importance to the First Nations peoples of the area.[6] Additionally, the Vancouver rail yards eventually became home to a settlement of men. By the end of the summer, City officials, as well as the public had grown uneasy with these unsightly communities. H.W. Cooper, who was tightly connected with those who kept a watchful eye on the homeless men living at the Harbour Board (near the old Hastings Mill site at the north end of Dunlevy), described the jungles as "a hot-bed for every form of disease, physical, moral and social."[7]

Automobile wreckage was a common shelter solution for the city's transient unemployed. CITY OF VANCOUVER ARCHIVES, CVA AM54-S4-: RE N3.2. PHOTOGRAPH BY W.J. MOORE.

Cooper had previously talked much differently of these men, particularly of those who assembled near the offices of the Harbour Commission. In J.S. Matthews's *Early Vancouver*, Cooper explains the compassion felt for these men:

> As the [Jungle] began to get bigger all three Harbour Commis-
> sioners began to take a private and personal interest, and one day
> a ton of potatoes was mysteriously found in the basement of the
> office [...] The fisherman at the wharf sent over fish everyday; P.
> Burns and Co. sent meat; Capt. Binks came down one day with

ten dollars worth of cigarettes; the Vancouver Club sent ten gallons of soup every morning, Sundays included, and all the bread, and rolls and buns left over from the day.[8]

Not every jungle was shown the same generosity. Though each site featured a number of capable men, many at the Harbour Board jungle had previously served in the First World War. The veterans' distinction would prove critical for these men for two specific reasons: many of them were accustomed to wartime food rationing, tough weather conditions, and living in crowded shelters. Moreover, their collective experience as soldiers meant that city officials saw them as more organized, more disciplined, and easier to identify with—not to mention they were predominantly white. There existed a sense of respect and favouritism towards these men that was not afforded to "jungaleers" elsewhere.

The somewhat sophisticated nature of the Harbour Board site and other jungle communities and developments indicates an important part of hobo culture in Vancouver: shelter, in many ways, was more important than food, and creating these squats meant that men were able to work together in a rudimentary hierarchy that allowed delegation of tasks (food procurement, building, etc.) and a place to call home. This autonomy afforded them a certain dignity and sense of proactivity. They were no longer at the mercy of government charity; they had constructed their own environments in which to weather out the storm of unemployment. Of course, the men also relied on charitable organizations. The popular Rev. Roddan, for example, played an important role in feeding the masses.[9] Moreover, the jungles contributed to a collective identity among the men that in turn established a political presence. Towards the end of the summer, socialist sentiment had taken root in the jungles.

Makeshift shelters could be mobile, as seen in this photo taken near the Georgia Viaduct, circa 1930. CITY OF VANCOUVER ARCHIVES, CVA 260-297. PHOTOGRAPH BY JAMES CROOKALL.

While Rev. Roddan and his volunteers handed out food and supplies to the men in the jungles, communist organizers were quickly spreading their agenda with leaflets and newsletters. Initially, Roddan was winning the popularity stakes: communist ideology was no salve for empty stomachs. Roddan, however, was not without goals of his own. His charity campaign drew on a strong Christian ethic, and he was looking for followers every bit as much as the Left. And while Roddan's United Church message was perhaps more benign than the communists' rhetoric, his efforts waned when he realized these men were not entirely swayed. Unfortunately for Roddan, the desperate men of the jungles were quick to accept food, but not as quick to accept his invitation to the church.

As summer came to an end, so too did the city's tolerance level for the jungles. Although percolating support (or at least sympathy) for the communist movement was likely the most pressing reason to eradicate the jungles, it was ostensibly a health issue that became the catalyst for action from city officials. The *Vancouver Sun* stated on September 4, 1931, that "Vancouver is in grave danger of an epidemic of typhoid or other disease resulting from filthy conditions in city 'jungles' ... "[10] Colonel Cooper speculated that "[M]any of the men are lying on the ground which is becoming damp, and they are certain to suffer from bronchial and rheumatic troubles."[11] The day before, a man had been removed from the jungle at the Harbour Board with symptoms of typhoid—though it is not known that typhoid was ever confirmed.[12] Members of the city Relief Department and Police Commission met almost

The unemployed living at the city dump line up for food and provisions supplied by the Rev. Andrew Roddan (fifth from right) and the First United Church. CITY OF VANCOUVER ARCHIVES, AM54-S4-: RE N4.4

immediately and were presented with a report by Medical Officer Dr. H.A. McDonald, calling for the closure of the jungles. Another man was removed from the Harbour Board site on September 4 suffering from abdominal pains,[13] which were taken as a further sign of typhoid. Fearful of a full-blown outbreak—not to mention terrified by growing unrest and the threat of political organization within the jungles—Alderman W.C. Atherton wrote to the federal minister of labour urging him to take immediate action and announce a relief policy.[14] His telegram noted that more than 15,000 people were registered as unemployed in the city, with 2,500 families in need of financial assistance. He also estimated that there were now more than 1,000 men in the jungles. Vancouver and its surrounding municipalities, without aid or indication of a federal strategy, had become unable to act, effectively "paralyzed" by the lack of organization.[15]

Relief Officer Cooper also wrote to the federal government urging immediate steps to find work for the increasing number of transient men. With more than 2,000

The spread of disease inside the jungles at the city dump as well as threat of political organization by the unemployed became a growing concern for city officials. CITY OF VANCOUVER ARCHIVES, CVA AM54-S4-: RE N3.1. PHOTOGRAPH BY W.J. MOORE.

men panhandling or relying on charity, the City was stressed to the point of breaking, and destroying the jungles meant more men would be forced onto the streets. The City might be able to police begging or provide some food or shelter relief, but it could not do both.

Though viewed as a threat to the social and political fibre of the community, the jungles also represented a unique opportunity for charitable intervention and assistance, as evidenced by the work of Rev. Roddan. Collectively, the many men within the jungles were viewed as a blight on society; however, as individuals they were still afforded help by numerous organizations and citizens. Once the call was made and the wrecking crew descended upon the jungles, clothing drives, meal tickets, and beds were assembled across the city. In all, 880 men were left without shelter when the jungles were razed. Each was provided with temporary meal and bed tickets from the provincial government on Saturday, September 5, 1931. It was reported, however, that days later a number of men were found still residing in the jungles at Prior Street when they were demolished, supposedly having been absent from the bed-ticket distribution.

These relief measures were just short-term: the bed tickets expired the following Tuesday, the meal tickets on Wednesday night. The City was not financially equipped to maintain relief for the jungle men, which initially stalled efforts to continue social support. The provincial government was expected to step in at some point to take on this burden. The City took a risk, and on September 9 announced that it would issue week-long meal and bed tickets, expecting compensation in full by the provincial government. At this point, it was still unclear when or how much the federal government was planning to donate to relief efforts.

The process of providing relief to the scores of unemployed following the closure of the jungles was disjointed at best. Since no level of government had officially assumed responsibilities for these men until the end of September, the measures taken by civic and provincial governments were noticeably makeshift and only suitable as temporary practices. Pressed into action, the provincial government introduced work camps in 1931 as a way to ship out the transient and unemployed away from the cities where they might congregate and cause problems and off to more remote locations in the province. The men would be put to work on projects that relied on low-wage labour, like building highways, roads, and the occasional private golf course. This work was often the epitome of a boondoggle; pointless routine calculated to keep idle hands busy. The men were provided with basic, military-style barracks in which to live, meager food, and—in payment for their hard work—20¢ a day, a sum far below the standard of living. By the end of May 1932 it was reported that nearly 5,000 men were living in relief camps across the province including Vancouver Island, Kamloops and Salmon Arm, Revelstoke, Cranbrook, Prince Rupert, and the Cariboo Region, in addition to the Lower Mainland. By June the number had risen to more than 5,600, with 22 percent of the men classified as transients from outside BC. Unsurprisingly, nearly 94 percent of those working in the camps were single without dependents; this disenfranchised group possessed no significant ties to their communities and presented the largest political threat.[16] In 1933, the federal government took over the camps and further enforced a pseudo-military work structure.

The relief camps, as well as the jungles, have come to symbolize not only the struggle for employment in Depression-era Canada but also the strength of its working class. Inside the camps various groups, including the communist-leaning Relief Camp Workers Union, established a foundation and political philosophy that would inspire men to act against a system rife with inequities. From the Hunger Marches of 1932 and 1933 to the On-to-Ottawa Trek in 1935, it was these men— including many jungaleers—who were at the forefront of changing the way Canadians approached the rights of the unemployed. Their efforts, and the eventual recognition of their demands for relief, would continue to influence political and social welfare programs well into the post-war period.

(Endnotes)

1   John Douglas Belshaw, "The Administration of Relief to the Unemployed in Vancouver During the Great Depression" (master's thesis, University of British Columbia, 1979)

2   "Advice on Jobless Aid is Awaited." *The Columbian* [Vancouver] April 16, 1931, 1.

3   "Fear Typhoid from Jungles." *Vancouver Sun*, September 4, 1931, 1. Courtesy of John Belshaw.

4   Major James Skitt Matthews, "Memorandum of Conversation, 23 August 1933, with Mr. W.J. Moore, Photographer, 420 Hastings Street West." Early Vancouver. Vol. 3. (Vancouver: City of Vancouver, 2011), 304.

5   "How They Live in Vancouver's Jungles." *Vancouver Sun*, July 25, 1931. 1. Web

6   For more information on the history of First Nations in Stanley Park, refer to Jean Barman, *Stanley Park's Secret: The Forgotten Families of Whoi Whoi, Kanaka Ranch, and Brockton Point* (Vancouver: Harbour, 2007).

7   H.W. Cooper to Alderman W.C. Atherton, September 3, 1931, file 18, box 15-D-4, series 20, City Clerks' Papers, City of Vancouver, VCA.

8   Major James Skitt Matthews, *Early Vancouver*, Vol. 1 (Vancouver: City of Vancouver, 2011), 178.

9   Todd McCallum delves into the work of Rev. Roddan in "The Reverend and the Tramp, Vancouver 1931: Andrew Roddan's God in the Jungles," *BC Studies* 147 (2005): 51–88. Also see Andrew Roddan, *Vancouver's Hoboes* (Vancouver: Subway Books, 2004).

10   "Fear Typhoid from Jungles," Vancouver Sun [Vancouver], September 3, 1931, 1.

11   Ibid.

12   Ibid.

13   Ibid.

14   Ibid.

15   Ibid.

16   Walker, P. Canada, BC Ministry of Labour; Department of Unemployment Relief, *Summary—Personnel in Relief Camps*, Victoria, 1932. Print.

RED SHADOWS: A SPY'S EYE VIEW OF VANCOUVER IN THE DEPRESSION

LANI RUSSWURM

The Red Shadow was a professional wrestler on the Pacific Northwest circuit in the 1930s. He was known for his famous "backbreaker" move and the signature red mask he wore to hide his identity and which his opponents unsuccessfully tried to remove. One theory was that the Red Shadow was actually Leo Nurma Anderson, a popular wrestler who many fans imagined occasionally donned the mask to become the theatrical wrestling-ring villain. But when the Red Shadow trounced Anderson in a Vancouver bout in 1936, fans realized Anderson couldn't have been fighting himself. The *Vancouver News-Herald* speculated it may have been Pat Fraley in the mask that night based on his wrestling style, which differed from other Red Shadow fights. "You pays your money and takes your choice," quipped the *Herald*, and the mystery remains unsolved to this day.[1]

Not only was the Red Shadow probably more than one wrestler, but he was also only one of several grapplers using that name in different regions and at different times. Various "Red Shadows" could be found on the professional wrestling circuits for much of the Cold War era. There was also a fictional Red Shadow in the 1920s operetta *The Desert Song*. This incarnation was a Zorro-like figure, a masked rebel leader in Morocco under French colonial rule. Hollywood film versions in the 1940s and 1950s changed his name to El Khobar, possibly because a heroic Red Shadow would have been awkward at a time when "Red" combined with "Shadow" had connotations of Soviet intrigue. In the late 1940s, readers of the *Montreal Gazette* were treated to "Red Shadow over Canada," a series of articles on communist machinations

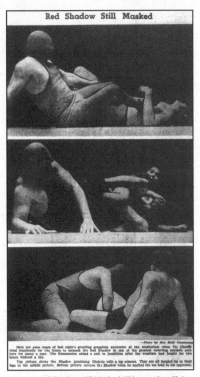

Red Shadow Still Masked

Red Shadow still Masked. This popular villain of the wrestling ring echoed the real-world conflicts of industrial relations before WWII. *VANCOUVER SUN*, JANUARY 8, 1937.

in this country. These were based on the revelations of Igor Gouzenko, the Russian cipher clerk whose defection from the Soviet embassy in Ottawa revealed communist spies operating in Canada and is considered a starting point for the Cold War.[2] Soviet-led or at least inspired activities had a longer pedigree than this, particularly on the west coast.

In the shadowy real-world of 1930s Vancouver, the "Reds" were organizers with the Communist Party of Canada (CPC) trying to mobilize workers under the Workers Unity League, a militant trade union umbrella organization. In response, business and political leaders employed their own "shadows": labour spies who gathered intelligence by attending meetings, hobnobbing with workers and union organizers, and posing as unemployed men. During the Depression years there were numerous Red Shadows in the city employed by the RCMP, the Vancouver Police Department, the British Columbia Provincial Police (BCPP), individual employers, the city's Relief Department, and private detective agencies contracted by the Shipping Federation, an association of waterfront employers.

One such labour spy was "Operator #3." He worked for the BC Detective Agency, a private firm run by J.G. Petrie, a former Saskatoon police detective. Operator #3 took over from Operator #5 in August 1934. Petrie sold his reports for ten dollars apiece to the Shipping Federation. Most of the information supplied by #3 consisted of names, addresses, and other details of individual activists working on the waterfront. Some of his inquiries reflected particular concerns of Shipping Federation bosses, such as who was behind the *Heavy Lift*, a militant newsletter distributed to longshoremen that was fanning the flames of industrial relations along the waterfront. One of Operator #3's missions was to find the location of the mimeograph machine used to churn out this and other communist propaganda sheets.

Through "discreet inquiries among certain Longshoremen," Operator #5 had reported on July 13 that the *Heavy Lift* was indeed printed in Vancouver and that its main writers were Blondie Moffat and Bill Ward.[3] In September, a Mrs. R.H. Flynn told #3 that the mimeograph machine was housed at 3411 Wellington Avenue. The

Heavy Lift, September 11, 1934. Publications such as this one promoting worker militancy on Vancouver's waterfront were a major concern for labour spies in the 1930s.

newsletter, she said, was brought there from a house at 1159 East 19th Avenue, where it was prepared. The *Heavy Lift* publishers, however, were preparing to move their equipment "as they are scared that the Police will soon get onto where the Machine is and seize it as they are doing quite a bit of printing for the Vancouver Communistic Party."[4] Sure enough, it was taken to a home on Lozells Avenue in Burnaby, but Operator #3 believed there must be a second machine. "Russian Alf," one of the distributors of the *Heavy Lift*, told #3 that he picked up bundles of the newsletter at the Toronto Apartments (today called the Astoria Hotel) on East Hastings Street. "I would suggest that a room be taken for a few days in the Apts," Operator #3 wrote, "to ascertain the correct room in which

The Toronto Apartments, now called the Astoria Hotel, was a hotbed of communist agitators in the 1930s and for a time the location of the mimeograph machine that printed the *Heavy Lift*. VANCOUVER PUBLIC LIBRARY #11463. PHOTO BY STUART THOMSON.

they keep the machine."[5] A couple of weeks earlier, #3 reported that "one of the main places for the sale of the *Heavy Lift* is a newsstand run in connection with a Shoe Shine Parlor at 163 Hastings Street West, and this is where Flynn gets in touch with the Russian known as Al or Allen."[6] This address, the Flack Block, appears frequently in the spy reports. At least eight union and communist-affiliated organizations are listed there in the 1935 city directory, including *BC Workers' News*, the main organ of the Communist Party's British Columbia chapter.

Petrie's spies identified numerous private homes connected with prominent and not-so-prominent Communists. Some were used as venues for secretive "Communistic" meetings. One of these was 4733 East Hastings, owned by a Burnaby relief recipient, described as a former longshoreman and "one of the main Red Leaders" who received one dollar per hour from the party for the use of his home.[7] There was also a cluster of agitators living in what is now the Hastings-Sunrise neighbourhood in the East End. Two radical unionists lived on Wall Street. One of them, Charles Hodgkinson, had been on relief but was now working in a shingle mill, also on Wall Street. He was "doing all he can to organize the men employed there," according to #3. His father, James, lived nearby on Pandora Street and sometimes gave his son support. "He is now retired and devotes all his time toward the Socialist movement," #3 wrote, before elaborating on the family's political history:

> In 1912 and 1913 James Hodgkinson was arrested as a ringleader in the Nanaimo Coal Strike, and stood trial with several others. Charles Hodgkinson was a draft evader during the War, his Father James Hodgkinson refusing to let him fight for the Union Jack, as he wanted him to fight for Russia.[8]

There was another "hot bed of reds out on Eton Street" in the same neighbourhood, not in houses or apartments, but in squatter shacks along the train tracks and in houseboats on Burrard Inlet. Operator #3 pointed out that this land was probably owned by the federal Harbour Board, perhaps to imply that this was one communist nest that could be easily broken up by the authorities.[9]

Public gathering spots were also good places to collect intelligence on subversive activities, such as the many beer parlors and pool halls frequented by workers. Operator #3 heard about one such place, "a certain pool room in the down town district that is supposed to be another hang out for waterfront Reds."[10] By his next report he had identified it as Sandy's Billiard Parlor at 443 Seymour Street: "This pool-room is used by some of the Red agitators as a meeting place for some of their talks and to pass the word around about their new activities."[11]

Sandy's Billiard Parlor at 443 Seymour Street, seen here on the right as "Nick's" in 1956, was identified by labour spies as a popular meeting place for "red agitators" in the 1930s. CITY OF VANCOUVER ARCHIVES, CVA #BU P508.68. PHOTO BY A.L. YATES.

There were other communist hotspots in Vancouver listed in Operator #3's reports, including what he referred to as another headquarters that had been set up on West 2nd Avenue in Kitsilano.[12] One of the more interesting places was the World Hotel in Japantown. If accurate, Operator #3's reports on this site should have been considered one of the more valuable pieces of intelligence, at least from a national security standpoint:

> I learned that the World Hotel at 396 Powell Street is quite the hang out for Reds, and a lot of the waterfront workers are now using it for their red element to gather; a man by the name of Charles Hanson is now using this Hotel for his headquarters. I learned from a most reliable source that this man Hanson has in the last fourteen months, made two trips to New York to get money and instructions as to carrying on of the Communistic movement in Vancouver.[13]

On October 5, Hanson's name came up again in #3's report:

> Talking to one man whom I am well acquainted with I find a lot of grief can be expected from Charles Hanson. This man is continually talking among the men and is telling them there is no doubt but the Reds will pull off a big strike in May or June 1935. He claims there won't be much difficulty as it's a cinch to get the lumber industry tied up, and that is where it will start. There was a meeting held by a few of the well-known Reds in the World Hotel last night October 4th 1934.[14]

And on October 20:

> Meetings are still being held at the houses I have mentioned in previous reports, chief among the agitators is Charles Hanson, World Hotel, A.J. Johnson, 3411 Wellington, J. Jacobson, Glen Apts.
>
> The above gang are still very optimistic and believe that a General Strike is not far off. They claim to have the Lumber Industry in such a shape that they can depend on them at very short notice.
>
> A further claim is made that a large fund is held in New York from Russia for the sole purpose of aiding in strikes. It is alleged that Hanson handles some of it.
>
> Personally I am of the opinion that if anything does happen it will be a show down among the waterfront workers as from my observations I find the majority of them are regular fellows and dead against the Reds.[15]

Charles Hanson doesn't appear to have caused much grief after all, since his name or activities don't appear again in the spy reports. It is possible that he funnelled "Moscow Gold" to fund labour agitation in Vancouver, but it's not likely. The VPD's chief constable, Colonel W.W. Foster, later concluded that local activism was precariously self-funded, and Foster would have had access to much more intelligence than what survives in the archives or what individual detective agencies had at their disposal.[16] The report on Hanson therefore raises two possibilities. First, it is possible that the Soviet Union did have a strike fund in New York but that it wasn't made available to Vancouver agitators after all. Second, it calls into question just how reliable these spy reports were, given they consist of opinion, hearsay, gossip, speculation, and information that may or may not have been true. If Operator #3's cover was slipping and he was suspected of being a "stool pigeon," for example, it's possible that his informants deliberately supplied him with misinformation.

Like the Red Shadow of the wrestling world, we know almost nothing for certain about Operator #3 himself, such as what qualifications or biases he brought to the job, although we could make some safe assumptions. He was male and whatever his own class background, was able to blend in to some degree with Vancouver's industrial workers. J.G. Petrie informed the Shipping Federation that #3 lived in the same general area as some of the most active communists, which, Petrie thought, would make it easier for him to infiltrate their organizations.[17] Nevertheless, in at least one instance Operator #3 aroused enough suspicion to get kicked out of a union meeting of unemployed seamen at 233 Main Street. "After answering several questions I was permitted to enter; when the meeting started the door was locked and the door-man remained by the door inside," #3 reported. Later on, however, "three men came over to me and after a long questioning I was gently but firmly requested to leave the hall … I would like to add that this Hall is situated so that I think it would be very easy to install a Dictaphone."[18] Operator #5 had a similar experience the previous month when he attempted to attend a mass meeting at Moose Hall on Burrard Street using the name "Bud Jackson." He was questioned by two men and "although I convinced them that I worked on the waterfront I was requested to leave."[19]

Operator #3's proposal to secretly record meetings using a Dictaphone was fully embraced by the VPD. Chief Constable Foster later admitted that all known left-wing public meetings in town in 1935 had been bugged.[20] He also introduced phone tapping to the VPD's arsenal, with mixed results. Police set up a listening post in the Carter-Cotton Building at the corner of Hastings and Cambie to record telephone conversations of allegedly corrupt police officers supplying information to Joe Celona, the notorious pimp and bootlegger. Poor sound quality on the recordings made them inadmissible as evidence in court and may have reinforced the preference for flesh-and-blood spies such as Operator #3 for gathering intelligence.[21] On the other hand, as imperfect as electronic surveillance was, it may have offset the unreliability of intelligence generated by labour spies, and vice versa.

Operator #3's reports were occasionally supplemented with research by his boss, J.G. Petrie. In August, 1934, for example, Petrie wrote to Shipping Federation manager Major W.C.D. Crombie:

> With reference to Operator #3 report of even date, I beg to state
> that I personally checked up the report that R.H. Flynn had been
> an employee of the C.P.R. through their investigation Department

and learn that R.H. Flynn was employed by the C.P.R. as a Clerk from 1908 to 1929, when he was fired for Agitating a General Strike and openly expressing his Radical ideas.[22]

Robert H. Flynn, according to Operator #3, was "a great Communistic worker and speaker and his house is where the executive Committee men meet."[23] Another time Petrie obtained intelligence from his old boss at the Saskatoon Police Department and furnished the Shipping Federation with the criminal record of Sam Scarlett.[24] Scarlett is one of the more colourful characters in western Canadian labour history. A charismatic public speaker involved in some of the biggest American labour struggles as a member of the Industrial Workers of the World, Scarlett worked alongside legendary union figures such as "Big Bill" Haywood and Joe Hill. He was arrested and tried hundreds of times and deported to Britain during the American "Red Scare" of 1919–20. Scarlett ended up back in Canada in time for the 1931 Estevan Coal Miners' Strike, which culminated in the death of three strikers at the hands of the RCMP in Bienfait, Saskatchewan. Petrie added to his report that "I know this man personally and he is a very dangerous character."[25]

As Operator #3's reports show, it appeared that communist agitators were attempting to pull together a general strike of BC's major industries, including waterfront workers, loggers, and streetcar workers. San Francisco's bloody "Big Strike" in 1934 was exactly that, and it wasn't something employers and authorities in Vancouver wished to see replayed in their city. At one point the Shipping Federation even contracted "Inspector S-9," a spy in California, to track down Harry Bridges, the leader of the American longshoremen's union, to find out if he was influencing developments in British Columbia. S-9 came up dry.[26]

Another area where the communists were making headway was in the relief camps that were set up throughout BC to warehouse the unemployed and keep them away from cities. Labouring and living under grim conditions, many of the men in camp were receptive to the communists' idea of a strike to push for a program of "work and wages" instead of what they referred to as "slave camps." In early April 1935, close to 2,000 unemployed men abandoned the camps and headed for Vancouver. Police spies were working in the camps, and Vancouver's Chief Constable Foster hired his own informants to keep tabs on the unemployed.

Some of the reports coming in from police spies were alarming. Before the relief camp strike got underway, an operative working undercover for the BC Provincial Police urged his bosses to take the relief camp strike seriously, as "all the men in the Camps are out to raise Hell and he expresses the view that there is sure to be some bloodshed."[27] Another unsigned BCPP agent report described the situation in Vancouver a couple of months before the strike. This spy hung around 52½ Cordova Street, the headquarters of the Relief Camp Workers Union that coordinated propaganda and organizing in the relief camps. Meetings there, he wrote, "are taking place daily and the strike is not far off now. The speakers ... are working them all up to a pitch where they go out to Camp and raise hell." This spy also recognized numerous men on the city's streets from the relief camps who had been blacklisted as agitators. "I think there must be two or three hundred thrown out of BC Camps since first of 1935," he wrote. As police spies often did, he offered his own opinion on how to deal with the situation: "I would think that the Department of National Defence should build one big camp, say up the Coast somewhere, and put barbed wire around. Then all these agitators, Reds and Communists could be gathered together and kept in one place."[28] This kind of advice did little to calm the authorities in Vancouver.

The police had cause to be nervous. If the longshoremen and workers in other industries went out on strike and joined forces with the unemployed relief camp strikers, the numbers would be overwhelming. A BCPP operative reported in March 1934 that the relief camp strike was being held off precisely so these forces could align, "so that when the Camps strike and come into Vancouver there will be an effort made to pull out all organized labour and unorganized as well. This, however, could not take place this month." Moreover, the unemployed who were already in Vancouver were getting antsy, and the BCPP spy reported that "there might be some violence this month even if the strike does not come off."[29]

May Day, 1935. Spy reports incorrectly concluded that local communists would launch a general strike on May 1, 1935. There was a large demonstration, but no trouble for the authorities. The Flack Block, the building on the left, was home to several radical labour organizations. PHOTO COURTESY VANCOUVER PUBLIC LIBRARY #8814.

Spy reports indicated that the general strike of longshoremen and workers in other industries was to be launched on May 1, 1935, while the relief camp strikers were in town. One of the VPD spies reported a few days earlier that the situation was getting serious because strike funds would be exhausted May 1 and "there would be hell to pay":

> There is sure to be a lot of trouble on Monday next as the Relief Camp strikers and Longshoremen, also all the unemployed Hoodlums in town, will be on the streets looking for a fight. Special care should be taken to have all firearms, ammunition and gunpowder, dynamite, etc. carefully checked up in the City for both Monday & Wednesday, May 1st. If the [May Day] Parade takes place to Stanley Park from Cambie St. Grounds on Wednesday, 1st, the Communists will be sure to make the best of it. I am afraid that in the present mood the Relief Camp strikers are in, also the 500 odd Hoodlums who have joined them now, that there is to be very serious clashes with the Police . . .
>
> Troops should be kept in readiness and martial law might have to be declared. I am making this very strong, I know, but after a year with these fellows, mostly Eastern toughs, I know their minds pretty well . . . Vancouver is now a seething caldron of discontent . . . Of course, the joke of the whole thing is the rank & file does not stop to think that the Communists are using them to blow the lid off Vancouver.[30]

Despite the alarm bells sounded in police spy reports, the 1935 May Day Parade was uneventful. With more than 20,000 people marching from downtown to Stanley Park, it was probably the largest May Day turnout in Vancouver's history, but was completely peaceful. What followed in the months to come was anything but.

The unemployed relief camp strikers left town in early June on what became known as the On-to-Ottawa Trek. It was a dramatic political statement, one that began with great promise but ended with bloodshed in the Regina Riot. Longshoremen in Vancouver were locked out shortly after in a labour dispute that culminated in the Battle of Ballantyne Pier, a three-hour-long riot triggered when police attacked a demonstration of waterfront workers and their supporters. We can't know for sure what role labour spies played in these confrontations, but can safely assume they were involved in some capacity. In any case, Vancouver's revolutionary moment had already passed.

Herbert Darling, one of the RCMP's top spymasters, was sent to overhaul the Vancouver Police Department, which included the establishment of the Communist Activities Branch. *REGINA LEADER-POST*, AUGUST 31, 1945.

Following the dramatic events of 1935, the Vancouver Police Department borrowed one of the top spymasters and anti-Communists from the RCMP, Herb Darling, to restructure the city police force. Darling found the spy department dysfunctional and inadequate, which may help explain the hyperbole found in spy reports generated by the Vancouver Police Department. In response, Darling "broke it up, disbanded it, and started afresh" with the creation of the Communist Activities Branch that he set up in an office in the Dominion Building on the corner of Cambie and Hastings Street.[31] The Shipping Federation continued to use labour spies to monitor union activity. One spy, known only as "The Fink" to members of the Inlandboatmen's Union, filed reports every other day in 1938 and 1939.[32]

There are many archetypal characters associated with the Great Depression: the hobo, the populist politician, the confidence man, the hard-boiled detective, the G-man, and the tommy-gun toting gangster are perhaps the best known. In many North American cities, "Red Shadows" were also commonplace, but the secretive nature of their work and the obfuscation of politics make them elusive historical figures. Still, the Red Shadow was hinted at in many pop culture expressions of the decade, from the wrestlers using the name, to comic book, pulp fiction, and radio serial characters such as the Phantom and the Shadow, who had his own secret network of operatives to help combat what he believed to be the evil that "lurks in the hearts of men." Vancouver had many Red Shadows in the 1930s and a surprising number of spy reports that they left behind have been preserved. They don't tell us much about the individual spies, but they provide a small window into the opaque world of political intrigue, suspicion, and deceit that helped define the decade.

(Endnotes)

1   *Vancouver News-Herald*, November 27, 1936. On the continuing mystery of the Red Shadow's identity, see J Michael Kenyon, ed., The WAWLI Papers (Wrestling As We Liked It), no. 452, April 1, 1999 [online], https://groups.google.com/forum/#!topic/rec.sport.pro-wrestling.info/Fh95NMNZ7_w.

2   The first article in the "Red Shadow over Canada" series appeared in the *Montreal Gazette*, September 9, 1946.

3   City of Vancouver Archives, Add MSS 279, Shipping Federation fonds, Loc 521-C-2, file 2, Pratt Secret Services [hereafter SF], "Re:-Communist Members," report from Operator #5 sent to W.C.D. Crombie, July 13, 1934. For more on the *Heavy Lift* and a detailed account of industrial relations on Vancouver's waterfront before WWII, see Andrew Parnaby, *Citizen Docker: Making a New Deal on the Vancouver Waterfront 1919-1939* (Toronto: University of Toronto Press, 2008).

4   SF, "Report," Operator #3, September 4, 1934.

5   Ibid., September 6, 1934.

6   Ibid., August 25, 1934.

7   Ibid., "Re:- Communist Members," Operator #5, July 13, 1934.

8   SF, "Report," Operator #3, September 20, 1934.

9   Ibid., August 29, 1934.

10   Ibid., October 1, 1934.

11   Ibid., October 3, 1934.

12   Ibid., September 6, 1934.

13   Ibid., October 1, 1934.

14   Ibid., October 5, 1934.

15   Ibid., October 20, 1934.

16   Lani Russwurm, "Constituting Authority: Policing Workers and the Consolidation of Police Power in Vancouver, 1918–1939 (master's thesis, Simon Fraser University, 2007), 55.

17   SF, Petrie to Crombie, August 6, 1934.

18   SF, "Report," Operator #3, August 28, 1934.

19   SF, "Re:- Communist Members," Operator #5, July 17, 1934.

20   Vancouver News-Herald, February 11, 1939. None of the recordings appear to have survived, although a transcription of a recorded meeting of the unemployed held at the Avenue Theatre on July 10, 1935, can be found in City of Vancouver Archives, Vancouver Police fonds, Series 199, subseries Communism, 75-F-2, file 9.

21   *Vancouver Sun*, December 2, 1936.

22   SF, Petrie to Crombie, August 25, 1934.

23   SF, "Report," Operator #3, August 21, 1934.

24   SF, Petrie to Crombie, September, 1934.

25   Ibid., October 3, 1934.

26   SF, "Re: Harry Bridges," CE Pratt to Crombie, March 4, 1935.

27   BCA, GR-1323, reel no. B02301, L-125-1-1935, McMullin to Attorney-General, March 22, 1935.

28   Ibid., Unsigned report, February 17, 1935.

29   Ibid., March 9, 1935.

30   Unsigned report, April 27, 1935, in Victor Hoar, ed., Ronald Liversedge, *Recollections of the On to Ottawa Trek* (McClelland and Stewart: Toronto, 1973), 155.

31 Russwurm, 157.
32 Ibid., 44, *n*.6.

CRIME AND ITS PUNISHMENTS IN CHINATOWN

ROSANNE AMOSOVS SIA

December 20, 1931

W aitress Grace Leslie was standing in the Pender Café in Chinatown chatting with a customer when she heard the front door jerk open. It was Dick Lee. He'd already been in earlier for dinner, when he'd ordered his regular ox-tongue-no-gravy with milk. But now here he was back again, just after 11 p.m., standing at the door in a long trenchcoat that went down past his knees, sopping wet from the rain barreling down outside. Grace watched as Dick avoided the smattering of Chinese-Canadian customers sipping coffee and reading newspapers, making his way to one of the corner booths. He looked so cold and miserable that Grace excused herself from her conversation and hurried over to the kitchen to get a warm cup of coffee for him.

She carried it over to Dick. "Back again?" she said, setting down the cup.

"Wanted to see you again, sweetheart," he said, winking at her, but it was half-hearted flirting, certainly not his best.

Grace had a lot of nights to compare this one to. She'd been waitressing for the past 18 months in Chinatown, first at the Yen Tong Café, where she'd met Dick, and now at the Pender. Dick came in for a bite to eat every night after work. He worked as a cook in Shaughnessy Heights, he'd told her in one of their first conversations. He was what she called "a quiet chap" who spoke so softly (though in good English) that Grace had to strain to hear him. Still, he livened up once Grace got to know him. It became a bit of a game, the flirting between him and all the waitresses. Grace didn't mind. It gave her practice figuring out how to get a good tip from the customers. And if she got called sweetheart, well, Dick called all the waitresses sweetheart, except for Marion, who was Chinese. He called Marion "sister" instead.

"Let me hang up your coat to dry," Grace said, pointing to the coat Dick had bundled up on the seat next to him. Dick shook his head. Instead, he reached into his pocket and handed her a small box. It was a box of face powder, just the brand Grace had requested a few weeks ago when he'd asked her what she wanted for Christmas.

"Oh, but it's still five days before Christmas!"

"Don't tell Mary," was all Dick said in response. Grace just shook her head.

By Mary, Dick meant Mary Shaw, who Grace had met at the Yen Tong over the summer. Mary'd come in one day, just 19 years old, desperate for work. At home Mary's mother, sister, and niece were all looking to her to bring in the money. The Depression made it hard times for all. Mary was good at her job, though; she raked in the tips. Never stopped smiling and could bring a smile to anyone's lips. She was always gossiping about her favourite talkies with the customers now that she worked at the Pender with Grace. Greta Garbo this or that. Grace didn't get out to the movies that often, couldn't afford it except when she'd go out on a date with one of the customers. But that was something Grace didn't do too often anymore, not like some of the others. She liked a few quiet nights at home, herself.

It seemed that Dick had taken a fancy to Mary, though. Mary'd shown Grace a few letters he wrote telling her he loved her. She'd heard him say it too, aloud, and Mary'd always tell him not to be crazy and walk away. It was only fooling; Grace was sure of that, and Mary'd just laugh and agree with her.

Grace stuck the box of powder in her apron pocket, and not a moment too soon. Mary'd just come in from the backroom to start her shift. She was powdering her nose in front of the mirror at the end of the aisle. Grace walked past her on her way to the kitchen, greeting Mary with a smile. She saw Mary smile back at her through the mirror.

Grace was almost at the kitchen, when a *bang* stopped her in her tracks. She swung around. Dick was on his feet, a gun in each hand. There was another flurry of shots, and then Mary crumpled to the ground. It had to be a joke. A toy gun. Except then Grace saw waitress Rose Munro and the rest of the customers scrambling for the door.

There was blood staining Mary's back, marring the pale pink fabric of her dress, Grace noticed. She was still too dumbfounded to move. And so she watched as Dick, staring down at Mary on the floor, slowly brought one of the guns up to his head. There was one more shot, and then Dick too dropped to the floor.

It'd been eight shots, Grace learned later when she read the coverage in the *Vancouver Sun*. Eight shots from a .38 calibre revolver and a .32 automatic taped to

Dick's wrists. He must have hidden them under that coat of his. "He was so decent. I can hardly realize he shot Mary and killed himself," the *Sun* quoted her as saying. Though it was true, Grace didn't remember saying that, nor any of the other things they reported in the papers.

"Chinese Slayer of Waitress Insane?" the front page of the *Vancouver Sun* asked its readers the next day. The verdict of the Vancouver coroner's jury was yes. The jury had examined the evidence and concluded that Dick was "temporarily insane." But that wasn't all. It also recommended: "If there be a bylaw or a law prohibiting the employment of 'white' female help by Orientals, it should be strictly enforced."

There was, in fact, already such a law on the books in British Columbia. Legislation that prohibited "Chinamen" from employing "white women and girls" was first passed in Saskatchewan in 1912. Two restaurant owners in that case, Quong Wing and Quong Sing, went to court to fight the law, taking their case all the way to the Supreme Court of Canada. They lost the fight. When the Supreme Court upheld the law, it set a precedent for similar legislation to follow in provinces across Canada including BC. But this law was not enforced within the City of Vancouver until 1936.

It took four years, but the 1935 appointment of Vancouver Police Chief W.W. Foster brought to power just the right man to carry out the coroner's jury's recommendation. Backed by Mayor Gerry McGeer, Foster sent his police force out onto the streets. On the labour front, he crushed the communist "Bolshevik" element in Vancouver. He ordered police to use tear gas and clubs against striking longshoremen in what became known as the 1935 Battle of Ballantyne Pier, injuring 60 people. Next, he turned his full attention to the "problem" of white waitresses in Chinatown.

In Foster's opinion, young white women were not to be trusted in Chinatown: "It was the practice of Chinese [men] to contact the girls in the cafés, and, in cases where the girls were already loose, make arrangements for the girls to come to their quarters after working hours, where immorality took place." His trusted Detective Sergeant Andrew S. Rae agreed. Rae claimed that the

Police Chief W. W. Foster in 1935, the year he was appointed Chief of Police. Still trim at age 59, he is the picture of British respectability. He wears a full military uniform with the rank insignia of colonel, a crown above two four-pointed Bath stars visible on his left shoulder and an impressive array of medals earned during the First World War on his left breast pocket. CITY OF VANCOUVER ARCHIVES, AM54-S4-: PORT P246.

typical Chinatown café was "a breeding place for crime and vice, and premises such as these, while they offer employment to white girls who may be in need of work, appear to be little better than a trap for the defilement of young girls."

Elite Vancouverites like Foster still saw themselves as representing the British Empire. At the very moment when an aging Britain was losing its grip on empire, young Vancouver aspired to embody its values in the Pacific Northwest. With Anglo-Saxon superiority as his central creed, Foster carved out a privileged place in Vancouver. Middle-class women were at the heart of this project: relegated to the home, they symbolized purity, both racial and sexual.

And so Foster sent his police force into Chinatown. They staged surprise inspections in the cafés. They interrogated waitresses on their way to work and on the job. They peered into Chinatown boarding houses, hoping to surprise waitresses "in bed" with Chinese-Canadian men. And they kept detailed reports on the women they found in these "immoral circumstances."

On August 5, 1939, police interrogated 15-year-old Wanda Woods on her first day at the Geck Lock Café in Chinatown. After making note that Wanda was a "rather pretty blonde," Detective Sergeant Rae took down the following statement:

> One of the Chinamen wanted me to go to his room with him. Another one wanted me to go out with him to a Beer Parlour. I did not go. Later, one of the girls named "Bunny" and I had some coffee. While there she introduced me to a young and well-dressed Chinese named Wing or Wayne Hope. He speaks good English. He took me out for a walk. We went to Chinatown and went to the Flying Dragon café.

On August 29, 1935, police caught waitress Jerry Wilson "in bed" with Toy Hong in his room at the New Harbour at 139 East Cordova. Jerry told police she'd been living for six weeks with Toy, who was chef and part owner of the BC Royal Café. Police reported that Jerry claimed Toy was "good to her, giving her nice presents, and that she was able to take a day off when she pleased."

On May 28, 1937, police found BC Royal Café waitress Jessie Pleasance "living with" Harry Chin in Room 217 of the New Lion Hotel. Police called Jessie a "well known prostitute" who had "once lived with a coloured man named Smith, later with a Chinaman named Jimmy Fong." A few months later, they reported that Jessie had "actually married this Chinaman."

By venturing into Chinatown and making a life there, women like Jessie Pleasance were seen as and labelled as prostitutes.

In 1937, Foster threatened to revoke the licences of the Hong Kong, BC Royal, and Gee Kong cafés if they didn't fire their "white" waitresses. Incensed, Hong Kong Café owner Charlie Ting told the *Sun*, "There's no reason why they should make those spasmodic attempts to clean up Chinatown. The excuse of closing the places because they hire white girls is too weak to fool anyone."

But appeals by the Chinese consul general, visits to city council by prominent Chinatown men, even hosting a dinner in Chinatown to schmooze with city counselors – none of these diplomatic niceties worked. Foster, now backed by Mayor George C. Miller, refused to budge. The owners of the three cafés, unable to risk losing their livelihood, finally fired their waitresses. The rest of the cafés in Chinatown followed suit.

It would seem that Foster had gotten his way. But the story didn't end there.

On the morning of Friday, September 24, 1937, waitress Kay Martin woke up early, giving herself extra time to do her hair and pick out her clothes. She took her usual route to work, but instead of tying on an apron at the Hong Kong Café, she assembled with 14 other waitresses on the streets of Chinatown.

Kay Martin was yet another waitress police had surprised when, in June 1936, they found her "living with" a Chinese-Canadian man named Roy Fong. At that time, the police didn't pursue Kay's case any further, but on this September day, they would hear from her again.

The 15 waitresses waving to *Vancouver Sun* photographer Stan Williams as they start their long march from Chinatown to Vancouver's city hall. *VANCOUVER SUN*, SEPTEMBER 25, 1937.

Photographer Stan Williams captured the waitresses in a photo that appeared on the front page of the *Vancouver Sun*. It showed them standing two-by-two in an orderly line. We can see Dorothy Crutchley in the front row, bobbed hair curled and topped by a stylish, pert hat. Next to her, Peggy Parker waves at the camera with a glove-covered hand. Kay Martin stands near the back of the line, clutch purse tucked under her arm and shiny black pumps on her feet.

Dressed in their best, and all smiles, these 15 young women marched on Vancouver's new city hall south of False Creek. But despite appearances, this was no friendly visit to Mayor George C. Miller. They had business to do.

The public, in their opinion, should know about this absurd attempt to take away jobs during the Depression. At a time when the unemployed filled the streets of Vancouver, "Why are individuals denied the right to work and forced to live on starving relief?" asked one waitress in a letter to the mayor. Waitress Margaret West told *Sun* reporter Christy McDevitt, "We are fired just at a time when Old Man Winter comes along. Many of us support families and are right up against it."

The Chinese-Canadian café owners understood the waitresses needed to work. Charlie Ting declared to the *Sun:* "The girls are able to look after themselves. They have to make a living." A few months later, Charlie Ting and Gee Kong Café owner Harry Lee risked losing their licences when they gave food to former waitresses in exchange for a few hours of work. Wong Foon Sien, Secretary of the Chinese Benevolent Association, defended their actions to city council, saying their Confucian beliefs had led them to feed the "hungry" waitresses.

The waitresses, for their part, seemed to have no problem with Chinese-Canadian men, not as employers, co-workers, or customers. They said they chose to work in Chinatown at least partly because of the good working conditions. Kay Martin made it very plain: "They treat us swell. We work eight hours each day, seven days a week and are paid good wages. There is never any trouble with the boss. I would much prefer working for a Chinese employer than for some other nationalities." Kay, for one, wasn't buying into the racist caricatures promoted by men like Foster.

Their bosses, the waitresses said, were unfairly targeted because they were Chinese. "[Our employer] could easily have fired us and taken on Chinese waiters, but that isn't the point. They feel that the present city bylaw on this question is not only illegal but an insult to their pride."

In short, city officials had stuck their noses where they didn't belong. In Kay's words, "They're a bunch of fussy old bridge-playing gossips who are self-appointed directors of morals for the girls in Chinatown."

Though these waitresses made their case to the *Sun*'s reporter, they didn't convince Mayor Miller. When they reached city hall, he refused to see them. Still, they persisted for two more years. In 1938, a group of former waitresses and Charlie Ting challenged the ban. When that didn't work, the waitresses tried again in 1939, but once more Foster intervened: "In view of the conditions under which these girls are expected to work . . . it is almost impossible for them to be so employed without falling victims to some form of immoral life." For Foster, to include white women in the Chinatown community was unthinkable.

The public record acknowledges the achievement of all the men involved, even the Chinese man Charlie Ting. After his death in 1939, Charlie Ting was recognized for his contributions to the Chinese-Canadian community. He was given the first public funeral for a Chinese official in Canada with a "monster procession" of two hundred motorcars and an estimated 1,000 people making the trek from Chinatown to Mountain View Cemetery in his honour.

The city authorities involved in the ban went on to have successful careers. Foster served in the Second World War and was promoted to major general. Later, he became chairman commissioner to the British Columbia Power Commission. After working in the federal government, McGeer's career in civic and federal politics ran through the 1930s and into the late '40s. Mayor George C. Miller, meanwhile, went on to become a member of the Legislative Assembly of British Columbia.

After their efforts in 1938 and again in 1939, the waitresses disappeared from view. There is no public acknowledgment of their struggle.

STREET KINGS: THE DIRTY '30S AND VANCOUVER'S UNHOLY TRINITY

CATHERINE ROSE

L.D. Taylor's Vancouver was a festering sewer, and Gerry McGeer couldn't wait to lift the manhole cover. When McGeer coasted to victory over his long-time rival in the 1935 municipal election, he won a law-and-order mandate and immediately set about investigating allegations of corruption at the highest levels of City Hall and the Vancouver Police Department. The police shake-up, launched by McGeer within hours of taking office, would ultimately expose Police Chief John Cameron and gangsters Joe Celona and Shue Moy as an unholy trinity and would reveal just how deep the sleaze ran in Mayor Taylor's office. By the end of the year, L.D.'s political career would be in ruins, Joe Celona in jail, and 17 police officers in disgrace.

When McGeer announced his mayoral candidacy in November 1934, he declared that, "Vancouver should not permit the open flaunting of the law by foreign, mercenary self-seekers. The condonement of the commercialization of vice and crime by public authority should be abhorrent to every Canadian. That kind of thing can and must be stopped." Weighing in on the mayoral race a few days later, the *Vancouver Province* asserted that, "This year is going to be different. We are going to have an interesting election. We are going to have a fight." The newspaper couldn't have known that the real fight would begin after McGeer was elected.

The election wasn't the first time Gerald Gratton McGeer and Louis Denison Taylor had squared off. McGeer played a leading role in the 1928 Lennie Commission investigations that heard from every rat in the criminal food chain, from petty thugs and beat cops to crime kingpins and VPD bigwigs. Tales of scandal, intrigue, and the cozy relationship between the mayor, the chief of police, and two of the city's most notorious gangsters took centre stage.

Joe Celona was known at different times in the press as King of the Bawdyhouses, King of the Bootleggers, Public Enemy #1, and the Mayor of East Hastings. Shue Moy, his Chinese counterpart, was the alleged King of the Gamblers, with lottery schemes and gambling dens throughout the East End. While McGeer had been unable to provide any conclusive evidence of a police payoff scheme, the Commission was enough to cost L.D. the next election, and the chief constable, his job.[1]

Fortunately for L.D., the people of Vancouver had short memories, and 1930 saw him safely ensconced in the mayor's office for a fourth and final term. Thanks to a divided upper-class electorate, the populist mayor was able to win the big prize in one election after another for years, despite the rampant prostitution and gambling, bootlegging and drug use that pervaded the city. His secret weapon was his popularity among the working stiffs of the East End, where the brothels, gambling dens, and back-yard beer gardens allowed the largely immigrant population to make a bit of extra dough on the side. L.D. could often be found in the watering holes of Hogan's Alley and spent more time on the job rubbing elbows with celebrities than with aldermen.

Taylor's final term was a turbulent one. Always at the centre of scandal, L.D. had been returned to office in the midst of a global depression, and now faced not just the old issues of vice crime and quibbling aldermen, but also the new threat of thousands of unemployed men demanding relief. Although he had long positioned himself as an advocate of the working man, the conditions of the 1930s tested his patience, and the police were tasked with breaking up one protest after another. By December 1934 Taylor appeared to have lost whatever control he had over conditions in the city, and the people of Vancouver had lost their patience.

Part of the problem was a lack of continuity at the helm of the Vancouver Police Department. The VPD had acquired a reputation as "the graveyard of police chiefs" after going through six of them in less than ten years. After the latest chief was sacked in 1933 for alleged "inefficiency," the chief constable's office received fresh meat in the form of John Cameron, the former chief of New Westminster Police, who had had a distinguished career with the VPD as a young constable. Sadly, Cameron's polished reputation and professional prestige wouldn't last long.

The 1935 election and subsequent shake-up was McGeer's personal vendetta, a chance to get the satisfaction that had eluded him in 1928 and a point of pride to show how crime had continued to infest the city in the years since the Lennie Commission. Energetic and deeply religious, McGeer stood in sharp contrast to the aging L.D.

He painted a picture of a city besieged by the criminal element and on the verge of financial ruin after years of fiscal mismanagement. McGeer was enjoying the battle and he even tossed out a catchphrase on the last night of his 1935 campaign: "We're going to Bar Celona." He dismissed a recent spate of police raids on known criminal operations as "election gestures" ordered by L.D. for political purposes.[2] McGeer won the election with nearly 80 percent of the popular vote.[3]

Once elected, McGeer didn't waste any time putting his ambitious plans into action. On December 30, a drunk and despondent Chief Cameron had allegedly turned up at McGeer's home, begging to be allowed to keep his job. McGeer didn't blink. On December 31, Cameron bid adieu to 1934 and to his brief term as chief constable by tendering his resignation, stating that, "In view of the announced statement of Mayor-elect McGeer that he proposes to institute a drastic plan of police reform, I feel that my continuance as chief of police might prevent the fruition of this undertaking." His resignation was unanimously approved, as was his request for an extra month's salary in lieu of the previous year's vacation time.[4] (McGeer complained, "he resigned before we got him.")[5] By January 3, just one day after McGeer was sworn into office, the Vancouver Police Department had a new chief constable, although he technically wasn't a constable at all. Colonel W.W. Foster was a military man and a politician, but his British birth and education, combined with his war medals and no-nonsense attitude, seem to have made him the right sort of chap for the job. Cameron wasn't the only casualty of the new regime. Acceptance of the chief's resignation was, ironically, the final act of two other members of the Police Commission: Magistrates J.A. Findlay and W.M. McKay, both of whom would soon themselves be investigated. Deputy Chief John Murdock didn't fare much better, reigning as acting chief constable for just three short days before being suspended pending further investigation.[6] In the same meeting of the revamped Police Commission, McGeer alleged that, "the demoralization of the police force and the open commercialization of crime resulted from a general laxity in law enforcement, ineffective police administration, incapable and slack prosecution of arrested offenders, feeble Police Court administration and a general attitude that Police Commission and magistrates' courts, working in co-operation with dishonest police officers, had the right to license crime."[7] This was only the beginning of the purges.

The department blacklist soon added 16 officers ranging in rank from detective to inspector. They comprised the majority of the department's elite Criminal Investigation Department (CID). Foster interviewed them all personally, and it wasn't long before they all started singing. The evidence presented of bribe taking and general corruption was so damning that the resulting report recommended dismissals of 12 of the suspended officers and a demotion for one other. The three officers who were spared the axe were kept on because they were junior detectives, and as such were felt to be "victims of a vicious system" controlled by their superiors.[8] John Cameron and his erstwhile cronies must have been sweating like a cold beer on a hot day when Foster recommended further investigation and indicated that criminal charges were imminent.[9] The details of the ensuing investigation confirmed what the people of Vancouver had long suspected: that the Vancouver Police Department, and the CID in particular, was ineffectual at best and downright dirty at worst.

According to Colonel Foster, every officer he interviewed—including the 17 under suspension—declared that vice conditions in Vancouver were "disgraceful." More significantly, there was a general consensus that the situation had been worsening steadily, and that L.D.'s "open town" policy was to blame. It was reported that "persistent interference" prevented officers of all ranks from doing their jobs, and that it was common knowledge that any officers who tried to get in the way of the crime bosses were moved to outlying stations in short order. Foster alleged dramatically that, "to such an extent has the system of protection for White Slavery [aka: prostitution], Bootlegging, Gambling, Dope, and confidence rackets developed, that Vancouver has become the International Headquarters of a revolting type of vice, and the natural refuge for criminals of dangerous character."[10]

The allegations in Foster's initial report to the Commission were dynamite, but the best was yet to come. When Colonel Foster became chief, he brought in a new legal advisor to assist in the reorganization of the VPD. Major T.G. McLelan's February 18 report to McGeer showed Cameron's VPD to be elbow-deep in sleaze. Reporting that "the Police organization was completely demoralized," McLelan alleged that:

> Commercialized vice and well organized crime thrived under Police protection. Well-known criminal groups to the knowledge and with the sanction of ex-Police Chief John Cameron, and several other of the Police Force openly carried on . . . white slavery and the operation of brothels, gambling, including slot machines, Chinese lotteries, book-making and all forms of card, crap, and other table games. Illegal sale of liquor, bootlegging joints were operating in almost every block of the downtown area, and the illegal sale of drugs was rampant. As a result of this the conditions that developed, robbery with violence, burglary and theft, became a nightly and daily occurrence.[11]

This was damning evidence that L.D.'s "victimless crime" was a sham.

Certain characters feature prominently in the McLelan report, most notably Shue Moy and Joe Celona. The rest of McLelan's list of infamy reads like a Noir-era crime novel: Mickey Tudor, Shorty Miller, Newsy Bernard, and "Tom the Greek," to name a few. Not only did these men have the run of the town, they also apparently had the run of the department, commanding immediate audiences with Cameron through means of a secret knock on his office door. It came out that on at least one occasion, Cameron and Deputy Murdock had spent the night cruising Howe Sound on the police boat in the company of Celona, his fellow "white slaver" Tony Lombardo, and certain "women of the underworld." Somewhat suspiciously, the captain of the police boat had been recommended by Cameron for promotion the previous fall.[12]

Shue Moy had had a varied career since his arrival in Canada in 1899. On the legitimate side, he was the Potato King, whose Fraser Valley operation was, by 1935, the largest potato farm in Canada. Over in the shadows, however, Moy had interests in dozens of gambling dens, lottery houses, and protection rackets, to name but a few of his activities. He also trafficked opium and even had a share in a brothel. While he was never convicted of a criminal offence, witnesses at the 1928 Lennie Commission drew unwanted attention to Moy when they testified that he was frequently seen at L.D.'s home. The Commission also heard that of the many raids made on the city's gambling dens in 1927, not one came to the door of any in which Moy had an interest.[13] Like Celona, he developed a cozy relationship with Chief Cameron: McLelan revealed not only that Moy enjoyed occasional use of the chief's car, but also that in August of 1934 Moy paid $150 of farmhands' wages at the chief's ranch in Haney. Few would have been surprised to learn that Moy complained directly to Cameron if any officer unwittingly interfered with his gambling operations, nor that there were "dire results to the officer in question."[14] That Moy managed to avoid prison is perhaps a testament to his ingenuity and insight, which may also explain his hasty departure for China at the end of 1934.

Moy wasn't the only beneficiary of Cameron's weak moral compass. The Taylor-era police chief had a tight relationship with a triumvirate of notorious bootleggers: Joe Alvaro, Wally Cole, and Eugene Valente. These three wise men of the East End each had their own special gift for Cameron: Joe Alvaro bore the gift of a truck that Cameron frequently borrowed for trips to his ranch. Wally Cole bore the gift of a gin joint on Kingsway, where Cameron would pass entire evenings drinking with brown-nosing beat cops bent on promotion. Eugene Valente, Cameron's "pet bootlegger," bore the most useful gift of all: his own taxi company, always on call to deliver champagne and whisky to the chief's office for illicit on-duty drinking parties.[15]

The problems didn't end with Cameron's shady relationship with gangsters. Administrative corruption abounded in the form of fraud, theft, and sloppy record-keeping. In what McLelan called "an appalling lack of co-operation between the Police and the Local Law Enforcement Departments," no records were kept by the Police Court clerks as to whether fines were paid or convicted offenders imprisoned.[16]

Liquor seizures presented a similar problem. Short of the Dry Squad logbook, no record was kept of liquor seized and disposed of, and even then it was typically entered a few bottles short. Sometimes bootleggers would simply come to the station to claim their own liquor back. As no record was kept as to why seized liquor might have been returned, the entire system was thoroughly open to abuse.

The corruption wasn't confined to the police department, either. Ex-Police Court Magistrates Findlay and McKay also came under fire surrounding the issue of sureties for bail. In both instances, it was found that the magistrates had allowed known criminals to post bail for one another without providing the necessary proof that they actually owned the property that they were posting as bail bonds. In many cases, the same characters would then claim that they could not afford to pay the imposed fines the next time they were "nicked." The police court clerk reported that when he had tried to raise the issue, Magistrate McKay had told him to "mind his own business and not to interfere."[17]

McLelan's report was the final nail in John Cameron's constabulary coffin. On February 19, 1935, arrest warrants were issued for the ex-chief and his five accomplices: Celona, Moy, Alvaro, Valente, and Cole. Cameron was easy enough to find, having been confined to hospital with a broken shoulder since early January, but both Moy and Celona were initially on the lam. Celona turned himself in the next day, and another $10,000 was added to the $30,000 bail he had already posted for the prostitution charges on which he had not yet been tried.[18] Forty thousand dollars was a lot of lettuce in the midst of the Great Depression, and more than a few heads were turned by Celona's easy willingness to part with that sort of change.

Celona would be spending a great deal of time in court in 1935. First there was the December 1934 charge of living off the avails of prostitution. In the dying hours of the L.D. regime, senior members of the VPD would take steps to improve their record. By the time the election results hit the newspapers, the CID had Joe Celona in its crosshairs. On December 14, just two days after McGeer's election victory, Celona was arrested in his Hastings Street brothel on prostitution-related charges. He was released on $30,000 cash bail. In March 1935 a second trial was added for a related charge of procuring the two young girls involved to work for him as prostitutes. These were followed by the requisite appeals. Finally, there was the trial for conspiring to cause a public mischief with co-accused John Cameron et al. Celona didn't make any friends on the stand, calling the prosecutor "cheeky" and denying every accusation levelled at him, from pimping to bribery. While he admitted to having once been on the police boat, he claimed that he was helping the police search for a wanted criminal and denied the presence of any women, liquor, or the police bagpiper who, it had been rumoured, provided entertainment. He cited McGeer's attack on his reputation during the Lennie Commission as the reason for his many aliases. Celona's lawyer also made the connection between his client's arrest and McGeer's election victory: "Doesn't it suggest that somebody is behind all this thing, somebody is out to get Celona? They knew what happened in 1928 and that the mayor and Celona crossed swords so they got busy in less than twenty-four hours. Every policeman got busy to save his job."[19] It wasn't enough.

While the prostitution cases were more sensational in content, the corruption trial was the far bigger event. Seventy witnesses were called to testify in the preliminary hearing in Police Court. In mid-April 1935, four more defendants were added to the case, although two were believed to have recently left the country. The most convincing evidence came from police witnesses, one of whom testified that he had been told by Cameron to "go easy" on certain establishments of a nefarious nature, including the two hotels linked to Celona's later prostitution charges. On another occasion, the same constable had been called to the chief's house, where he found him drinking champagne with Celona and a former department employee. Cameron's ranch was a frequent weekend getaway for crime bosses and underage girls. Other beat constables working the East End claimed that gambling dens run by Moy always seemed to be closed on days that police raids were planned.[20] Cameron could even be petty on behalf of his friends: one witness claimed that he had been instructed to raid a brothel kept by Josephine Celona, right around the time she obtained a divorce from her husband, Joe.[21]

A picture rapidly emerged of a chief of police (and a good portion of the department) beset by alcoholism and financial difficulties, freely flaunting their power at the expense of those officers with professional integrity, and at huge cost to the community at large. Officers testified to having seen known criminals drinking in the offices of the chief and the morality squad, and having been given money by the chief for "satisfactory performance" after keeping him company at all-night parties in Wally Cole's bar.[22] Inspector Charles Tuley had been harshly reprimanded in a 1934 meeting of the Police Commission for making a report of liquor infractions at an event attended by the chief, L.D. Taylor, and Magistrate McKay, which had "caused their names to be bandied about in a disrespectful manner."[23] During Celona's trial, Tuley stated that he had once "reasoned with the chief to cut out the booze," to which the chief replied, "What business is it of yours?"[24] After being caught by Moy's doorman watching officers and criminals coming and going from the gangster's offices, Tuley was suddenly demoted and moved to "the sticks" of South Vancouver.

In late May, after a brief adjournment, Cameron, Celona, and another pimp, Lou Barrack, were ordered to stand trial in a higher court, their accomplices' cases having been disposed of in Police Court. When Cameron himself finally took the stand, he used his exemplary record prior to his time as chief as evidence and adhered to Celona's explanation of the Howe Sound cruises, stating that they were searching for suspects in a hold-up; he did not explain why the deputy's wife was present, nor how he was expecting to sneak up on a pair of fugitives in a marked police boat, their arrival announced by the wailing of bagpipes. He also failed to elucidate why the chief of one of the largest police departments in the country was personally investigating relatively minor vice crimes by attending parties in gangsters' homes, or why he would have thought it wise to take a room in the Maple Hotel after an all-night drinking binge. The Maple was home to Celona's brothel, and there was a gambling den downstairs that Cameron himself claimed to have raided on numerous occasions.

Despite overwhelming and damning evidence to the contrary, Cameron emerged triumphant. Several points were noted by his counsel, including the fact that both Celona and Lou Barrack had been arrested on Cameron's watch.[25] Presiding Judge McIntosh observed that while several instances of moral delinquency had been at

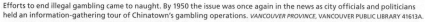

Efforts to end illegal gambling came to naught. By 1950 the issue was once again in the news as city officials and politicians held an information-gathering tour of Chinatown's gambling operations. *VANCOUVER PROVINCE*, VANCOUVER PUBLIC LIBRARY 41613A.

issue, none of them in and of themselves proved that there had been any overt agree-
ment among the three accused. More importantly, he stated, the police force was
notoriously undermanned and underfunded: even Chief Foster documented numerous instances of officers not having access to functioning handcuffs and revolvers. In
such circumstances, McIntosh declared, failure to control vice crime could not be
considered the same thing as enabling it.[26]

Joe Celona was eventually sentenced to 22 years in prison for the prostitution
charges and for keeping a gambling den in the Maple Hotel. His sentence was cut in
half on appeal, and he was ultimately released on "good behaviour" after only six
years. Unfortunately for him, he was an Italian national, and his release came in
1941; when word got out, there arose such a public outcry that his parole was revoked
and he was sent back to prison to finish his sentence. Lou Barrack, also convicted of
prostitution-related charges in the spring of 1935, was sentenced to 10 years. Shue
Moy prudently remained in China for the duration of the trial and never was convicted of any criminal offence.

From the earliest days of the Vancouver Police Department, vice crimes had
been seen as more or less harmless. Records show that one police chief after another
had publicly advocated for a red light district. In a September 1935 meeting of the
Police Commission, even Chief Foster himself had argued that eradication of the sex
trade was impossible, and that its suppression and mitigation were the best that could
be hoped for. It seems that all forms of vice were seen more or less the same way by
the police, and occasionally by politicians. The exception to the rule was drug
offences, which may be partly explained by the impact on the VPD of the 1917
murder of Chief Malcolm MacLennan by a crazed addict in the East End.

Given these attitudes, it is not surprising that the VPD was rife with graft. The
morality movement that had begun to gain steam in the late nineteenth century was
largely a middle- and upper-class preoccupation; the working-class origins of the
vast majority of men and women on the police force meant that most probably
sympathized with the industry and ambition of the city's most notorious immigrant
communities. Add to the mix a City Hall that openly downplayed the harm of vice
enterprises, the total absence of formal training, and two significant pay cuts to a
force that was already earning significantly less than their counterparts in other
jurisdictions, and it becomes easy to see how—individually and collectively and at all
levels—the police could have justified the systematic harvesting of bribes.[27]

If there had been a shadow of a doubt in anyone's mind at the end of 1934 as to
the complicity of L.D. Taylor, that doubt should have been thoroughly extinguished
by the summer of 1935. Although Cameron and his motley crew of gangsters were
acquitted on the conspiracy charges thrown at them by Foster and McGeer, the

allegations of corruption levelled at Cameron and the Police Court magistrates were entirely substantiated and corroborated by multiple witnesses. As all three men had comprised the Board of Police Commissioners alongside L.D. since at least 1933, it stretches the bounds of credulity that L.D. could have been unaware of the state of affairs in the Police Department and in the city as a whole.

While it may be said that the worst that can be proven against Taylor is "laxity of law enforcement and ineffective police administration," at a certain point "laxity" becomes complicity. The strongest evidence in L.D.'s favour is that he retired from politics in apparent poverty, although this is perhaps not terribly surprising, given his history of fiscal mismanagement at the civic level. And yet, a few days after his final political loss in the 1937 aldermanic election, noted East End defence lawyer Angelo Branca (who had defended Celona in his 1935 pimping trial), sent L.D. a letter informing him that a group of anonymous well-wishers had established a "pension" for him of $25 per week, for life.

Dirty '30s, indeed.

(ENDNOTES)

1   Daniel Francis, *LD: Mayor Louis Taylor and the Rise of Vancouver* (Vancouver: Arsenal Pulp Press, 2005), 154.

2   *Vancouver Province*, December 12, 1934.

3   Francis, *L.D.*, 189.

4   Minutes of a Special Meeting of the Board of Police Commissioners, December 31, 1934. City of Vancouver Archives, S180, File reference 75-A-2 #3.

5   David Ricardo Williams, *Mayor Gerry: The Remarkable Gerald Grattan McGeer* (Vancouver: Douglas and McIntyre, 1986), 172.

6   Minutes of a Special Meeting of the Board of Police Commissioners, January 3, 1935. City of Vancouver Archives, S180, File reference 75-A-2 #3.

7   *The Vancouver Province*, January 3, 1935, 1.

8   Chief Constable W.W. Foster, Report to the Chairman and Members, Vancouver Police Commission, January 18th, 1935.

9   Ibid.

10   Ibid.

11   Letter from T.G. McLelan to Mayor G.G. McGeer, February 18, 1935. City of Vancouver Archives, file reference Box 33-B-5, RG 3, Vol. 12, File 1.

12   Meeting of the Board of Police Commissioners, September 13, 1934. City of Vancouver Archives S180: Board of Police Commrs. Minutes (Feb 33—Dec 36). File Reference: 75-A-2 #3

13   Schneider, Stephen, *Iced: The Story of Organized Crime in Canada* (Mississauga: John Wiley & Sons, Canada, 2009), 139.

14   Letter from T.G. McLelan to Mayor G.G. McGeer, February 18, 1935. City of Vancouver Archives, file reference Box 33-B-5, RG 3, Vol. 12, File 1.

15   Ibid.

16   John Clough, the city's first gaoler, had been caught running a similar scheme before the Great Fire of 1886. Citing borderline illiteracy for the error, he had been caught collecting fines from prisoners then "accidentally" entering records showing that they had done time in the clink instead.

17   Ibid.

18   *Province*, February 21, 1935, 1.

19   *Province*, April 12, 1935, 2.

20   *Province*, April 25, 1935, 26.

21   She was later acquitted. *Province*, April 24, 1935, 5.

22   *Province*, April 25, 1935, 26.

23   Meeting of the Board of Police Commissioners, November 8, 1934. CVA S180 75-A-2 #3.

24   *Province*, April 26, 1935, 1.

25   *Province*, July 16, 1935, 1.

26   *Province*, July 19, 1935, 1

27   Before 1937 officers were not paid for testifying in court on their days off, a further disincentive to arrest criminals and lay charges.

JAMES CROOKALL'S
VANCOUVER[1]
JOHN BELSHAW

T here's one photograph in particular, one big black-and-white shot of two newsboys joyously shouting out the headline: "PEACE." It feels like New York, perhaps Chicago, maybe San Francisco. It's Vancouver. The study of mid-century Vancouver photography has become something of a cottage industry. The list of well-known practitioners grows longer every day. But we tend to see the more recent photographers with greater clarity than those who preceded them. Before the Curt Langs and Fred Herzogs,

there was James Crookall and a small contingent of street photographers who helped nurture his talent. Some of Crookall's photos are well known, although he himself is not. He doesn't make the cut in many surveys of Vancouver and British Columbian art, nor is his work featured in studies of local photography. He is not to be found in *Visions of British Columbia: A Landscape Manual* nor is he in *The Visual Arts in Canada: The Twentieth Century*. Like many of

Probably the most oft-published of Crookall's photos. Newsboys announce the end of WWII. CITY OF VANCOUVER ARCHIVES. CVA 260-1455. PHOTOGRAPH BY JAMES CROOKALL.

his peers' photographs, his work shows up anonymously in collections of historical Vancouver photographs. Several Crookalls illustrate Aynsley Vogel and Dana Wyse's *Vancouver: A History in Photographs* but no attribution is made. No one seems to notice his handiwork specifically. This is likely because, almost uniquely among his contemporaries (including the photojournalists Stuart Thompson, Jack Lindsay, Gord Sedawie, and the partnership known as Artray, or the street portrait snapper, Foncie Pulice), he was not a professional photographer.

Crookall was born in 1887 in Preston, Lancashire, the very centre of the world's textile industry. He had two sisters, Lizzie and Gertie, and a younger brother, Joe. Crookall secured a scholarship to Preston Grammar School, an old and distinguished institution. Performing especially well in writing, drawing, and mental arithmetic, Crookall stood out enough to obtain a glowing reference from his headmaster, who described him as "a bright, intelligent youth, quiet in his manner, gentlemanly in his bearing, neat in person, punctual and methodical in his habits." The reference continues, "He is quick-witted and resourceful, thoroughly trustworthy and I have much pleasure in saying he has my unqualified respect and confidence."

After completing his education in 1902 Crookall went to work as a junior clerk in the offices of the Ribble Navigation Corporation, an ill-fated canal-building company in Preston. The year that followed found him employed as a telegraphist for the post office and then, in the summer of 1904, he and his family emigrated to Canada on board the *SS Bavarian*. They stopped first at Moosomin, Saskatchewan. Like so many English immigrants, the Crookalls were likely not prepared for prairie winters; balmy Vancouver beckoned. By 1908 Crookall could be found at the Union Steamship Company (USC) where he was employed as company secretary under Gordon Tyson Legg, the firm's chairman.

Crookall wryly puts himself in the frame in this self-portrait, combining black and white with the illusion of oils, ca. 1928. CITY OF VANCOUVER ARCHIVES. CVA 260-30. PHOTOGRAPH BY JAMES CROOKALL.

Not long after he arrived on the west coast, Crookall joined the 6th Regiment of the Duke of Connaught's Own Rifles, a rifle brigade with a new drill hall on Beatty Street. But when war came, Crookall spent most of his two years of active service at Camp Taliaferro near Fort Worth, Texas, in the Motorcycle Section of the Royal Flying Corps (still in its infancy), and not in the trenches with the Connaughts. Photographs of crash landings fill the pages of two albums: the early days

Flying machines and their mishaps continued to fascinate Crookall long after the Great War. CITY OF VANCOUVER ARCHIVES. CVA 206-243. PHOTOGRAPH BY JAMES CROOKALL.

of weaponized flight were highly dangerous for pioneering pilots, and Crookall's collection includes bitter marginal notes like "Crash 82" and the names of flyers who died. The experience cemented a lifelong interest in aircraft that would complement his professional fascination with shipping. Returning to Canada, Crookall rejoined the Steamship Company, becoming the house bookkeeper and all-rounder. He would occupy several positions of increasing importance—rising to comptroller—at the company's office near the Burrard Inlet docks in downtown Vancouver. Almost every day for the next 40 years he would be at the city's hub.

Despite his apparent authority and influence in the firm, he remained an inconspicuous office-body: there are at least five histories of the Union Steamship Company, but only two mention Crookall. What's more, each of these volumes is sumptuously illustrated, and the likelihood is great that Crookall's photographs are included in all, yet this aspect of one of the company's longest-serving employees mostly goes unacknowledged. The exception is Tom Henry's *The Good Company*, which includes an early photo of a cocky-looking Crookall with his employer and his colleagues. The caption describes him as "company secretary (and later renowned photographer)." If Crookall ever achieved any "renown," those days were far ahead of the Edwardian youth seen leaning against a porch by the waterfront.

The photographic facet of Crookall's life seems to have started in the pre-War years. Anticipating the habits of later generations of tourists, Crookall documented a voyage across Canada, filling albums with slightly blurred 3" x 2" pictures of classic subjects like the Château Frontenac. By 1918, however, he was more serious, effective, and curious at the same time, displaying an interest in the crowd. Decades before American pioneer Robert Frank and a good ten years ahead of French photographer Henri Cartier-Bresson, Crookall was experimenting with what would become more widely known as *street photography*.

The defining feature of street photography involves the pairing of public spaces and people in unposed and unguarded situations. Crookall would, throughout his life, document shipping, aircraft, and bridges—he was, like many of his contemporaries, mightily impressed by the engineering accomplishments of the early twentieth century. He especially liked making a photographic record of large-scale construction projects and grand openings. By 1930 Crookall had emerged as a modernist with a keen interest in the angularity of architecture, industry, and steelwork. As well, he would from time to time assemble individuals and groups for self-conscious portraiture. But what is outstanding about Crookall's photographic archive is his attempt to capture Vancouverites unbound and in their urban environment. The city's natural beauty and its dramatic setting have confounded visual artists throughout the city's history. The sea, the mountains, the forests—these are the subject matter of tourism brochures and tourist snaps. But the scale itself defies capture in a still photograph. Photographers like Crookall, Curt Lang, and Fred Herzog turned away from the landscape with which Vancouverites profoundly identify and focused their lenses on the cityscape. It was during the Dirty '30s and the Second World War that Crookall hit his stride in this respect.

Twelve years after he had begun observing the street and its people, two developments came along that would change the texture of Crookall's photographs: small handheld cameras and the Great Depression. Interwar changes in camera technology made photography a much more portable and discrete proposition. Crookall's go-to device was a 35 mm "miniature camera," an innovative model that appeared first in 1924. According to Helga Pakasaar, the curator at Presentation House Gallery, the camera's "rapid exposures, finer optical equipment, and range finders providing sharp focus, allowed for unaccustomed angles, cropping, freedom with light, and capturing motion." As for the economic crisis, it put more people onto the streets, looking for work or taking advantage of sunny days and inexpensive pleasures in public spaces.

Crookall's Depression-era archive is dominated by crowds: at the cenotaph, at Lumberman's Arch, watching parades. These are records of events, some of which were scheduled, some of which (like the photograph of men watching trees being cut down through the middle of Stanley Park and leading to the new bridge) were not. The year 1937 finds Crookall photographing electric-lit streets and coffee bars, shacks and shanties around downtown, Chinese market gardeners at work in massive

Crowd in front of sideshow attraction, Happyland/PNE, 1938. Crookall captures the array of "Oddities" on display but his focus is on the posture of the people taking in the barker. CITY OF VANCOUVER ARCHIVES. CVA 260-933. PHOTOGRAPH BY JAMES CROOKALL.

vegetable patches on the edge of the city, and the Japanese-Canadian fishing community at Steveston. Two years later his portraiture of both people and urban settings had become more romantic and haunting. Contrast his landscapes from Stanley Park and the Interior of BC with the street scenes from the late 1930s and the surface hardness of the city and its sharp edges; the human need to insulate oneself from the environment—in warm coats, under awnings, in huddled poses with hands in pockets—leaps out.

Thematically, Crookall's record is simultaneously conservative and radical. His fascination with transportation technologies results in some profoundly conventional photographs. But then we have his street scenes (almost as often they are, really, *dock* scenes) that are sometimes highly geometrical and very often highlight the contrasts between private and public spaces. Small groups of men mooching on the waterfront. Huge throngs racing to watch the city's main pier reduced to smouldering stumps in a massive fire. There is the intimate—a clutch of men looking at news and job postings on the outside of a building, a cook and his assistant in a midway concession, a man carefully repairing fishing nets—and there is the anonymous—dockworkers trying to rescue a horse, a crowd outside a fairground. People in Crookall photographs seem to have purpose—they are often at work and sometimes actively at play, which reminds us that they have inner lives, concerns, stories. Crookall was sensitive, too, to the stillness of the city in the midst of bustle. His photographs invite the viewer to

The Lions Gate Bridge under construction, ca. 1934. CITY OF VANCOUVER ARCHIVES. CVA 260-809. PHOTOGRAPH BY JAMES CROOKALL.

slow down and listen to the stories that Vancouver wants to tell. These are private tales, confidential stories that define individual lives and capture the soul of the city. Because he was *not* a journalistic photographer, Crookall rarely captured anything newsworthy, and yet something important is implicitly happening in his pictures.

Crookall was self-taught, an amateur photographer. Insofar as he achieved any fame in his lifetime, it was through local photography groups. In the 1930s and into the 1940s, Crookall (and his wife-to-be, Doris Hacking) were part of an entourage of gregarious amateur photographers who scoured the city and its margins on two wheels; they called themselves the Cycling Circus. Despite the heavy bicycles they used, this group made ambitious forays into the Fraser Valley and further north, especially in the wartime days of gasoline rationing. The Circus had but one rule: every member had to be capable of pedaling 100 miles in a day: more than a GranFondo run to Whistler! These journeys enlarged Crookall's subject matter (and, presumably, his legs) while enabling him to pick up better techniques from his peers. Percy Bentley, the founder of Dominion Photograph Company, was a friend and photographer whose work Crookall particularly respected. He was active in the Vancouver Camera Club and Vancouver Photographic Society. He exhibited his work at their "international salons" into the 1950s. Crookall benefited, as well, from the patronage and moral support of John Vanderpant, an immigrant from Europe whose careful and canny cultivation of photography as a legitimate art form included promoting modernist perspectives. Crookall's photographs of grain elevators echo subjects explored by Vanderpant.

St. James Church, ca.1936.
CITY OF VANCOUVER ARCHIVES.
CVA 260-430. PHOTOGRAPH BY
JAMES CROOKALL.

Crookall's private life reveals little in the way of glamour or recklessness. He was a diligent company man and never worked for anyone other than the Union Steamship Company from the time he arrived in Vancouver until he retired 50 years later. He lived in the same house at 3746 Eton Street in North Burnaby from 1921. He enjoyed hiking along Burrard Inlet below Vancouver/Burnaby Heights and he is recalled as someone who could easily strike up a conversation with strangers. Crookall married only once and rather late in life, at 58 years. He nevertheless had time for a family: two daughters, Ruth and Joyce, arrived in 1948 and 1952 respectively. By this time, although he was still exhibiting his photos, he was now far more likely to turn the lens on his young family than crowds. The advent of colour film (more glitzy and trendy but more finicky and expensive to process) eclipsed black and white. Crookall experimented but couldn't justify the additional cost of processing, and his darkroom remained a shrine to monochrome. He explored other lifelong interests, including hiking, golfing, drawing and painting, marksmanship, stamp-collecting, sailing, and gardening (he grew prize-winning dahlias). He retired in 1958 and was promptly cheated of his pension when the Union Steamship Company ceased operations the following year.

Death came for Crookall on July 27, 1960. His collection of photographs was donated to the City Archives nearly 20 years later by his widow and collaborator, Doris Crookall. The periods during which he was active as a photographer were interrupted by long stretches of negligible output. It is impossible to know today whether he was continuously active and the fruit of his labours has been lost or if, from time to time, he set down his camera and shut the door on his little dark-room. A mostly unassuming man, Jim Crookall saw the city as few before or since have been able. Anticipating the street photographers of the second half of the twentieth century, he found geometry and humanity in the everyday. Crookall's Vancouver was both extremely humble and staggeringly proud. He saw individuals where others saw "types"; he saw human beings where others saw ... nothing. Crookall's great accomplishment is to make visible the many invisible men, women, and children who occupied the mainstages of the city from one end to the other.

The Marine Building reflected in pools of rain in the rail yards, ca.1939. CITY OF VANCOUVER ARCHIVES. CVA 260-999. PHOTOGRAPH BY JAMES CROOKALL.

Longshoremen tying up the "Empress of Canada" to dock, ca. 1939. CITY OF VANCOUVER ARCHIVES. CVA 260-1003. PHOTOGRAPH BY JAMES CROOKALL.

Children playing on a dock, Steveston, ca.1936. Six years later the whole community would be interned. CITY OF VANCOUVER ARCHIVES. CVA 260-605. PHOTOGRAPH BY JAMES CROOKALL.

Woman at drinking fountain at the beach, 1937. The textures and lines of this photograph make it one of Crookall's most important. CITY OF VANCOUVER ARCHIVES. CVA 260-670. PHOTOGRAPH BY JAMES CROOKALL.

Man painting the side of a ship, ca. 1936. CITY OF VANCOUVER ARCHIVES. CVA 260-426. PHOTOGRAPH BY JAMES CROOKALL.

A man and woman walk across
the still-relatively-new Lions Gate
Bridge, 1939. CITY OF VANCOUVER
ARCHIVES. CVA 260-995. PHOTOGRAPH BY
JAMES CROOKALL.

Men playing giant checkers, 1937. CITY OF VANCOUVER ARCHIVES. CVA 260-645. PHOTOGRAPH BY JAMES CROOKALL.

Sailor with crab in net on dock, ca. 1938. CITY OF VANCOUVER ARCHIVES. CVA 260-835. PHOTOGRAPH BY JAMES CROOKALL.

Women and children sneak a peak through knotholes and from treetops, 1938. CITY OF VANCOUVER ARCHIVES. CVA 260-937.
PHOTOGRAPH BY JAMES CROOKALL.

Men reading posted newspapers in Chinatown, 1937. CITY OF VANCOUVER ARCHIVES. CVA 260-758. PHOTOGRAPH BY JAMES CROOKALL.

The car barns illuminated at night in the BC Electric Building at 425 Carrall, 1937. CITY OF VANCOUVER ARCHIVES. CVA 260-779. PHOTOGRAPH BY JAMES CROOKALL.

SOURCES

City of Vancouver Archives. The photography of James Crookall. *AuthentiCity: The City of Vancouver Archives Blog:* http://www.vancouverarchives.ca/tags/james-crookall/

Cornwall, Claudia. *At the World's Edge: Curt Lang's Vancouver, 1937–1998.* Salt Spring Island: Mother Tongue, 2011.

Grenville, Bruce and Scott Steedman. *Visions of British Columbia: A Landscape Manual.* Vancouver: Vancouver Art Gallery and Douglas & McIntyre, 2009.

Henry, Tom. *The Good Company: An Affectionate History of the Union Steamships.* Madeira Park: Harbour Publishing, 1994.

Leonoff, Cyril E. *Bridges of Light: Otto Landauer of Leonard Frank Photos, 1945–1980.* Burnaby: Talonbooks, 1997.

Pakasaar, Helga. "Formulas for the Picturesque: Vancouver Pictorialist Photography 1930–45." *Vancouver: Art and Artists 1931-1983.* Vancouver: Vancouver Art Gallery, 1986.

Presentation House Gallery. *Unfinished Business: Photographing Vancouver's Streets, 1955–1985.* North Vancouver: Presentation House, 2005.

Presentation House Gallery. *In Transition: Postwar Photography in Vancouver* (North Vancouver, ca.1986).

Pullan, Selwyn. *Positioning the New.* West Vancouver: West Vancouver Museum, ca.2011.

Rushton, Gerald A. *Whistle up the Inlet: The Union Steamship Story.* Vancouver: JJ Douglas, 1974.

Thirkell, Fred and Bob Scullion. *Frank Gowen's Vancouver, 1914–1931.* Vancouver: Heritage House, 2001.

Thirkell, Fred and Bob Scullion. *Philip Timms' Vancouver, 1900–1910.* Vancouver: Heritage House, 2006.

Vogel, Aynsley and Dana Wyse. *Vancouver: A History in Photographs.* Vancouver: Altitude Publishing, 1993.

Whitelaw, Anne, Brian Foss, and Sandra Paikowsky. *The Visual Arts in Canada: The Twentieth Century.* Toronto: Oxford University Press, 2010.

THE IMMOVABLE OBJECT
WILL WOODS

Mayor Gerry McGeer stood on the steps of the cenotaph in Victory Square. His trembling hand clutched a single sheet of paper. A line of city police separated him from more than 1,000 cold stares. These were the eyes of destitute, unemployed men, some as young as 15, many of whom had engaged in hand-to-hand combat with the city's police barely an hour before. The Relief Camp Workers Union strike of April 1935 was two weeks in, and things had come to a head. The paper held by McGeer was the Riot Act. Once read, the implication was "not clubs, but bullets" for any who did not disperse.

The occupants of the surrounding office buildings leaned out their windows, watching the scene below. Newspapermen at the nearby offices of the *Daily Province* had a bird's eye view.

For a moment, Victory Square, a small urban park and World War I memorial in downtown Vancouver, became the eye of the storm in Canada's arduous and at times brutal response to the Great Depression—a storm that had by now raged for five long years and appeared no nearer to abating. Witnesses would recount that McGeer read the Riot Act in low, wavering tones that day, struggling under the weight of pressures bearing down on him in the square.

Gerry McGeer would later become a federal MP and senator. He also casts a long shadow over the city's history as an enemy of civic and police corruption. Yet his reading of the Riot Act in 1935 was, for many Vancouverites, his defining moment. It was either a brave stand against an incipient communist uprising or a heartless spit in the eye of Canada's most needy. So what led a former iron moulder, union man, self-avowed conquistador of poverty, and now mayor of the City of Vancouver to read the Riot Act to a group of hungry young men?

Gerald ("Gerry") Grattan McGeer was born in Winnipeg on January 6, 1888. He was the third eldest of 11 children in a large Irish family. The McGeers moved to Vancouver, via Langley, when Gerry was still a small boy. His father, Jim, worked in the dairy business, at turns a farmer, delivery man, and dairy inspector. Born a Catholic in his native Ireland, Jim had become an Anglican seemingly in protest at the hegemony of the priesthood. Jim was well known and generally well liked; gregarious, generous, terrible with money, and fond of a drink. He was a passionate Liberal, a political creed he would pass onto his son Gerry, along with his affection for the bottle and a love of public debate. Yet while the father was in his element pontificating over a whisky in a smoke-filled Vancouver saloon, the son was most at home berating opponents in courtrooms or parliamentary committees. His drinking usually kept to midnight indulgences in his backyard, away from any scrutinizing eyes.

The Vancouver that Gerry McGeer grew up in was a fledgling town of around 20,000. Gerry enjoyed a childhood of riding on his father's milk-delivery truck, picking wild berries, and playing in streams now running forgotten under Vancouver's streets. Gerry attended Mount Pleasant School, which he decided abruptly to leave, aged 14, much to his father's disappointment. Jim expected his children to be

Gerry McGeer the iron moulder (2nd from right).
CITY OF VANCOUVER ARCHIVES. CVA 9AM54-S4-PORT P1130.

well read and educated. He himself had studied at the prestigious Trinity College, Dublin, where many of the brightest minds of his countrymen had studied, from Oscar Wilde to Samuel Beckett. Jim McGeer was an articulate, intelligent man, even if his career had followed a potted path. Gerry's decision to leave school betrays the impulsiveness that marked much of his life. The lure of earning a day's pay was too much for 14-year-old Gerry to turn down.

A series of odd jobs followed for McGeer until he settled on the trade of iron moulding. He would spend his days toiling inside the dangerous, noisy confines of the Letson, Burpee and Company foundry on the Vancouver waterfront. Occasionally the smoky darkness would become illuminated by sparks and flames pouring from an open blast furnace. McGeer earned 25¢ a day beating red-hot metal into shape. He quickly made a name for himself in his union, the International Iron Moulders Union of North America. By 1909 and aged only 21, McGeer had initiated and led a number of strikes to protest the long working hours and poor conditions in

Vancouver's foundries. The whole of the Vancouver waterfront of 1909 was fostering a militant unionism that would pit union men against business owners, labour spies, and police. It was a situation McGeer would become all too familiar with later in his career, but under drastically different circumstances.

At some point Gerry McGeer realized that practicing lawyers could make $25 for writing a single letter and that the two-bits he was getting for a day's hard slog in the foundry compared rather badly. He quit the foundry and blazed through his high school matriculation in less than six months. Following a period of study and articling, McGeer was called to the bar in 1915, aged 27, a testament to his powerful work ethic. The path was not a smooth one for McGeer however. His father Jim died in 1913, aged 58. A reckless real estate investment had left Jim penniless when he died. As the eldest son, McGeer became the main breadwinner for the family. In this light, Gerry's decision to see through his legal education was the act of a young man determined to meet extraordinary responsibilities. He would never look back.

Vancouver's legal profession in the early twentieth century was dominated by political patronage. With an allegiance to the Liberal Party inherited from his father, McGeer quickly secured a nomination and election in 1916 as a Liberal MLA, aged 29. McGeer's 1916 election campaign was marked by vigorous support in public for prohibition, despite his notorious bouts of heavy drinking in private. (According to his biographer, David R. Williams, McGeer's wife, Charlotte Spencer, extracted from him a promise that he would never drink at home again. Barely skipping a beat, Gerry hid bottles of liquor in the garden of their Point Grey home and crept out for illicit midnight swigs.) McGeer served only one term in office, returning to more lucrative work in the legal profession. But the political bug had bitten.

McGeer would find the success of his practice ebbed and flowed with the successes and failures of the Liberals at the ballot box. And the post-war era was a good time to be a Liberal—provincially and federally. His most notable legal work came in the 1920s when he represented the province in a multi-year legal battle with the Canadian Pacific Railway (CPR) and the federal government over freight rates. The matter was of huge significance to the province. Inequity in freight rates had meant grain from the prairies—a major export—could be shipped far more cheaply from eastern ports than from Vancouver.

McGeer battled the "powerful and ruthless" CPR with considerable vim and revelled in the devilish complexity of the legal wrangling. His bombastic speeches in front of various committees succeeded in making him a household name. "His bursts of rhetorical pyrotechnics at times send a gale of laughter ringing through the railway court" reported *Saturday Night* magazine. His adversaries in court were not always so amused by McGeer's oratory. At one hearing the commissioner F.B. Carvell interrupted McGeer in mid-flow to caution, "There is too much politics in this to please me." McGeer shot right back: "Mr. Chairman, if we don't get a removal of discrimination, there'll be a great deal more politics in it before we're through."

McGeer's legal work also included his role as the star prosecutor in the 1928 Lennie Commission into police corruption in the Vancouver Police Department. McGeer took great glee in exposing the weak, inconsistent, or just plain false testimonies of the various witnesses. Even the head of the commission, Robert S. Lennie, was not spared McGeer's acid tongue. At a critical point in the proceedings McGeer let fly: "I want to tell you that organized lawlessness has taken charge of this town and it is an outrage and you can't get away with it. You are a coward and a quitter ... You are acting for crooks and scoundrels and you will not get away with it. Lennie you are no good." The outburst against Lennie stands as another fine example of McGeer's tendency toward both impulsiveness and dramatic public appearances. His grovelling apology to Lennie the day after his outburst—published in Vancouver's newspapers— betrays a peculiar willingness to admit wrongdoing in McGeer, who was usually so convinced of his own righteousness: "I find it difficult to express the very sincere regret I feel over my most unfortunate attack on you yesterday . . . I have made mistakes and I know that I made a great mistake yesterday ... I tender to you my most sincere apology for the wrong that I have done."[1]

While McGeer harangued both railway executives and crooked Vancouver police officers during the 1920s, his efforts to enter federal politics during the same period fell flat. He fought and lost on a Liberal ticket in the federal election campaigns of 1925, 1926, and 1930; first in the Vancouver-Centre riding, then in North Vancouver, and finally Fraser Valley. McGeer's trademark tub-thumping speeches attracted large crowds and much newspaper coverage. "He has the sprightliness and vivacity of a prancing steed coupled with the quick temper of an Irishman," observed the *Vancouver Star* during the 1926 election.[2] Yet in each instance McGeer's opponents cut his legs out from under him by drawing attention to the enormous legal fees the lawyer charged the province in his various rail freight-rate cases. McGeer had made enemies on his own side as well, including a few in high places. Provincial premier John Oliver had famously labelled McGeer "a son of a bitch" after receiving an invoice for $60,000. McGeer could loudly proclaim his success in battling the rail companies on behalf of the province, but could not shake off a reputation for avarice.

The fat years of Liberal contracts ended locally with the 1928 election of a Conservative government and, in 1930, with the rise of R.B. Bennett's Tories federally. It was the Great Depression, however, that would define McGeer's life's work. Within weeks of the Wall Street Crash of 1929 the crisis had spread across the globe. Canada's economy collapsed along with international demand for commodities. Once-dependable foreign orders for lumber, grain, and minerals disappeared. Within a year nearly 30 percent of Canada's workforce was unemployed. British Columbia was hit particularly hard, with so much of the economy dependent on resource extraction.

Both the mainstream Conservative and Liberal parties were fixated on the merits of "self-reliance" in times of economic hardship. Young single unemployed men often left home, reluctant to place a burden on their struggling families. Now homeless and jobless, these "hobos" were typically threatened with arrest for vagrancy by the police and denied any kind of financial assistance from the government. "Relief payments" were only available to married men.

Men as young as 15 years took to "riding the rails," stowing away illegally on trains in a restless journey from town to town in search of food, shelter, and work. Vancouver became a popular destination. The city was the last stop on two transcontinental rail lines, and as it was the hub for BC's resource-based industries, many unemployed men felt it offered better odds for work than elsewhere in Canada. Upon arrival, and finding work as scarce in Vancouver as elsewhere, many of the men took refuge in the hobo jungles that had sprung up around the city soon after the start of the depression. Eventually the City of Vancouver closed them down, and the men were encouraged to take up residence in a number of relief camps established in remote areas of BC. Relief-camp work included clearing forests, building roads and constructing military buildings. Conditions were usually inhospitable, and boredom was epidemic. Enrolling into a relief camp was voluntary, but the threat of arrest for vagrancy was an unwelcome alternative for most unemployed single men.

While the unemployed continued to arrive in Vancouver by the boxcar-full, many destined for relief camps, McGeer sat alone in his private study at home in Point Grey. His ego was bruised by his third federal election defeat. Besides, with the Great Depression on, lucrative legal work was more difficult to come by. McGeer's family was effectively immunized from the travails of the Depression by the wealth he had generated through his work in the 1920s. In addition, Charlotte herself was of wealthy lineage, being the daughter of department store chain founder David Spencer. The days of delivering milk with his dad were a distant memory for McGeer, firmly ensconced as he was among Vancouver's most affluent. And yet, without a courtroom or parliamentary session in which to talk the loudest or to know the most, McGeer had only his ideas for company.

A new direction did not take long to materialize. McGeer set himself the task of solving the great political conundrum of the time: unemployment. It says much about McGeer that he felt entirely able to single-handedly construct a theory that would—"within 24 hours," as he liked to say—resolve the terrible conditions of the

Great Depression. This was no small feat: it was a problem that had stumped the world's greatest economists and political leaders.

With typical doggedness McGeer spent most of 1931 in feverish study, mastering the intricacies of banking and finance. His inspiration came primarily from economist John Maynard Keynes, along with a cast of historical figures from Abraham Lincoln to Jesus Christ. He had, since his youth, fastened onto the notion that all the evils in Canadian political and social life could be traced to the door of the commercial banks and their role in issuing currency. McGeer believed absolutely that lending at any rate of interest was immoral. Indeed, the biblical story of Jesus knocking over the moneylenders' stalls in the temple was one McGeer would often reference in his speeches. "We have allowed paganism, the love of gold, the worship of money, to destroy the peace, order and progress of a Christian nation," he declared.[3] It is possible the root of McGeer's antipathy towards banks and his deep-seated loathing for bankers was a visceral response to the death of his debt-ridden father years earlier.

With obsessive attention to detail, McGeer put together a theory that Canada should become a "planned economy," wherein the government could print money at will by lending to itself at a zero-percent rate of interest. In tandem, all foreign trade would be managed via a barter system. As an example, when trading with France, the Canadian government might swap BC lumber for Beaujolais wine (without any actual currency necessarily being involved). The challenge of the Canadian government negotiating myriad barter arrangements with every single trading partner was a daunting prospect at best. Yet McGeer was certain such drastic monetary reform was required to finance infrastructure projects and create jobs and thus—overnight—solve the problem of mass unemployment. In fairness to McGeer, the idea of publicly funded infrastructure projects was not a million miles from the heart of American President Franklin D. Roosevelt's Depression-era New Deal.

Throughout 1932 McGeer gave countless speeches and wrote endless letters on his monetary reform ideas, even writing a book grandly entitled *The Conquest of Poverty*. In truth the book details a dense (and utterly incomprehensible) home-baked economic theory, which was publicly disparaged by many economists of the day. Professor J. Friend Day of the University of British Columbia asked of McGeer's theories, "whether it is now possible . . . to reverse ordinary rules and get something for nothing?"[4] McGeer flew into attack mode, decrying economists who "teach a mumbo jumbo they call economics" and who would "be better engaged reading Grimms' fairy tales to their students."

McGeer's efforts in defending his theories had little effect. R.B. Bennett's Conservative government in Ottawa was closely aligned with banking interests and

Communist propaganda, 1932. *The Worker.*

had not the slightest intention of taking instruction on monetary policy from a loud-mouthed West Coast Liberal like Gerry McGeer. He did find common ground with the federal government on another, very different, feature of the Great Depression however: the perceived threat of communism from the ranks of the unemployed.

Military Chief of the Canadian General Staff Andrew McNaughton perhaps best summed up the mood of officialdom at that time: "In their ragged platoons, here are the prospective members of what Marx called the 'industrial reserve army, the storm troopers of the revolution'."[5] In 1933, with politicians on all sides terrified of a communist insurgency led by thousands of jobless transients, Prime Minister Bennett instructed the Department of Defence to establish a series of federal relief camps across Canada. The existing provincially run relief camps in BC were subsumed into the federal program. In the process the BC relief workers' pay was slashed to 20¢ a day, a tenth of what an employed labourer could expect for the same work.

Hiding away the prospective "storm troopers of the revolution" in remote camps was not the antidote to communism that McNaughton and his supporters in the BC and federal governments hoped for. It did not take long for relief-camp workers to tire of the camp's military discipline, prison-like conditions, and pathetic wages. Ron Liversedge, who worked in a number of relief camps in BC, summarized the spirit of the camps: "In those bunkhouses, there were more men reading Marx, Lenin and Stalin than there were reading girlie magazines."[6]

As the camps became increasingly politicized many of the men joined the Relief Camp Workers Union (RCWU), which had close ties to the Communist Party of Canada. Most RCWU organizers themselves were blacklisted from the camps but they nevertheless succeeded in spreading left-wing propaganda among the residents. Vancouver became a centre for anti-relief–camp activity, with most men en route to the camps passing through the city and the RCWU's offices housed at 52½ West Cordova in Gastown.

With large numbers of militant RCWU organizers active in the city, rumours began to percolate. Vancouver's business elite heard that a mass walk-out in sympathy with the RCWU was being planned by local unions. The stakes were highest on Vancouver's waterfront. The fear of striking longshoremen made palms sweat in the boardrooms of even the most powerful Vancouver business magnates, such was the importance of shipping to the city's economy.

In the fall of 1934 one waterfront business owner decided to take action. Career Conservative politician and lumber baron Colonel Nelson Spencer (no relation to McGeer's wife, Charlotte Spencer) established the Better Vancouver League. Ostensibly the Better Vancouver League's purpose was to "rid Vancouver of Taylor rule" in light of incumbent Mayor L.D. Taylor's inability or unwillingness to tackle crime.[7] Ridding Vancouver of prostitution, gambling, and illegal liquor was certainly one goal of the Better Vancouver League; another was to confront communism and prevent militant unionism gaining ground on Vancouver's waterfront.

Spencer had no trouble in recruiting powerful allies but was reluctant to run for mayor himself. He was unlikely to attract the working-class votes needed to win. The Better Vancouver League needed a "virile, hard-hitting, clear-thinking man,"[8] someone able to appeal to the working man and the business owner. But who would fit the bill? Step forward one Gerald Grattan McGeer.

The political courtship between Spencer and McGeer did not take place overnight. McGeer was readying himself for a fourth attempt at running for federal MP.

He was likely convinced of his destiny to rescue Canada from the Great Depression and probably felt the trivialities of municipal politics were beneath him. Indeed, it is remarkable that Spencer was able to convince McGeer to even consider running for mayor. Spencer was a dyed-in-the-wool Conservative, a member of the party McGeer had publicly lambasted at every turn throughout his career. Tories, McGeer liked to say, "merely decorate the memory of the past and stand obsolete in the way of progress." But Spencer was able to tap into the one fear that united Conservatives and Liberals alike, the fear of the "Red Revolt."

Mayor McGeer, 1935. CITY OF VANCOUVER ARCHIVES. CVA PORT P965; PHOTOGRAPH BY GEORGE T. WADDS.

According to Better Vancouver League sources, whose information McGeer was made privy to, communist elements in Vancouver were planning a general strike. This was to be "the start of the rebellion."[9] Horrified, McGeer made an about-face and agreed to run, perhaps feeling that the glory that would come from saving the Dominion from a communist uprising would make a term as Vancouver's mayor bearable.

McGeer won the December 1934 election by a landslide, obliterating L.D. Taylor at the polls. The influence of the Better Vancouver League had made sure no right-leaning candidates would split the anti-Taylor vote by running against McGeer.

McGeer was sworn in as mayor on January 2, 1935. The following day he launched an unprecedented attack on the Vancouver Police Department (VPD). Retired army Colonel W.W. Foster (who, notably, also happened to be on the executive of a waterfront lumber company) was installed as the new chief. Foster set up a permanent police intelligence branch, outside the existing police hierarchy. Viewed with deep suspicion by the police union who perceived the branch as labour union spies within the VPD, the branch was supposedly charged with investigating confidence tricksters. The branch's actual agenda became apparent when they were later renamed the Communist Activities Branch.

As winter thawed in April 1935, approximately 2,000 relief-camp workers from across western Canada went on strike. In a coordinated effort led by the RCWU, the men departed the camps (by now commonly referred to as slave camps by the workers who occupied them) and rode boxcars to Vancouver, intent on raising their grievances. Striker Matt Shaw said "the biggest quarrel was working for 20¢ a day, eight hours a day with nothing ahead of us but a blank wall, day in and day out . . ."[10] Once in Vancouver, the strikers crammed into any available accommodation, including

Arthur "Slim" Evans. COURTESY OF THE GLENBOW ALBERTA ARCHIVES; NA-36334-7.

labour halls, boarding houses, and the private homes of supportive Vancouverites. One building at 380 Cordova Street was said to hold 200 men, all sharing a single washroom.

The strikers' leader was long-time Communist activist Arthur "Slim" Evans. His mood was not conciliatory: "I am very patriotic to this country. I want to see it become a beautiful place for people to live in, but not for those men that take these utilities and close them up, who close up mills and factories, and who have elevators filled with food stuff to overflowing with every good thing, and denying the possibilities of sharing in these good things to the people who are not given work."[11] Evans was in Vancouver to make sure the unemployed of Canada were heard at last. Organizing the men into four military-style divisions, overseen by a strike committee, he crafted a set of demands, including a work and wages program, a minimum wage of 50¢ per day for unskilled workers, workers' compensation, non-contributory unemployment insurance, and the right-to-vote for relief-camp workers. The demands were deliberately moderate and devoid of communist rhetoric. Evans and his peers were conscious that widespread public support would be necessary to force change. Most Canadians were not exactly gunning for a communist revolution, despite the hardships of the depression.

McGeer made it very clear that under his watch the City of Vancouver would not provide any support to the strikers. "We in Vancouver have our own problems, and this is not one of them" he was quoted in the *Daily Province* as saying. He went on: "We have to maintain civic payrolls, now in grave jeopardy, and to continue paying relief to Vancouver people." However, McGeer did agree to occasional meetings with RCWU leaders. Indeed, the RCWU HQ at 52½ West Cordova was a mere stone's throw from City Hall, then situated in the Holden Building at 16 East Hastings. In all likelihood, the short walk to City Hall and back was the most enjoyable part of the experience for the RCWU representatives. Striker Ronald Liversedge recalled "A visit to the mayor . . . was always a little frustrating . . . a rather arrogant corporation lawyer . . ." The RCWU always left McGeer's office empty-handed, with McGeer adamant the city was not responsible for feeding and housing the newly-arrived strikers. Liversedge recalls that "Gerry would, while passing the buck, go into a long, tedious, incomprehensible explanation of monetary reform."

When McGeer was not busy explaining his economic theories to whomsoever would listen, he led his council in taking severe steps against the strikers. McGeer closed off any possibility of relief payments to the men from city funds and even denied the RCWU's permit applications for "tag days"[12] a popular fundraising method of the day. Not only would City Hall refuse to buy these homeless men a single meal, a blanket, or a roof for the night, they would do what they could to prevent the general public paying for the men's food and shelter too. While City Hall tried to starve out the strikers, the VPD Intelligence Branch set about infiltrating the strikers' ranks, as did federal agents and even newspaper journalists keen to get an inside scoop on the strikers' next move.

Faced with hostility from all levels of government, the RCWU was effectively engaged in a PR battle for public support. One tactic of the RCWU was to hold "snake parades." Men would walk two-by-two or four-by-four in zigzag fashion through downtown, often taking a detour through a department store. The parades were non-violent and aimed to cause mild disruption to shoppers and drivers, without provoking confrontation with the police. The strikers also held a highly successful illegal tag day on April 13, 1935, raising more than $5,000.

Vancouver's citizens showed much sympathy for the men. More than 100,000 men across Canada had spent time in the camps by 1935 and Vancouver had sent

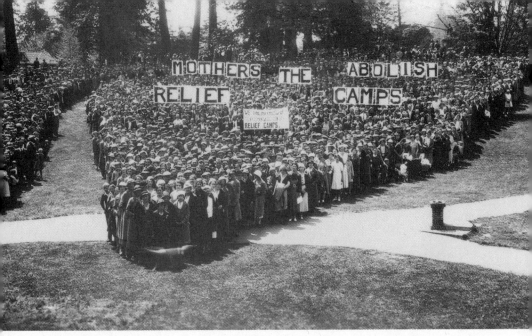

Mother's Day in Stanley Park, 1935. COURTESY OF THE *VANCOUVER SUN*.

more men as a share of population than any other major city. Plenty of Vancouverites had sons, brothers, uncles, and nephews in the camps. And a peaceful parade through downtown by hungry men chanting requests for food and shelter did not look much like a Bolshevik threat. Touchingly, an event in Stanley Park on Mother's Day 1935 saw more than 1,000 strikers encircled by some 300 women in the shape of a heart. Sentimental, but evidence that there was considerable goodwill in Vancouver toward the strikers.

On Tuesday, April 23, all four divisions of the strikers gathered at Water and Carrall Streets. Numbering around 1,400 in total, they commenced a snake parade. Each division soon split off in different directions, so as to avoid being a concentrated target for the police. Division Three, comprising around 300 men, went west along Cordova, then Hastings, up to Georgia and finally over to Granville. Here they rushed into the Hudson's Bay Company department store, marching about the store chanting "work and wages." Previous similar occupations had lasted approximately two hours and then ended peacefully when the strikers had marched off to carry on their parade elsewhere. This time, the police arrived after about 30 minutes and a stand-off soon became a violent battle. Glass display cases crashed "like firecrackers" as strikers and police officers traded blows: batons versus 18-inch iron railroad-brake shoe pins, the weapon of choice for the strikers.[13] Several of the police officers and the strikers suffered serious injuries, with the Bay recording thousands of dollars in damage.

The men eventually fled the store en masse and ran to Victory Square, the unofficial public meeting place of the strikers. A crowd of citizens and fellow strikers from the other three divisions greeted them, along with strike leaders Evans and Shaw. Both the RCMP and VPD encircled the square, many in riot gear and on horseback. A decision was quickly made by the strikers to send a delegation of 12 men to meet with Mayor McGeer at City Hall. McGeer welcomed the delegation by refusing their demand for relief and having them arrested for vagrancy. Before a second delegation could make it to City Hall, McGeer himself arrived at the square, Riot Act in hand.

As McGeer stood on the steps of the cenotaph and looked into the whites of the strikers' eyes, one might wonder if any unemployed iron moulders stared back. He was uncharacteristically subdued, but if he suffered a crisis of conscience, it didn't stop him from reading the Act:

> Our Sovereign Lord the King charges and commands all persons assembled immediately to disperse and peaceably depart to their habitations or to their lawful business on pain of being found guilty of an offence on conviction of which they may be imprisoned for life. God Save the King.

McGeer was flanked by Colonel Foster and Vancouver East MLA Harold E. Winch, a member of the left-leaning Co-operative Commonwealth Federation (a forerunner of today's New Democratic Party). Winch was at Victory Square that day to support the strikers; he was certainly no friend of the mayor. After McGeer had read the act and departed for City Hall, Winch addressed the crowd and warned the men that the order "meant not clubs, but bullets."[14] The crowd dispersed only to reconvene later that night on Hastings and Carrall for a pitched battle against the VPD. Again the result was smashed glass and injuries to both strikers and police.[15]

Days later McGeer made a public address claiming that the confrontation had been of historic magnitude. He announced that "no more vicious violation of the peace, order and good government of a Canadian city has taken place" and had it not been for the actions of the police "a condition of uncontrollable riot and rebellion would have engulfed our city."[16] McGeer was,

Gerry McGeer reads the Riot Act, April 23rd, 1935.
COURTESY OF THE ON-TO-OTTAWA HISTORICAL SOCIETY.

however, forced eventually to offer the strikers six days of relief payments after they staged a sit-in at the unlikely location of the Vancouver Museum at Hastings and Main. Further protests and fruitless negotiations continued for about six weeks, before the strikers departed on their "On-to-Ottawa Trek," culminating in the Regina Riot on July 1. This was a black day in the history of the RCMP, one that saw a city police officer and a trekker killed, scores injured, and 120 arrested.

From their offices at 140 West Hastings the reporters of the *Daily Province* had a bird's-eye view of McGeer in action. The April 24 edition offered steadfast support for McGeer, who "calmly read the Riot Act." The newspaper laid the blame squarely at the door of the strikers: "The striking camp men must realize that they can not take part in mass demonstrations which take the form of invading department stores and still keep the peace . . . It is a form of intimidation . . . we advise the strikers to go back to the camps."

The paper published verbatim McGeer's account of events, where he took the opportunity to blame "communistic elements" among the striking men: "It is now perfectly clear that Vancouver is being victimized by an organized attempt to capitalize, for revolutionary purposes, the conditions of depression."[17] He went on to lambast the federal and provincial governments for refusing to implement a "work and wages" program based on national credit—that is, their refusal to countenance his own monetary reform proposals. Ironically, McGeer's wholehearted support for a work and wages program echoed the demands of his foes, the relief-camp strikers' "communist" leaders.

Despite McGeer's tough stance and his deep conviction that his actions halted in its tracks a communist revolution, he certainly saw himself as a true friend to the poor. He continually referred to his monetary reform proposals as a means to end poverty. A drinker who supported prohibition, a rich corporate lawyer who demonized bankers, McGeer readily wielded the twin threats of starvation and police violence while calling for a more caring state.

In fact, McGeer's monetary reform obsession helped him rationalize his response to the strikers. As far as he was concerned Ottawa had wilfully failed to remedy the Great Depression. If the feds would only implement his monetary reforms then the depression would be cured "within 24 hours."[18] But suppose, for a moment, the relief-camp strikers had angrily demanded reform of the banking system, rather than shelter and food? How

Relief Camp Strikers' caricature of Gerry McGeer reading the Riot Act. COURTESY OF THE ON-TO-OTTAWA HISTORICAL SOCIETY.

would McGeer have responded to a parade of eager monetary reformists marching along Hastings Street, perhaps forcing entry into the Bank of Montreal and staging an occupation in protest at the bank's usurious ways? It is entirely plausible McGeer would have interpreted the events as legitimate protest, not a riot. He may even have led the charge himself. Barely a month before the relief-camp strike McGeer thundered at a parliamentary committee in Ottawa: "If any sheriff comes into my city, I will organize a riot and lead it to throw him into the bay."

The statement was part of a typically vociferous address by McGeer, in which he put forward the case for the City of Vancouver to be partially forgiven its debt given the dire financial straits it found itself in. Specifically, McGeer was campaigning for the city's interest payments to be reduced, a proposal entirely consistent with his monetarist ideology. As one might expect McGeer's debt-reduction scheme was met with utter disdain by bond holders and disinterest by the federal government, which had its own financial woes with which to cope. McGeer's threat was met with general derision and was certainly more figurative than real. It was designed to illustrate his argument rather than stoke the fires of civil unrest. Yet as a footnote in Vancouver history it is curious that the man who read the Riot Act to a group of striking men had only the month before threatened to start a riot himself.

Later in 1935 Gerry McGeer finally won his coveted seat as a federal MP, taking the Vancouver-Burrard riding while still serving as Vancouver's mayor. He would later become a federal senator. He continued to promote his monetary reform theories throughout the remainder of his life, but found little discernible support among policy-makers or the general public. McGeer also had a second stint as Vancouver's mayor, winning the 1947 election—as before—on a law-and-order ticket. McGeer died in office while at his Point Grey home in 1947, aged 59.

(ENDNOTES)

1   David Ricardo Williams, *Mayor Gerry: The Remarkable Gerald Grattan McGeer* (Vancouver: Douglas & McIntyre, 1986), 81.

2   Ibid., 66.

3   *Globe and Mail,* April 1, 1935, 11.

4   Williams, *Mayor Gerry,* 118.

5   Don Gillmor, Pierre Turgeon, and Achille Michaud, *Canada: A People's History, Volume 2* (Toronto: McClelland & Stewart, 2001), 145.

6   Ronald Liversedge, *Recollections of the On-to-Ottawa Trek,* ed. Victor Hoar (Toronto: McClelland and Stewart, 1973), 39.

7   Lani Russwurm, "Constituting Authority: Policing Workers and the Consolidation of Police Power in Vancouver, 1918–1939" (master's thesis, Simon Fraser University, 2007), 70.

8   Ibid.

9   Ibid., 72.

10   Victor Howard, *"We Were the Salt of the Earth!": A Narrative of the On-to-Ottawa Trek and the Regina Riot* (Regina: Canadian Plains Research Center, University of Regina, 1985), 37.

11   Ibid., 24.

12   A tag day usually meant a charity posting people around downtown to collect money in tin cans from passers-by and to distribute paper "tags" with catchy slogans or messages. In the case of the relief camp strikers, the message printed on the tags was "When do we eat?"

13   Howard, *"We Were the Salt of the Earth"*, 51.

14   "Riot Act Read to 2,000 Vancouver Relief Strikers," *Globe and Mail*, April 24, 1935, 2.

15   A curious personal connection McGeer had to the events of April 23, 1935, concerned Spencer's, the department store, founded by McGeer's father-in-law, David. The chain included a flagship store on Hastings Street, two blocks west of Victory Square. Throughout their married lives, Gerry and Charlotte made ample use of their account at Spencer's. It is estimated the McGeers ran up more than $37,000 in unpaid bills at the store over the course of a 30-year period. The Spencer family apparently thought the McGeers fair recipients of such benevolence, given Charlotte had not been granted any ownership of the chain of stores in her father's will. Prior to entering the Hudson's Bay Company, the marching strikers had made an attempt to enter Spencer's but had been repelled after staff locked and barred the doors. Whether or not McGeer's decision to read the Riot Act was influenced by the strikers' attempt on Spencer's will remain unknown, although the attempt would not have softened McGeer's attitude towards the strikers.

16   "McGeer Gives Warning of Red Revolt Plan," *Globe and Mail*, April 29, 1935, 10.

17   "Extra Burden on Taxpayers," *Daily Province*, April 24, 1935, 4.

18   "Divine Aid Only Hope of Nations: Mayor McGeer Points to Way out of Depression," *Globe and Mail*, April 1, 1935, 12.

ADDITIONAL SOURCES

Barnholden, Michael. *Reading the Riot Act*. Vancouver: Anvil Press, 2005.

Douglas, Stan and Reid Shier. *Stan Douglas: Every Building on 100 West Hastings*. Vancouver: Arsenal Pulp Press, 2003.

Francis, Daniel. *LD: Mayor Louis Taylor and the Rise of Vancouver*. Vancouver: Arsenal Pulp Press, 2004.

Lonardo, Michael. "Under a Watchful Eye: A Case Study of Police Surveillance During the 1930s." *Labour / Le Travail*, Vol. 35 (Spring, 1995): 11-41.

McGeer, Gerald Grattan. *The Conquest of Poverty, or Money, Humanity and Christianity*. Gardenvale, Quebec: Garden City Press, c.1935.

Waiser, Bill. *All Hell Can't Stop Us: The On-to-Ottawa Trek and Regina Riot*. Calgary: Fifth House Limited, 2003.

NEWSPAPERS

Daily Province

Globe and Mail

Vancouver Star

Vancouver Sun

CITY OF FEAR
AARON CHAPMAN

S tanding at the shores of Tower Beach, at the most western part of the Point Grey peninsula and the city of Vancouver, are two abandoned concrete towers built to defend an enemy that never came.

Like two Ozymandian statues, their feet covered with rocks, brush, and driftwood, the towers stand nearly ten metres high with an observation deck at the top that looks out onto a wide panorama of the Strait of Georgia and the portal to Burrard Inlet.

Built at the beginning of the Second World War, the misnamed "gun towers" were part of the Point Grey Battery Fort that sat at the top of cliffs that rose from the beach below. The battery was the most heavily armed of the five coast artillery forts built in 1939 to defend the port of Vancouver from a Pacific invasion. The Tower Beach relics did not hold cannons but artillery searchlight towers instead. Each housed a 6-inch searchlight with 800-million candle-power efficiency that could project light three to five miles into the night and sweep the entrance of Burrard Inlet. These powerful beams would help aim the artillery guns in the battery above at potential naval targets. Identical searchlights were found at a battery position in Stanley Park and also across the water at the northern end of the Second Narrows on the North Shore. *Vancouver Defended,* Peter Moogk's exhaustive account of Lower Mainland military history, notes that "It was also a favourite trick of the soldiers to flick the beams onto Prospect Point after midnight and, with the aid of binoculars, watch surprised lovers disentangle themselves to escape the all-revealing glare."[1]

The Point Grey prominence in particular has had a long history of military significance. The Musqueam First Nation used the site as a lookout for the northern tribes—in particular the Squamish, and the Laich-kwil-tach from further north—whose approaching war canoes could be easily spotted.

In the 1960s, when Vancouver became a haven for political radicals, draft dodgers, and artists, one of the towers even became a temporary home for future environmental activist and *Sea Shepherd* captain Paul Watson. Newly arrived from Montreal, with sleeping bag in hand and nowhere to stay, he kept warm with fires made from driftwood gathered along the beach.

The City long ago caged the observation deck and sealed access to the towers for any campers or curiosity seekers, most of whom were likely more interested in the nude Wreck Beach nearby. Today the only attackers are graffiti artists who have used these structures as a unique canvas for their elaborate designs. But the towers are among the few visible relics of the Second World War left in Vancouver, where little suggests that the war even touched the city at all.

They stand as two monuments to a time in Vancouver—a city without battlefield memorials or the scars of war—when the city suddenly considered itself threatened. It was an era when Vancouver was subject to a sense of fear it had rarely felt before or has since. That fear of attack was used to censor and direct its populace toward some of the harshest decisions in the city's history.

On the home front in Vancouver, the Second World War was a very different one for soldiers stationed here than it was for those fighting overseas. The Point Grey Battery that sat above the towers was the largest of the five battery stations in the city that hugged Burrard Inlet. For those soldiers in the 58th Heavy Battery of the 15th Coastal Brigade who manned the battery during the war, part of the fight was to keep up morale and quell boredom as they sat on the edge of a theatre of war. To enlisted men—particularly from 1939 to late 1941, before Japan entered the fray—it would have seemed that the war was passing them by. The now-declassified "War Diary" of Point Grey Battery in the National Archives in Ottawa gives some idea of what life was like both on the base and off.

The battery was comprised of separate living quarters for officers and ranks below, a mess, recreational quarters, engineer's workshop, and observation post. By April 1940 there were 29 officers and 441 enlisted men. Most of those who had volunteered for the military had done so with the hope of going to Europe and seeing some action. With little to do beyond basic routine, officers wrote up the men for such infractions as walking about with their coats unbuttoned, hands in their pockets, and for "considerable slackness in saluting."[2]

These disciplinary measures were used to keep soldiers mindful that there was still a war going on. The troops on guard at the base were instructed to deal with onlookers in no uncertain terms, even curious students at the University of British Columbia who might have wandered near the barbed-wire fences of the base after dark. Orders were given that the sentries were to yell, "Halt, who goes there?" in "the loudest possible manner" and that "the sentry must remember his responsibility but he will also use common sense when deciding whether to shoot."[3]

Troops practice a beach landing, not in the north of France but at Kitsilano. CITY OF VANCOUVER ARCHIVES, CVA 1184-3496. PHOTOGRAPH BY JACK LINDSAY.

Vancouver's soldiers were often reminded of the need for secrecy and discretion when dealing with the public. As noted in one memo, "Officers and other ranks are forbidden to correspond with strangers. While many of these offers and requests may be bona fide, it is pointed out that such correspondence might provide a means for obtaining information of value to the enemy, or of [use] for enemy propaganda."[4]

When soldiers were up for weekend leave, the men were reminded in weekly memos of "No Go" areas in the city. Soldiers were forbidden to go to the New Orleans Café at Granville and Drake and the Alexandria Ballroom at Hornby and Robson. These venues are listed in the memos of the War Diaries without explanation as to why they were regarded as beyond the pale for soldiers. It is possible they were regarded as locations where fighting was commonplace, or where drugs or people of ill-character could be found. The reasons might have been common unspoken knowledge among the enlisted men. The most often listed no-go address is 303 Union Street, described in James Johnstone's account of Lucille Mars's East End as one of the city's busiest brothels. There's no question in that case why the location was forbidden. That the address was so often cited as a no-go area was perhaps the best advertisement going for the brothel.

The strategic value of coastal defences like the Point Grey Battery could be debated, but to a nervous population they were evidence of some protection against a surprise attack. They were simultaneously a cause for comfort and, of course, proof that all was not well. There were other signs of the war on this home front. Vancouverites today might be surprised to learn that blackouts and rationing more usually associated with wartime London during the German blitz were a fact of life in the Terminal City as well. A full six months before Pearl Harbor, on May 22, 1941, at ten o'clock in the evening, with five short blasts repeated three times on the city's air-raid sirens, which had been installed back in 1939, the Lower Mainland experienced its first significant wartime blackout. Lights in homes and storefronts were turned off, blackout curtains were pulled across windows, and streetlamps and traffic light signals were turned off across various districts in a city that was described in the newspapers as being "like a tired man wandering from room to room dousing the lights of his home for the night."

Beyond Vancouver, the blackout test included the North Shore, Burnaby, New Westminster, and Delta, as well as Victoria, Oak Bay, and Saanich on Vancouver Island, covering some 600 square miles of British Columbia and affecting some 400,000 residents.

Military brass such as Major General R.O. Alexander (commander in chief of the Pacific Air Command), Group Captain C.R. Slemmon (the officer in charge of Western Air Command), Commodore W.J.R. Beech (the senior naval officer on the Pacific), and representatives from the BC Provincial Police were on hand to comment on the success of the 15-minute blackout test. Vancouver police headquarters and the fire department reported there were no calls or alarms during the blackout period. Coverage of the event even reached the *Ottawa Citizen*, which reported that "Vancouver lay as black as a country village after midnight."

With the war thousands of miles away in Europe, the blackout might have seemed like a curiosity, even a novelty to some citizens in early 1941. But when the Pacific War opened and the war progressed, regular blackouts, air-raid tests and further civil-defence measures contributed to the overall fear that an attack on BC shores was imminent. Vancouver motorists were warned to cover their car lights so that only a slit was visible or to paint the headlights blue to reduce their light. And while the first blackout was a 15-minute test with some warning, in the coming months, air-raid blackouts lasting as long as three hours became commonplace.

Those who did not comply with the precautionary air-raid blackouts were subject to fines by roaming auxiliary police, who checked neighbourhoods for blackout compliance, as well as ARP (air-raid precaution) teams that watched those in their own community. Four Vancouver citizens who kept their lights on during a surprise blackout on September 28, 1942, were fined, and their names and addresses were printed—as was customary in those years—in the pages of the newspapers that covered the daily police blotter. C.A. Jordan, a proprietor of an antique shop at 1015 Robson, was fined $25, with the alternative of a month in jail, after he left a light on in the rear residential part of his store while he was in it. Likewise Frank Dahl at the Balmoral Hotel, who had continued to display a light on in his room during the blackout. Leaving your lights on while you were out during a blackout netted no compassion. Seeing a light on at 1927 West Third, police forced their way through a back door into Mr. R.L. Walker's home, while he and his wife were out of the house. They were fined $5 or five days in jail for the infraction. Mrs. G. Martin of 1740 Victoria Drive explained to the magistrate that she rushed home as soon as the blackout was announced and turned off the offending light—a 15-watt bulb she left on because she was afraid to enter the house in the dark. She was given a $5 fine or ten days in jail.

Tourists in Vancouver during the war years were not exempt from blackout rules either. Behind the bureau of every room in the Hotel Georgia, guests would find a heavy sheet of black paper marked "Blackout Material," and under the glass top of the room's dresser lay instructions on how to tack up the paper to the glass window pane. Guests were warned to use just a single weak light in the event an air-raid siren was heard. If a five-minute steady tone on the two-tone siren was heard—the "Imminent Danger Signal"—guests were instructed to take the stairs down to the hotel basement, where an air-raid shelter had been devised. The Georgia had its own fire-alarm bells, which it would ring in chorus with the city's sirens. This was hardly necessary because, as the *Vancouver Sun* noted, the city's air-raid sirens were "huge, throaty and many in number." Spread out across the city and tested at odd hours, they gave "pause to hurrying Vancouverites at high noon or dusk."

The prospect of shortages of essential goods added another layer of fear to life during wartime. Rationing cards were issued, and food supplies—sugar in particular—were among the first to be affected. Gasoline, too, was rationed, and gas station business hours were cut from 12 to 10 hours a day. Beer rationing also began, and the hours that beer parlours could stay open were reduced. The production of new automobiles and even telephone service was effected. While it's difficult to imagine in the age of ubiquitous mobile phones, up until the 1980s the installation of a phone in the home was left to telephone-company servicemen, who visited your home and hard-wired phones to a wall. In May 1942, the British Columbia Telephone Company (later to become BC Tel) drastically curtailed the installation of new telephones in residential homes, noting, "By limiting the growth of our telephone system, we use less of the materials that are urgently needed for the war effort." And by not ordering more telephones from the factory, "We allow the workers and machines to spend more time in making things for war … This is just one more sacrifice that must be made on the road to victory." The scarcity of comforts and the belt tightening expected of Canadians across the nation was to be endured so industries could focus on the war effort.

Even veterans too old to serve in the war were expected to join the belt tightening. Vancouver in the '40s was still home to soldiers who'd fought for the king in battles largely forgotten today. Four aged survivors of the 1882 Bombardment of Alexandria who had served in the British Mediterranean fleet, and who had celebrated the anniversary of the battle every summer, cancelled their get-together in July 1940. Local newspapers announced that they were patriotically donating reunion funds to Canadian war-drive collections.

The concept that the war was a world away from Vancouver must have been shattered after the Japanese attack on Pearl Harbor in December 1941. As Japanese forces swept through Hong Kong, Burma, Malaya, Singapore, Borneo, Java, and the Philippines in the first months of the Pacific War, a growing sense of vulnerability flourished in Vancouver. To a population that might have assumed any new conflict would have been like the First World War—that is, dominated by trench warfare overseas—these developments suggested an altogether uncertain and threatening new world. That even Vancouver could be a potential target must have seemed a clear and present danger by June of 1942, especially when the Japanese launched an aircraft-carrier raid, bombing Dutch Harbor in the Aleutian Islands in Alaska on June 3 and 4.

A little more than two weeks later, on the evening of June 20, the small community of Estevan Point on Vancouver Island was to experience Canada's first direct attack since the Fenian raids of the 1860s. Japanese submarine *I-26* under the command of Commander Yokota Minoru had hunted throughout the North Pacific and the Strait of Juan de Fuca since the beginning of the war and had been involved in the Aleutian campaign. Around 10:30 p.m., the vessel surfaced and attacked.

Lighthouse keeper Robert Lally had just finished lighting the lamp atop the 125-foot lighthouse for the evening when he spotted a curious vessel he could not identify steering towards the point. Suddenly the submarine opened fire from its deck guns, and a shell crashed into the surf below him. Lally ran down to alert his wife to take cover, then ran back up the tower to extinguish the lighthouse lamp that he reasoned was illuminating the point as well as the radio tower. The few residents of the small Estevan Point community fled into the woods for the night, believing that the Japanese had begun a land invasion, only to emerge in the morning to find some small shell craters at the beach and the submarine long gone.

Back in Vancouver, the *Daily Province* reported on the story using the opportunity to depict Lally as a hero, with all the poetry of wartime excitement: "The solid, concrete lighthouse building trembled from the first explosions and several windows were broken by the concussion ... the quick action [by Lally] in climbing the tower to extinguish the powerful beacon while shells screamed all around and the raiders elevated their range . . . is credited with saving this remote little settlement from serious damage."[5]

In reality, the time of night that made for poor visibility might have saved the day. Commander Yokota, when interviewed after the war, recalled the attack. "Because of the dark, our gun crew had difficulty in making our shots effective. At first the shells were way too short, not reaching the shore. I remember very vividly yelling at the crew, 'Raise the gun! Raise the gun!' to shoot at a higher angle. Then the shells went too far over the little community toward the hilly area. Even out at sea we could hear the pigs in a farmyard near the lighthouse squealing as the shells exploded."[6]

While the Estevan Point attack is often viewed now as a trivial incident in Canadian war history, Japanese submarine *I-26* itself was no trivial ship in the Imperial Japanese Navy. Some military historians now agree that *I-26* may have taken the first American sea casualty with the notable sinking of the merchant ship *Cynthia Olson*, torpedoing the lumber-filled ship as it travelled between Seattle and Honolulu and sinking it more than an hour before Japanese planes first fired upon Pearl Harbor.

And while local livestock and the residents of Estevan Point (then just a hamlet of 33 people) were no doubt frightened by the Second World War arriving so briefly at their door, the notion that the Japanese forces were potentially at least close enough to launch a hit-and-run raid remained on the minds of many Vancouverites. Prime Minister Mackenzie King took the opportunity to galvanize the country into vigilance, stating the Estevan attack "only goes to bear out what has been said so often: That no one can take too seriously both the immediacy and the extent of the danger which all parts of the world are confronted, and our own part in particular at this time."[7]

Fear and a kind of paranoia were used to motivate populations in many wartime settings, at home and abroad. That loose lips could sink ships was a message drilled into the wartime citizens of Vancouver. They were cautioned to be wary of the information they shared in public. What mail they sent to family overseas was also observed, lest the information and potential secrets in the correspondence fell into enemy hands. New wartime regulations forbade individuals from sending newspapers overseas. The local papers answered by printing a short, sanitized summary of weekly local news, written in an informal, almost folksy tone, that could be clipped out and sent to loved ones overseas. With a "Dear _____" at the top of the page, newspaper subscribers had only to write the name of those who they sent the summaries to. That the news contained mostly positive everyday local chatter and not any substantive news was probably of little concern to those that received the summaries. One might imagine that those on the front likely found pleasant or trivial mail from home a welcome relief. On October 3, 1942, the *Vancouver Sun*, in that week's "Letter from Home," published a shot of Stanley Park, described the pleasant fall weather, and

Ships loaded with Canadian troops head off to an uncertain destiny, ca. 1942. CITY OF VANCOUVER ARCHIVES, CVA 1184-3491. PHOTOGRAPH BY JACK LINDSAY.

provided various morale-boosting news items about which visiting military officials had spoken in recent appearances. It also included which new Clark Gable and Lana Turner movies were playing downtown, the local sports highlights, and an item about a worrying rise in purse snatchings.

The internment of citizens of Japanese origin across Canada but most prominently on the West Coast is perhaps the most tragic and arguably best-known legacy of the war years in Vancouver. Across the country 22,000 Japanese Canadians (14,000 of whom were born in Canada and most of them in BC) were interned, with more than 8,000 detained between March and September of 1942 at a camp built on the grounds of the Pacific National Exhibition. They were housed in the PNE barns, which had previously held livestock, before being shipped off to other camps across BC and Alberta.

This initiative was sustained by a combination of elements. Outright anti-Asian sentiment had persisted for decades, as well as a fear that Japanese Canadians who held dual citizenship were not loyal to Canada. Even the lukewarm racism of many residents who felt that the government "had to do something with them" for their own safety contributed to a period that may in fact be the saddest in the city's history.

Far less well known are the names of those who ordered those measures. Nor do many recall the language of discrimination they freely exercised to magnify such fear to mobilize and perhaps even convince fence-sitting citizens that Japanese Canadians were a threat that had to be dealt with.

There was certainly no one individual responsible for such actions. At the federal level, there were plenty of voices pandering to anti-Asian sentiments. Men like Burnaby Liberal MP Thomas Reid stated in January 1942 that all Japanese should be deported. Ian MacKenzie, also a Liberal member of Parliament and British Columbia's senior member of the cabinet, was an advocate of permanent expulsion of the Japanese from Canada. These were just two voices in a chorus that would lead Prime Minister Mackenzie King, in February of 1942, to use the War Measures Act to intern "all persons of Japanese racial origin."

But those who turned local fears into internment orders were not just BC parliamentarians at work in Ottawa. They were on Vancouver city streets as well. And there was one individual more than any other at the time whose vehemence against the Japanese won him headlines as he sat in chambers at City Hall.

When the Japanese bombed Pearl Harbor, Halford Wilson was driving his car, listening to the radio. He felt no surprise whatsoever. He knew all about the Japanese.

Born in 1904, Wilson was elected as an alderman to Vancouver City Council in 1934 on the Non-Partisan Association ticket when he was aged just 29. Had it not been for some experience as a bank clerk and later an insurance agent, it might be said that racism had been the Wilson family business. He was from an old Vancouver family, the son of the Reverend George H. Wilson, a chief speaker and rabble-rouser at the notorious anti-immigration rally of 1907 that exploded in violence and vandalism on city streets. Following in his father's footsteps, Halford Wilson submitted a proposal to council in 1938 that all Japanese carry identification cards. He also suggested the closure of Japanese-language schools as they represented "a menace to Canadian national life."

Along with concerns about illegal immigration and accusations of espionage, Wilson was convinced the enemy was not only on land but also the sea. He warned that even Japanese fishermen posed a threat and suggested their occupations gave them intimate knowledge of the BC coastline and of the best areas to stage an invasion. In addition he stated that "Japanese fishing boats could be readily transformed into torpedo-carrying war craft by a hostile group."

On February 16, 1942, Wilson put forward a landmark motion to city council imploring "the federal government to remove all residents of Japanese racial origin and enemy aliens to areas of Canada well removed from the Pacific Coast." City council passed Wilson's motion unanimously.

Throughout the war Wilson continued his charges against the Japanese. He formed the Pacific Coast Security League in 1942, an organization that was sharply critical of what he saw as Ottawa's moderate stance toward the Japanese population. The league urged mass evacuation of all Japanese to other locations in Canada "where no danger to national defenses could exist from their presence," even though Canadian military intelligence and the RCMP found no legitimate seditious activity that could be attributed to the Japanese community at the time.[8]

The motions Wilson championed stripped Japanese citizens of their rights and had widespread consequences. In addition to Japanese proprietors losing their businesses, Japanese honours students at the University of British Columbia had their studies ended when they were sent to the camps. Wilson also contributed to the effective eradication of the "Japantown" area around Powell Street.

The city got some respite from Wilson's vocal anti-Japanese proclamations only when, having enlisted in the Canadian army in 1940, he was finally sent to Britain in 1942. He eventually won a *Croix de Guerre* during the liberation of France in 1944. When the war ended, Wilson ran unsuccessfully for the mayor's office, losing to Gerry McGeer in 1946. Instead, he was re-elected to city council in 1947 and served until 1953. On April 1, 1949, the Canadian government finally removed the restrictions on Japanese Canadians, and they regained their freedom to live anywhere in Canada. One might have thought a politician like Wilson, whose name had become synonymous with the anti-Asian sentiments of the war years, might have been regarded as coming from the politics of the past, as Vancouver moved on with more modern sensibilities. That was not to be the case.

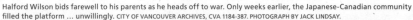

Halford Wilson bids farewell to his parents as he heads off to war. Only weeks earlier, the Japanese-Canadian community filled the platform … unwillingly. CITY OF VANCOUVER ARCHIVES, CVA 1184-387. PHOTOGRAPH BY JACK LINDSAY.

Wilson won re-election in 1955 and served as an alderman throughout the 1960s under Mayor Tom Campbell. Wilson supported some of what is now considered some of the city's worst developer proposals, such as a Four Seasons Hotel complex built at the entrance to Stanley Park, and true to form, a proposal to run a freeway through Chinatown. It was only in the 1972 civic election that Wilson's political career came to an end. Wilson—with his xenophobic past—shamefully remains one of the longest-serving members of Vancouver City Council.

He remained unrepentant in political retirement, stating in a 1981 interview, "I was personally of the opinion that the best thing that could have happened to the Japanese was their removal from the coast. They spread across to different parts of the country where they would be assimilated. I have no feeling of remorse." The enemy had always been there, he maintained. "I'll swear to this day, I saw a fish boat [near Steveston] with a Japanese in uniform."[9]

When Wilson died on April 23, 1988, the provincial legislature took a moment in afternoon sitting of the house to acknowledge him. Former Vancouver mayor and then premier Mike Harcourt paid "tribute to Halford Wilson, who served on the Vancouver city council for over 30 years and knew the city, loved it and served in many capacities. He will be missed."[10] That the sins of Alderman Halford Wilson are not better known in Vancouver and that he is not recalled as one of the city's great political monsters is perhaps surprising. Instead, his political durability is remembered—that, and a golf trophy named in his honour by the Strathcona Park Golf Club, which is competed for annually by current and retired City of Vancouver employees.

On September 25, 2013, more than 70 years after Halford Wilson had made his hateful 1942 motion, Vancouver City Council would take a more measured response to Wilson's legacy. At a special council meeting, 78-year-old Mary Kitagawa (one of the many survivors of the internment who attended the council meeting, and who had been a little girl in 1942) recalled to council the experience of being removed from her home on Saltspring Island by an RCMP officer with a gun who loaded her father onto a truck, leading her to believe her father was being taken away to be shot. The Kitagawas were among thousands sent to the PNE grounds. Mary recalled the internment at the meeting: "Going to Hastings Park was one of the most degrading experiences of our lives. The reason I continue to speak about this is because my parents were deeply affected by the internment. Their voices are silent, so I use mine."

As with Wilson's 1942 motion, Vancouver City Council voted unanimously in 2013. This time it was for an official apology for its complicity in the forced internment of thousands of former residents.

The sense of immediate danger of a Japanese attack in Vancouver became less likely by the summer of 1942. After the battles of the Coral Sea and Midway, Japan's navy had lost much of its potential to hit distant targets like the west coast of North America. The remaining war years coasted by for many of those in the city, who would come to find the rationing and blackouts more of an annoyance and less of a novelty. By 1948 the Point Grey Battery and the other battery stations around Burrard Inlet were removed. The gun decks that once sat at the Point Grey Battery would, in 1973, finally lose the war against the University of British Columbia's new Museum of Anthropology, which annexed much of their space. Only their concrete decks and the entrance to the tunnel that connected the magazines of the heavy artillery-gun emplacements remain.

Coast Artillery Search Light Tower #9 - built for an enemy that never came. PHOTOGRAPH BY AARON CHAPMAN.

The air-raid sirens have also fallen silent, though it was not long ago that they occasionally went off accidentally during thunderstorms, triggering panicked thoughts of nuclear war. The sirens were finally removed in the early 1980s. Those who live near Estevan Point no longer keep watch for Japanese submarines. Today they are more likely to find debris washing ashore from the aftermath of the massive tsunami that hit Japan in 2011.

For now, the two towers at Tower Beach still stand, two concrete sentries waiting and keeping watch over the waters of Burrard Inlet.

(ENDNOTES)

1   Peter N. Moogk, *Vancouver Defended: A History of the Men and Guns of the Lower Mainland Defences, 1859–1949* (New Westminster: Antonson Publishing Ltd., 1978), 62.

2   Ibid., 102.

3   War Diary, June 8, 1940.

4   War Diary, April 6, 1940.

5   "Estevan Point Saved By Light Keeper in Japanese Raid" *Vancouver Daily Province*, June, 22, 1942, p. 2.

6   Bill Twaito. *Espirit De Corps* "The Sub That Couldn't Shoot Straight" February 2004, p. 2.

7   "Estevan Point Saved By Light Keeper in Japanese Raid" *Vancouver Daily Province*, June 22, 1942, p. 2.

8   Ken Adachi, *The Enemy That Never Was: A History of the Japanese Canadians* (Toronto. McCelland Stewart. 1991), 202.

9   "Pearl Harbor Raid Brought Anguish to BC Japanese," *Montreal Gazette*, December 7, 1981, p. 31.

10   Hansard, 1988 Legislative Session: 2nd Session, 34th Parliament, April 28, 1988. http://www.leg.bc.ca/hansard/34th2nd/34p_02s_880428p.htm

ADDITIONAL SOURCES

Cramp, Beverly. *100 Years of Fun*. Echo Memoirs Ltd., 2010.

Globe and Mail. "Tsunami Debris Litters BC Beaches." January 28, 2013.

Khatchadourian, Raffi. "Neptune's Navy." *The New Yorker*. November 5, 2007.

Omatsu, Maryka. *Bittersweet Passage and the Japanese Canadian Experience*. (Toronto: Between the Lines, 1992).

Ottawa Citizen. "Spectacular Blackout Staged in Vancouver." May 23, 1941. p. 3.

Spokane Daily Chronicle. "Vancouver Eyes Japs Skeptically." August 7, 1940. p. 17.

Vancouver Sun. "Four Fined; Had Lights on in Blackout." October 8, 1942.

Vancouver Sun. "Reunion Cancelled." July 11, 1940. p. 1.

Public Archives of Canada. 15th Coast Brigade/Regiment. RCA Vol II, Point Grey Subsection.

Public Archives of Canada. 58th Coast Brigade/Regiment. RCA Vol. II, Point Grey Subsection.

Public Archives of Canada. 58th Independent Coast Battery. Vol. 1, Part 1, Orders.

Public Archives of Canada. 15th (Vancouver) Coast Brigade. Headquarters, Folder 1, File 6, Orders.

"WOOLRIDGE DRIVEN TO KILL WIFE": LESSONS ON HOW TO GET AWAY WITH MURDER

DIANE PURVEY

O n the afternoon of Saturday March 1, 1947, Malcolm Woolridge, a 20-year-old ex-navy veteran, husband, and father, shot to death his wife of three years, Viola Woolridge, age 22, in a downtown Vancouver boarding house. His guilt was never disputed. After firing three bullets into her body at close range he walked into a neighbour's room and called the police. Almost four months later, on June 28, 1947, Malcolm was found guilty of manslaughter by a 12-man jury. Minutes later he walked away from court, a free man.

We will never know for certain what prompted Malcolm Woolridge to kill his wife, nor are we able to fully reconstruct the months and years of the Woolridges' relationship that led to that fateful day. But the murder of Viola Woolridge sheds light on one of the most shocking stories of the city.

After the stagnation of the 1930s and the disruptions of the Second World War, Vancouver was finally growing again. The population increase was part of an economic boom, shared with the rest of the post-war western world. Sparked by demand for the province's natural resources during the Second World War, BC's economy rapidly recovered from the Depression and experienced expansion and diversification. Rising foreign investment, the decision of unions to trade off unfair labour practices in exchange for steadily rising wages, consumer confidence, and government spending meant anticipation and often realization of "the good life" for many British Columbians, especially Vancouverites.

As the city grew, there was a perceived "crime wave," and the civic government launched a campaign to control and assuage citizens' fears and restore law and order. What's more, the year 1947 was near the zenith of a rising homicide rate, so awareness of murder and concern for its rise was widespread. This sensibility was fed by civic election campaigns that preyed on public fears of police incompetence, crumbling social mores, and the possibility of random violence. In the midst of this homicide binge, the Woolridge case was one of the more publicized domestic murders.

Reports of random and even erratic violence are splattered throughout the pages of the city's newspapers in 1947.[1] For example, on the front page of the February 4 edition of the *Vancouver News-Herald* one headline proclaims, "Thugs Slug, Kidnap Vet." A former soldier was "held up, robbed, slugged and kidnapped in his own auto, and later thrown from the vehicle by a pair of armed and masked bandits." In March, under the title "Woman Thug," the newspaper details the "strongarm team of a man and a woman [who] robbed [their victim] of $30 at 2:30 a.m. Sunday in the 300 block Dunlevy . . . [the victim] said the man struck him on the jaw and held his arms, while the woman searched his pockets." And in May, a married couple allege they "were the victims of an 'unprovoked' attack" on an early Saturday evening. The husband "told police he and his wife were en route to a Davie Street dancehall when the three men stepped from an auto and accosted them." This was a serious and vicious attack: the man was treated in the hospital for facial lacerations. Violence was more than threatened; it was dished out. What's more, one did not need to have gang "membership" to be a victim of violence. Seemingly respectable couples were attacked, not just lone individuals caught in the wrong part of town.

Who was behind these attacks? The newspapers liberally used the term "thugs" to describe the perpetrators. Although the identity of most thugs is seldom revealed, typically they are male, usually white, and often identified as veterans. There is an assumption of heterosexuality, although the attacks are not sexual in nature. There is also a certain opportunistic and spontaneous quality to these attacks, which suggests a lack of planning. Moreover, this impression is carried over into a sense of rootlessness on the part of the attackers. Perhaps after returning from the war they have not yet been able to find employment and have "drifted" into a life of random, violent crime.

Not only were daylight muggings commonplace in Vancouver, there was also a surprising amount of gunplay in the streets. In February 1947, a 67-year-old woman who was waiting for a streetcar in downtown Vancouver was shot through the leg when one of two policemen chasing a suspect fired a warning shot. A second warning shot was discharged. Significantly, the "warning shots" were not fired into the air but horizontally at a height of about three feet. "Mrs. Annie Campbell . . . is reported in good condition in hospital, suffering from a flesh wound where the bullet tore through her left leg above the knee and grazed the right leg." What was the villian's crime? The two constables "were running after the suspect from a café on Granville where he was reported to be begging." This individual had asked the cashier for seven cents, while "lounging" near the cash register. The constables justified their volley of bullets by claiming "they had been led to believe [the suspect] had a gun, but no weapon was found."

In April, there were two incidents of people at home who "miraculously escaped death from wild-flying bullets." The first occurred in the West End living room of a mother and her young son. "Death in the form of a rifle slug fired through their front room window nearly took the lives at 8 p.m. of [the victims], as [they] sat side by side on the living room sofa in their small, new home ... The bullet missed [the boy] as he bent forward a split second before the missile pierced [the mother's] left cheek as she sat reading the paper." A youth was held in connection with the incident; he admitted to using a .22 caliber rifle for target practice in the basement of his home directly behind the victims' residence. On the same evening, a policeman was sitting in his suite in downtown Vancouver "when a bullet smashed through a window behind him, glanced off the back of the chesterfield, a foot from his head, and fell to the floor." Although the officer raced outside in search of the "gunman," no suspect was found.

These incidents beg the question: where did the guns come from? The newspapers of the day don't give the issue much concern. Anecdotal reports tell us of veterans who brought unlicensed weapons home from war as souvenirs. Many veterans' homes, and those of families in and from a rural background, were repositories of firearms. What was the impact of war on society's acceptance of these weapons as part of the veterans' lives? Certainly the war increased people's familiarity with guns. In a 1947 newspaper piece on Vancouver vital statistics, it is reported that "[f]irearms were responsible for five accidental deaths in November of last year compared with two during the same month of 1945." Firearms were available and they were being used with some abandon by both cops and robbers.

Before turning to the Woolridge case, there are three other murders in 1947 that led to trials and very different outcomes. The first is the "Lost Lagoon Murder," in which a 27-year-old married woman (estranged from her husband for five months but reconciled two months previous) was found murdered by strangulation on the eastern edge of Stanley Park in June. An "unnatural" sex act had been committed upon her body. She is described as having being "slight," "sensitive," and "quiet." She was employed at a local bakery, and one of her co-workers was charged with the murder. He was found guilty of manslaughter, for which he received a sentence of 12 years in jail. The murderer is described as a diminutive man, five feet tall, and weighing little more than a hundred pounds. Although both Johnson, the convicted murderer, and

Burton, his victim, were married (although not to each other), the trial reveals that after arranging to meet in a beer parlour on a Saturday afternoon with another couple, they later went to Stanley Park where they "necked." Johnson left before Burton at 2:45 a.m. Although the morality of the two is not explicitly questioned, clearly the behaviour reported in the newspapers is morally unacceptable: the depiction of drinking, especially in the public space of a beer parlour, and of sexual contact, not only outside the parameters of marriage, but adulterously. The trial generated substantial public interest, apparently among women particularly. "The courtroom was packed . . . to its utmost capacity. Many women were present." Prurience aside, this murder was of interest because it highlighted women's vulnerability and the danger that might overtake them if they transgressed moral codes. It served to remind them of their permissible roles. How many spectators at the trial felt that in murder the woman received her due? The narrative of the trial certainly confirmed the public perception that ill befalls "bad" girls. Similarly, in Johnson's conviction and sentencing, the murderer was seen to be treated justly.

Another 1947 murder of significance took place in Victoria. A well-known and prosperous businessman was found fatally stabbed and his wife unconscious from knife wounds to the throat. His wife was charged with his murder while recovering in the hospital. She was later found not fit to stand trial due to a "paranoid condition." Psychologists determined that as her actions placed her outside of the norms of acceptable female behaviour, she was not accountable for the fatal slaying of her spouse. The violent female was thus equated with insanity.

The most sensational murder trial of the year involved Harry Medos, 22, and William Henderson, 17, who were both charged with the killing of two on-duty police officers on February 27. In an attempt to foil a bank robbery the constables met death in a "wild gun battle" in the Great Northern Railway yards on Vancouver's east side. The civic funeral of the officers and the subsequent trial of Medos and Henderson served to highlight crime in the city. As fate would have it, the incident occurred shortly after Mayor Gerry McGeer's civic electoral victory, won on the promise of smashing crime. Medos was found guilty and hanged October 1, 1947. Henderson, although found guilty and sentenced to death, received a stay of execution and a subsequent prison sentence, mainly due to his youth and the fact that he willingly disarmed himself prior to the shootout. Being young and foolish saved his life.

Which brings us back to the Woolridge case. Unlike the others explored here, this was a married couple and both spouses were gainfully employed. This was not a random act of violence involving strangers. This case tore at the very fabric of Vancouver society. What's more, in Canada in 1947 a guilty verdict would require the death penalty. Small wonder that the city watched the trial closely.

Viola May Godfrey and Malcolm Woolridge met in 1943 at a dance in Edmonton. After dating for eight or nine months they married when Viola became pregnant. Malcolm was 17 years old, Viola was 19. After three months of married life Malcolm joined the navy in 1944. Although originally stationed on the Atlantic coast, Malcolm was transferred to the Pacific coast, at which time Viola moved to Vancouver with Butch, their infant son. Marital bliss seems to have been elusive for the couple: between 1944 and 1947 they apparently separated several times. They cared for Butch intermittently. In his first year of life, Butch was either living with his paternal grandparents in Alberta or boarding out for seven months in Vancouver to a Mrs. Wells. Wells was under the impression that Viola had been referred by the Children's Aid Society due to marriage breakdown. After the war, Malcolm worked as a bundle-staver at Sweeney's, a local cooperage. Viola, who had been in the wartime armed services, found employment at a cleaning establishment. Malcolm's kin, who lived in Edmonton, joined him during the trial and sentencing. His mother testified in court. Although the trial testimony indicates that Viola's parents cared for Butch as a baby, there is no other reference to them.

On the day preceding the murder, Malcolm and Viola had arranged to meet at home at 10:30 p.m. The plan was to go dancing in celebration of their third wedding anniversary. Malcolm waited for Viola, but she did not return home until the next morning at 5:30 a.m. A lengthy and violent row ensued. When Viola refused to disclose her whereabouts, Malcolm slapped her across the face, injuring her to the extent that she sought assistance from a neighbour for a bleeding nose. Her neighbour testified that Viola "rolled up her sleeves—she was wearing a red sweater—and said, 'I'm going up and throw him out.'" When she returned to their room ten minutes later, their quarrel resumed, culminating in a struggle during which Malcolm pulled out a .38 calibre Smith and Wesson revolver from his coat pocket and shot her three times at a range of 6 to 12 inches—point blank. All three shots struck her: one lodged in her heart, a second passed completely through her body, just below the throat, and the third grazed her forehead. She died instantly. The time between Viola's return to the room and her death was a matter of minutes. As we know, Malcolm then left her in their room, in a spreading pool of blood, and called the police.

The Woolridge trial attracted substantial media attention. All of the province's major newspapers covered the trial. They all strike the same tone. The media perceived Viola Woolridge as the culprit. She transgressed acceptable notions of motherhood and womanhood, and their accounts are steeped in the language of judgment. Viola is condemned by the media, while Malcolm is exonerated.

The press reports appeal to the readers' emotions. Malcolm is a "frail, small, slight, trembling youth"; he is "mild-mannered, pale, haggard, and nervous" and commonly referred to as a "boy." By contrast, Viola is "muscular, stocky and heavy . . . well-developed and well nourished." She is an "untidy and resentful housewife" and "dirty." Viola is "nagging" and "quarrelsome"; while Malcolm is "subdued." Viola's intimidating size and strength as well as her "very violent temper" are illustrated in a story told by one of the witnesses. The Woolridges had a quarrel at a local dance: "She was a very heavy woman compared to Mac," the witness said. "She was about twice his size. [...] Once at a dance she got annoyed at him and literally threw him down the stairs. She followed him down to the first landing. The ticket-taker stopped her." The contrast between Viola's muscular frame and Malcolm's slight and frail physique is critically important: it tilts the scales, giving Malcolm permission to even them with a sidearm.

To damn Viola further, she is portrayed as an uncaring mother. First, she allowed her son to be boarded out, sufficient proof in and of itself of her maternal failure. "The child was boarded out because she didn't want to look after him," asserts one witness. We are also told that just days before Viola's death, she was informed by Butch's caregiver, Mrs. Wells, that the infant had an eye infection. Viola did not tell Malcolm, and when he did find out and asked her to go with him to the hospital with Butch, she apparently retorted, "I don't give a damn what you do with him." Also, Mrs. Wells testified that when she first received Butch, he "had a mastoid and was in a very run-down condition," implicitly further proof of maternal neglect. By contrast, Malcolm is shown to be deeply concerned for Butch: while he was waiting for the police to arrive immediately after the shooting, he wrote a letter to his "Mum" in Edmonton, asking her to "please come and care for my little boy." This story was repeatedly related in the newspapers as proof of Malcolm's strong paternal instincts. What is not addressed is the testimony of James W. Buchkan, Viola's date on the night before she was murdered. He said he left her at 5 a.m. on March 1 at the corner of Georgia and Hornby Streets, less than a block from her home, because "she was separated from her husband, and if neighbours saw her and Buchkan together, it might spoil her chance of getting custody of her baby." Such testimony suggests that Viola wanted her child and weakens the caricature of her as a "neglectful" mother, but of course the evidence was tainted because of its association with apparent infidelity.

Not only is Viola a poor mother, she also refused to fulfill her wifely duties. A witness testified that Malcolm "was the one who kept the house . . . When he came home from work there was no supper for him, only a pile of dirty dishes. When he asked where his supper was, she told him, 'If you want your supper you'll have to get it yourself!'" Courts have a track record of assessing people on the basis of their work ethic. The witnesses in the Woolridge case were repeatedly asked to comment on the work ethic of Viola. In judging her against dominant expressions of married women's femininity, namely her wifely and motherly roles, she was a *bad* worker. From this characterization, the jump to *bad woman* was very short indeed. It almost goes without saying that Malcolm was portrayed as a hard-working man, intent on supporting his family.

Other barometers of morality were invoked in the trial. Malcolm was asked by the judge to recount the swear words Viola commonly hurled at him. "When asked what names she called him, he told the Judge 'she swore often.' 'What was swearing?' asked Mr. Justice A.M. Manson. 'Very foul words, sir,' replied the accused. I don't like to repeat them.' 'Boy, you are on trial for your life,' encouraged the justice. 'Don't mince matters. Don't worry about it. Be frank with us.'" The impression is that Malcolm is so polite and decent that he has great difficulty uttering a swear word even when requested by a court of law. Nor would Malcolm criticize Viola directly. Later, Judge Manson told the jury: "It is highly to the credit that this boy would not slander his wife. Even to the hour of her death, it seems, he was still in love with her, though why he should be, I do not know." While on the stand during the trial, Woolridge "is on the verge of collapse as he sobs out evidence." These examples show that normative gender roles are reversed: Malcolm is infantilized while Viola is presented as callous and domineering.

Evidence to support this characterization of Malcolm-the-good and Viola-the-bad is provided by the neighbours, Stanley and Geraldine Lowe. They are the chief witnesses in the trial and in the newspaper accounts. "The slain woman was described by witnesses as bad-tempered, neglectful of her two-year-old son, and interested in other men." Stanley Lowe characterizes Viola Woolridge as "a woman with a violent temper [who] had 'frequently' fought with her husband." He describes an argument between the Woolridges during which "he had seen Mrs. Woolridge 'get so mad she stamped her feet and screamed and swore.' She . . . always antagonized Mac," testified Lowe. "He was very quiet but his wife was quarrelsome. She drove him to do it."

The final nail in Viola's figurative coffin is her sexual immorality. Much is made of her supposed relations with men other than Malcolm. Witnesses testify to her entertaining other men in the Woolridges' home. "She (the dead woman) had other men in her room when her husband was out and went out with other men." The reason offered for her failure to meet Malcolm to celebrate their wedding anniversary on what became the night before her death was her rendezvous with a presumed lover. As well, Viola apparently had a letter-writing relationship with a man imprisoned in Oakalla, the provincial penitentiary. In fact, it was Malcolm's reading of a letter sent by this man to Viola—"couched in language suggestive of an improper relationship"—that set off the fatal argument. Viola's extracurricular activities carry the stamp of infidelity: she had clearly crossed the lines drawn for women in the postwar era.

If Viola is a strong, large, sexual woman, Malcolm comes across as frail and susceptible. Wartime placed a premium on classic masculine traits of power and self-discipline; the emergent Cold War asked for the same. In 1947 when concern over national security in the face of a growing Red Scare was ramping up, effete, weak-willed men were seen as vulnerable, dangerous, and intolerable. In the act of killing Viola, Malcolm is seen to abandon his feeble tendencies as he defends the patriarchal family and, by extension, the very foundations of the Canadian nation. Failure to do so would be a sign of weakness, perhaps even deviancy. Malcolm's recourse to violence, according to the press and the courts, was a legitimate means by which to defend his reputation and to regain his masculinity. Viola's aggressive, non-feminine personality and her physical size overwhelmed Malcolm and threatened his manhood. In the face of this diminishment, as the court observed, and even in the face of Viola's betrayal, Malcolm persevered, trying to create a stable family environment by being a hard-working husband and a caring father. Within this context, Malcolm's murder of Viola was an acceptable next step, a way to restore the natural order of things.

What was glossed over throughout the trial by both the defence and the prosecution, however, was the most glaringly obvious fact: Malcolm had a gun. The blasé attitude of everyone in the courtroom regarding Malcolm's .38 revolver reflects the post-war profusion of weaponry in the city that went largely unquestioned. During the trial, Justice Manson was the only participant to draw any attention to the side-arm, stopping cross-examination to ask Malcolm where he got the gun. Malcolm's response was that he found it in a paper bag on Broadway the previous day. This explanation was sufficient for all present and the cross-examination resumed.

At the end of the day it was the villainy of Viola Woolridge that mattered most in the trial. Justice Manson's judgment, in which he calls for the release of Malcolm Woolridge, brings into focus the case against Viola:

> Upon the evidence, the jury doubtless found that after a preliminary quarrel, she returned to your room with the avowed intention of throwing you out, and it would seem clear that . . . [being] a much bigger woman than you a man, you had resort to a revolver which you had found by sheer accident the night before while walking the streets as you did for hours looking for her. Your shooting, I am satisfied, was entirely unpremeditated, and was a shooting by a man who had, for the time being, lost control of himself. The provocation was very clear.

Justice Manson further argues that Woolridge has suffered enough: "The memory of your harrowing experience so far as you are concerned will be with you a long, long time. That will be your punishment." He advises Woolridge to move on and "forget the past." A jury of his peers found Malcolm guilty of manslaughter (a homicide committed "in the heat of passion caused by sudden provocation"). The jury also "recommended and pleaded" for and won the utmost clemency for the man who murdered his wife: his sentence was only a seven-year probation.

Throughout the Woolridge trial the innocent character of Malcolm Woolridge remained intact. Viola, in contrast, is retroactively condemned to death because she did not appear to fit the only mould available to her—that of a virtuous, self-sacrificing and dedicated wife and mother. In this case it appears that the criminal was not so much defined by what *he did*, but by what *she was*. Viola was the one on trial, not Malcolm.

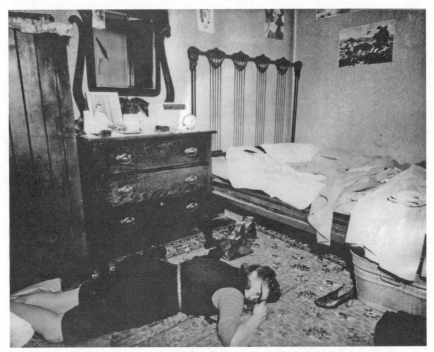

Viola Woolridge, who went on trial for her own murder. COURTESY OF THE VANCOUVER POLICE MUSEUM.

(ENDNOTES)

1   While all three Vancouver newspapers were consulted, the *Vancouver Daily Province*, the *Vancouver Sun*, and the *Vancouver News-Herald*, the bulk of the newspaper quotations come from the *Vancouver News-Herald*, Vancouver's only morning daily.

THE LONG WATCH

JESSE DONALDSON

The night of August 11, 1949, was darker than most. It was a little after eleven o'clock in the evening, with the moon not shining and a sticky, heavy warmth blanketing the North Shore mountains. The couple in the car were well dressed, and if you'd only laid eyes on them for a second, they would have seemed no different from the countless others who used the remote darkness of the city's downtown thousand-acre Stanley Park for romance and sex. The man was handsome, masculine, and well built. The woman too would have seemed masculine after a fashion, though from a distance her most striking features would have been her bright red hair and exaggerated bosom.

After pausing briefly to talk to a passing Vancouver Police Department patrolman, the pair began cruising the park's most secluded locations, making stops for an hour or more at each, quietly wiling away the darkness along the stretch sometimes known as Lovers' Lane, settling regularly into a quiet spooning routine no different from any other couple.

. But this was no couple. For starters, they were both men, one dressed in a Halloween wig, a tight, borrowed sweater, and a pair of fake breasts. They were also both armed. The one in the suit carried a Colt .45 tucked under one arm. The one in the wig had a billy club borrowed from the traffic division. This couple hadn't come to the park for romance.

The events of that night would come to be known among locals as the Stanley Park Caper, and by the time it was over, the two men in the car had subdued the leader of a gang of serial rapists who had been terrorizing couples in Lovers' Lane for more than a year. These crime fighters were determined, ambitious, sharp, and sober. They were *Province* reporters Don McClean and Ray Munro, and tonight they were calling on a predator.

Exactly how it all began is anybody's guess. Assembling an accurate portrait of the events that culminated that night in Stanley Park is, ironically, made more difficult by the fact that the only detailed account that survives was written by Munro himself. Twenty-seven years old, muscular, good-looking, charming, and popular with the ladies, Munro's work—whether behind the camera or a typewriter—would make international headlines throughout the 1940s and '50s. Unfortunately, despite his credentials, the 27-year-old wasn't, strictly speaking, in the news business—he was in the legend business: specifically his own. Egocentric and volatile, he was not above exaggerating, bending the truth, or outright lying when it suited him. He once shot multiple rounds into the wing and cockpit of his own airplane, claiming he'd been fired on by avowedly pacifist Doukhobors while covering a story from the air. ("Douk Terrorists Fire on Sun Photo Plane," screamed the headline. "Craft Forced Down with Bullet Holes.") Whether it was deliberate or accidental is unclear. He had transformed his automobile into a "personal press emergency car," which contained first-aid equipment and which he declared a "special ambulance." Boasting that he'd received death threats, he carried a gun as often as he was legally allowed (the majority of the time, he wore an empty holster). Munro was also notorious for mean-spirited pranks. On more than one occasion he cut off a colleague's tie with scissors and once had now-legendary journalist Pierre Berton carted off in a straitjacket. After spending an afternoon with a professional hypnotist, he managed to hypnotize a copyboy into believing he was the editor-in-chief (a change which lasted several hours, before Munro returned to undo the damage). He even weaseled his way into a photo with none other than Marilyn Monroe.

"Raymond Munro is one of the most honoured Canadians in history," he later claimed, with characteristic bluster, on the jacket of his autobiography. And that he "has had enough adventures and brushes with death to fill ten lifetimes. Here is the story of a man whose legendary exploits have not only made headlines on both sides of the Atlantic but earned for him countless civilian and aviation awards."

In spite of his flair, Munro was in good company. Like the city it covered, the news business in the late 1940s and early 1950s had more than its share of characters. Gar MacPherson, the *Sun*'s crime reporter, also regularly wore a gun and was known to accompany the police on raids. Religion editor Ivers Kelley, who started at the paper in 1950, had been charged with attempting to murder his wife with an axe. Newsmen could be a hard-living lot, and drinking at work was commonplace. Some, like MacPherson, kept booze right in their desk drawers. Others, such as photographer Dave Buchan, would duck out in the middle of the day to visit one of the city's many illegal speakeasies. In fact, the practice was so widespread that when the darkroom of the Sun Tower was being renovated in the early 2000s, crews found hundreds of empty liquor bottles stashed behind a built-in filing cabinet.

How McClean and Munro came to be jointly involved in this particular case is uncertain. In fact, little is known of McClean other than his age (25), and the fact that he spent some time in the Royal Canadian Air Force.

The press's relationship with the police department could be shaky at times, but by the summer of 1949, Munro had taken it to an openly adversarial level. It became personal. *Sun* photographer George Diack recalls an incident where a VPD inspector gleefully confiscated Munro's brand new pistol. In light of this tension, it's unclear where Munro first got his information about the Stanley Park case. All that's certain is that Munro, in his capacity as a police photographer, somehow got wind of a series of rapes, assaults, and robberies that had been taking place in the secluded area known as Lovers' Lane since late in 1948. The police, faced with a serious manpower shortage, had thus far come up empty-handed, and Munro, always looking for ways to bolster his own reputation, and hoping to give the VPD a serious black eye in the process, aimed to do something about it.

Or, as McClean explained succinctly in the pages of the *Province*, "Munro and I heard about the reports and rumours of robberies and of women being attacked in lonely spots in Stanley Park by two men posing as police morality officers and decided we would try to get them."

The assailants' modus operandi was always the same: men, sometimes as many as four or as few as two, would wait until dark, and then descend on couples in remote stretches of Stanley Park. They would shine flashlights through the car windows, announcing that they were members of the RCMP Morality Squad. Once the doors were opened, the men would be hauled out and viciously beaten while the women were raped and sodomized, their mouths often being stuffed with sand. According to Munro's sources in the police department, these incidents had been going on for more than 18 months.

At first, the *Province* investigation went nowhere. The local dailies and the police occurrence sheets were silent on the subject. Munro was of a mind that the information was being willfully kept from the public. In typical Munro fashion, rather than directly asking someone at the VPD (an action he believed would have resulted in "a total news blackout, followed by a snow-job from the public relations officer and a series of restrictive measures being placed on all police reporters"), he resolved instead to get hold of hard copies from the VPD document vault. This action failed to produce new leads, and the investigation into the Lovers' Lane assaults (said by Munro to number more than 100) stalled. Then one afternoon the telephone on Munro's desk rang, and a well-known North Shore auto dealer told the photographer a chilling tale.

"He was unhappily married and had entered into a sexual liaison with another woman," Munro explains in his autobiography. "To secure a private location for a romantic interlude, he had driven with her to a small side-road deep in Stanley Park and half-hidden the car under huge fir trees. Feeling safe in their darkened retreat, they had settled into a hugging and squeezing routine that generated enough heat to require the shedding of their outer garments. Lost in desire, neither of them heard a sound from the three rubber-shod stalkers who listened unseen through the partly opened windows."

Suddenly, both doors were pulled wide open, and the pair were bathed in the glare of flashlights.

"This is the Morality Squad!" shouted a voice. "Both of you get out of the car, now!"

They were both pulled from the vehicle. The man was kicked repeatedly in the face and genitals. The woman was said to have been raped and sodomized.

According to Munro's account, neither had contacted the police, fearful of the publicity that any revelation of their illicit affair might generate. Thus armed, Munro and McClean went to *Province* publisher Bill Forst, with a plan pulled from the pages of a Raymond Chandler novel.

"Only way to trap them, we figured, was to be decoys," McClean explained, in the *Province*. "I had felt that my training in the RCAF, though forsaken long ago for a typewriter, would come in handy. It did. And Munro, a handy man with his fists himself, took along his automatic."

Incredibly, Forst agreed to endorse the scheme, and, on the night of August 11, the pair put their plan into action. The weather was unseasonably warm as McClean and Munro met outside the *Province* building at a little after 9 p.m. McClean was dressed in a wig, grosgrain skirt, and sweater with, in Munro's words, "big boobies inside." As a precaution, he had lashed to one wrist a billy club borrowed from VPD traffic constable Ed Comiskey. Munro and McClean made their way into Stanley Park just before 10 p.m., and began their long watch. They parked in a few locations known as part of the Lovers' Lane stretch: near the English Bay Tennis Courts, along Pipeline Road, and at both Third Beach and Lumbermen's Arch. After several unsuccessful hours, they stopped for coffee, and as they drank, they met a police detective who told them he too was on the lookout for a group of park prowlers who had evaded the police for months. He'd seen them earlier that evening, he said, and even fired shots before they had escaped in a battered green pickup. The reporters shared their scheme for snaring the gang, and, surprisingly, the detective endorsed their plan, even suggesting tactics and hiding spots.

Encouraged, Munro and McClean returned to Stanley Park and continued making their rounds. It was pitch black by then. The stars had all but winked out overhead, and by McClean's estimation, visibility wasn't more than 25 feet in any direction. There they waited. Two hours passed in relative silence. Finally, around 2 a.m., as they dragged to a stop near Brockton Oval, they noticed the shade of a vehicle parked ahead—a green pickup, unmistakably framed in the glare of the headlight's filaments. They pulled past it by 100 feet or so and killed the engine. Then, with Munro's .45 tucked under one arm, and McClean's billy club securely in hand, they settled against one window together in their spooning routine.

A few moments passed and then the beam of a flashlight stabbed in through the partially opened windows.

"Stay where you are! This is the Morality Squad!" someone shouted.

Then chaos erupted.

McClean took a swing into the darkness, connecting with his unseen assailant. There was a grunt. Munro leapt from the vehicle, pulling his .45 from its holster as one of the men outside knocked McClean to the ground. Confusion descended, and Munro's Colt fired a slug into the darkness. Two of the assailants fled into the bushes. The third wasn't so lucky.

"I didn't waste time yelling at him to stop," Munro later explained. "I just pulled out the .45 and thumbed off one shot at his legs, just as his fleeing form melded with the ebony night. I heard the bullet strike something solid and saw the almost invisible form rear upright, clutch one leg, and fall to the ground. I was on him in a moment, bent on smashing his face with my gun barrel if he moved."

McClean and Munro pounced on their attacker, beating him mercilessly as he struggled. Munro pounded him with his fists, and McClean with the club. (Munro's autobiography will claim he subdued the man completely on his own.) After a furious minute, they managed to wrestle their opponent into the back seat of the car. However, not before they paused to snap a picture which would run on the front page of the following day's *Province,* and eventually in papers and magazines across the continent: McClean, club in hand, still wearing a wig, sweater, and bra, wrestling with their bloodied, wincing assailant, framed against the darkness of Stanley Park. It was an arresting image, one which would garner international coverage, even getting the pair a mention in *TIME* magazine.

In the six weeks that followed, the case would wend its way through the legal system. The captured suspect, a Coquitlam labourer named John Kenneth Clark, would be positively identified by six women. A search of his belongings would produce a notebook containing a series of licence plate numbers, alongside lurid descriptions of the violent sexual acts inflicted upon their occupants.

Held initially on charges of impersonating a police officer, Clark would be remanded to Oakalla Prison in Burnaby. And on August 20, 1949, he would be charged with the rape of a 25-year-old woman from Courtenay, a woman left so badly injured that surgery was required. During his trial in mid-October Clark would be found guilty on four counts and sentenced to 15 years in prison, with an additional penalty of ten lashes—five on the way in, and five on the way out. His three accomplices were never charged. According to Munro, even though they were known to police, there was no evidence with which to proceed.

As for the two crusading journalists, their lives split off in very different directions. McClean returned to relative obscurity following the incident. Munro's life, on the other hand, became even more colourful. In late 1955 he would quit the *Province* to publish a series of stories with the sensationalist Toronto tabloid *FLASH Weekly,* exposing rampant corruption in the Vancouver Police Department. Munro's allegations ultimately led to a full-scale investigation of the VPD, and in the wake of the resulting scandal, one senior officer committed suicide, another shot himself (and lived), and Police Chief Walter Mulligan was forced to flee the city in disgrace.

Munro's tenure as editor of the *Chatham Daily News*, beginning in 1956, was marked by a number of bizarre journalistic "experiments." He forced cub reporters to stage a fake UFO crash, and he printed a single issue of the paper dedicated entirely to good news. Always too headstrong and never an easy man to work with, he was later fired by Thomson Newspapers, at which point he took up hot air ballooning, and embarked on a career as a hypnotist. A man desperate to be remembered, today he has been all but forgotten.

"As head of the West Coast bureau of the tabloid *Flash*, Munro was responsible for launching a royal commission investigation into the Vancouver police," his 1994 obituary remarks blithely. "During the probe two police officers shot themselves and Chief Walter Mulligan quit ... In Vancouver, he broke a number of major stories. One of them involved him and a reporter dressing up as women to capture a molester in Stanley Park. Papers across North America reported the case."

The Lovers' Lane marauder may have been caught that night in 1949, but this would also not be the last time Stanley Park played host to a grisly or high-profile crime. In fact, as the city around it changed, so too did the essential character of the park, revealing a dark underbelly that contrasted with its increasingly manicured facade. Whether it was the 1953 discovery of two children's skeletons (known popularly as the Babes In the Wood) near Park Drive, or the 2001 beating death of Aaron Webster near Lost Lagoon by a team of thugs not unlike Clark and his accomplices, the park would time and again provide a secluded space for generations of the city's most violent impulses.

By that time, of course, most of the key players in the Lovers' Lane caper were themselves dead in the ground: the reporters, the photographers, the police officers, the news editors, the North Shore auto dealers, and their mistresses. To them, it no longer mattered who was guilty or who was innocent, who became president, or who made the Fortune 500. No longer concerned with making headlines or making deadlines. Their thoughts were as dark and empty as a Stanley Park night in August. Their long watch was over. Everybody except for the criminals. Their names and faces might change, but we haven't figured out a way to get rid of them yet.

Don McClean captures the Lovers' Lane Marauder, August 11, 1949.
VANCOUVER PROVINCE, AUGUST 12, 1949. PHOTOGRAPH BY RAY MUNRO.

ARSENIC AND OLD SIGNS
AARON CHAPMAN

Vancouver Broadway 1965…
The summer heat slithered and crept and the asphalt was breaking a fever of 102.
Coup de Villes and Buicks and swimming up and down the street at night
floating like Manta rays under the warm amber of a traffic light.
And down at The Cave there's a playbill for Mitzi Gaynor coming soon
and man that gal has legs from here to who hid the broom.
Out on Kingsway a street cleaner is mopping up the street
while inside the E&B Steakhouse a guy is mopping up the gravy from his plate
with a slice of
Wonderbread so white you could clean a piano with it.
Others are at home fallen asleep
asleep in the glow of the Indian Chief TV test pattern
asleep in front of their Curtis Mathes or Zenith Electrohomes.

Broadway's lit too.
Broadway's bathed in red and blue.
Ruby and sapphire neon tubes glowing ten storeys high from the BOWMAC sign.
Glowing and buzzing and flickering at a 60-cycle hum
standing tall in front of the BOWMAC car lot every night
pouring neon light down the street and reflecting off all the chrome in the lot.
And maybe that old neon sign sizzled a bit more in that 1965 summer.
Rene Castellani was his name. Rene Castellani.
A radio man from CKNW who got on top of the sign and vowed to stay on top
until all the cars were sold from the lot.

". . . Folks I'm going to stay up here until BOWMAC sells every car it's got. So come
on down here and get me off this sign . . . Come down and see a new Fleetwood
Eldorado hardtop, with four white feet, music and heat, wheel skirts and opera
lights, with a comfort tilt steering wheel with a walnut trim, and a V8 engine that
purrs like a hymn. You can drive one off the lot today, so come down to BOWMAC
on Broadway..."

And you could drive down Broadway and see Castellani that summer
making friends with the seagulls and tune into AM98
and listen to old Rene with traffic and news on the hour,
and all the while the sign would be glowing down on every car there
each two tons of iron made back when Detroit used to care . . .

And not even the two-piece suit car salesmen
in their Ingledews that shined like mirrors
knew that in the dark of the night,
Castellani would climb down from the top and sneak away for an hour or two
Nobody except the boys back at the radio station he'd innocently ask
if they'd fill in and play a record at the top of the hour to cover his ass.

When he'd sneak away
he'd drive home to find his plump wife Esther
with her hair in rollers eating bon bons in bed
chain smoking Winstons . . .
·But on other nights
his friends would notice his company car outside the home of Miss Miller
the station's strawberry blonde switchboard operator

And while he sat there day and night on top of the BOWMAC sign
between playing commercials for Honest Nat's Department store
and Woodward's $1.49 Day
as he daydreamed out onto the horizon
maybe it's easy to imagine the choice in his mind
the suburbs, his wife, and leftovers
and a marriage he knew the honeymoon was over
or over to Miss Miller's around nine
with a smile on her face and a bottle of wine.

So he started to sneak down from the sign each night
and bring home to Esther a milkshake, her favourite treat.
But she never bothered to ask why her husband was being so sweet.
And slowly Esther started to get sick
but never suspected her doting husband of any trick.
And the lonely late-night coffee patrons of the Knight & Day diner would never notice him,
and never notice his halfway grin
reflecting off the arborite counter as he came in,
as he came in to get another milkshake to go.

Esther got sick.
She got worse and worse.
Until one day they called in a hearse.
That night Esther died
one of the boys from the station came by to see if Rene was OK
But Rene wasn't in tears.
No, he has his feet up on the couch having a beer
eating a Stouffers Turkey TV dinner,
laughing at some comic on the *Ed Sullivan* show.

Now Esther might have died without another word.
Some said Rene never seemed to grieve
and others said he never wore his heart on his sleeve.
But the neighbours began to talk over fences and coffee shops
and the coroner's hunches went to suspicions
and suspicions became questions.

Like why two days after Esther was in the ground
he'd taken off with Miss Miller to Reno on vacation.
And when the police found the half empty bottle
of weed killer arsenic under Castellani's sink
when everybody knew Rene was never a gardener
and never gave a damn about weeds.

Rene must have felt doom
when the coroner opened Esther's tomb.
And when arsenic in the body was tested
he was arrested
for murder.

The newspapers splashed his name
and called him The Milkshake Murderer.
But Rene with his head held high in the stand
said through it all he was an innocent man.
When the judgment came down
they found him guilty and hit him with a life sentence . . .

He did his time
and rarely talked of the crime
and nobody came to visit him in jail.
The station scraped his name off his office door
and soon nobody cared anymore
and even Miss Miller married someone else and turned tail.
As he sat out his years in that cell
maybe Rene Castellani thought until he died in '82
that maybe crime doesn't pay as good as it used to.

Now if you go uptown Broadway today
now the car lot is gone.
There are no more Coupe de Villes or Buicks driving by.
There are no more radio waves pulsing from there.
A big kid's store has moved in
and the only cars they are now selling are toys.
The BOWMAC sign is half covered up but it still stands tall there.
Right where Rene Castellani stayed in that summer of 1965.
A free-standing charged memory with not a volt running through it.
But where Rene dreamt of Miss Miller
and dreamt up a plan
Where it all began
Fuelled by blood red and sapphire blue neon
buzzing into a Vancouver night.

BOWMAC I, 1996. PHOTOGRAPH BY PAUL CHUI.

"Arsenic and Old Signs" originally appeared on the Aaron Chapman album *Last Chance Gas.*

Arsenic and Old Signs © (SOCAN/ASCAP)

CONTRIBUTORS

John Belshaw is a historian, writer, consultant, online university professor, and a runner. He is the author and co-author of several books and articles on Canadian history, including *Vancouver Noir: 1930–1960*. Belshaw is a fellow of the Royal Historical Society, which sounds rather grand.

Tom Carter is a Vancouver artist, musician, producer, and historical researcher specializing in the city's vaudeville and early music scenes. He lives in an old warehouse surrounded by the bits and pieces of theatres he has rescued from oblivion.

Aaron Chapman is a writer, historian, and musician. Born and raised in Vancouver, he has been a contributor to the *Vancouver Courier*, the *Georgia Straight* and CBC radio. His 2012 book *Liquor, Lust, and the Law: The Story of Vancouver's Legendary Penthouse Nightclub* was shortlisted for the 2013 Roderick Haig-Brown Regional Prize (BC Book Prizes). *Live at the Commodore: The Story of Vancouver's Historic Commodore Ballroom* is forthcoming from Arsenal Pulp Press. A graduate of the University of British Columbia, he is a member of Heritage Vancouver and the Point Roberts Historical Society. (www.aaronchapman.net)

Jesse Donaldson is an author, journalist, performer, and playwright who has contributed to such publications as *VICE*, *SadMAG*, *subTerrain*, *The Tyee*, openfile.ca, and *The Dependent Magazine* (where he served as editor). His first book, *This Day in Vancouver*, was published by Anvil Press in 2014 and recently shortlisted for the Bill Duthie Booksellers' Choice Award (BC Book Prizes).

In a former life **James Johnstone** edited edgy international short-fiction anthologies and worked in Japanese tourism. Today he is a home history researcher, house and neighbourhood heritage advocate, popular history walk guide, and an obsessive blogger based in Vancouver's East End, when he's not exploring the back roads of rural Italy. His blog, *Sabina: A Stunning Land – My Secret Italy* has readers in more than 70 countries worldwide.

Eve Lazarus is an award-winning business reporter, historian, and author. She has written three books on popular history: *Sensational Vancouver*, *Sensational Victoria: Bright Lights, Red Lights, Murders, Ghosts & Gardens*, and *At Home with History: The Untold Secrets of Greater Vancouver's Heritage Homes*, which was a City of Vancouver Book Award finalist. Eve blogs regularly about places and their stories at http:// evelazarus.com/blog/

Diane Purvey is the Dean of Arts at Kwantlen Polytechnic University, as well as a historian and a specialist on teacher and leadership training. Her research interests include the history of deinstitutionalization and restorative justice practices in schools. She is the co-editor of *Child and Family Welfare in British Columbia: A History* and co-author of both *Private Grief, Public Mourning: The Rise of the Roadside Shrine in British Columbia* and *Vancouver Noir: 1930–1960*. She was born and raised in Vancouver.

Catherine J. Rose is a crime analyst and recovering goth, whose interest in Vancouver's seedy side stems from her family's own long history in the East End and her role as tour guide for the Vancouver Police Museum's "Sins of the City" walking tours. She received degrees in history from Simon Fraser University and the University of Western Ontario, following which she immediately sold out to "the man." She now studies vice and violence in a more contemporary context through her work with the Vancouver Police Department.

Lani Russwurm is a Vancouver historian living in the city's Downtown Eastside. He holds degrees from Simon Fraser University in history and political science and has been sharing his history finds on his blog, *Past Tense Vancouver*, since 2008. His first book, *Vancouver Was Awesome*, was published by Arsenal Pulp Press in 2013.

Rosanne Amosovs Sia has a M.A. in history from the University of British Columbia. Since graduating in 2010, she has worked as an English language teacher in France, a story gatherer with Aboriginal and immigrant communities for the City of Vancouver Dialogues Project, and a researcher for UBC and SFU Library's Chinese Canadian Stories. She has worked with Pivot Legal Society and the Vancouver Planning and Coordinating Table funded by the Welcoming Communities Project. She currently lives in Los Angeles, where she is studying towards a PhD in the Department of American and Ethnic Studies at the University of Southern California.

Jason Vanderhill is an amateur historian and collector of art and ephemera, with interests in fine art, architecture, and graphic design. He received a degree in image arts from Ryerson University in Toronto. As a tribute to Vancouver's 125th birthday, he created the website *Illustrated Vancouver*, compiling 1,000 local works of art and ephemera. He was a member of the organizing committee of the Vancouver Historical Society's "City Reflections" film project in 2007, a tribute to the oldest surviving film shot in Vancouver.

Terry Watada is an accomplished novelist, poet, playwright, essayist, and historian whose publications include *Kuroshio: The Blood of Foxes*, *Daruma Days*, and *Bukkyo Tozen: A History of Buddhism in Canada* and whose play, *Vincent,* was produced at the National Arts Centre in Ottawa and the first and second Madness and Arts World Festival in Toronto and Muenster, Germany, respectively. His essays have appeared in *Maclean's* magazine and he maintains a monthly column in the *JCCA Bulletin*. The Robarts Library at the University of Toronto recently installed his work as the Terry Watada Special Collections. His manuscripts and papers are stored in the Thomas Fisher Rare Books Library. He also received the Queen's Diamond Jubilee Medal in 2013. He lives in Toronto.

Stevie Wilson is a writer, editor, and historical researcher specializing in public history and memory studies. A graduate of the University of British Columbia, she is part of the editorial team at *Scout Magazine* and writer of the award-winning documentary, *Catch the Westbound Train*. Stevie lives in East Vancouver and is often seen with her dog, Lyle.

Will Woods is the founder and chief storyteller at Forbidden Vancouver Walking Tours. Driven by his twin passions of history and theatre, Will is found either buried in a book in the Vancouver Public Library, rehearsing lines to himself on a streetcorner somewhere, or dressed as a Victorian gent while merrily leading tour guests around Gastown.

INDEX